Causes of the Civil War

CORE DOCUMENTS

Causes of the Civil War

~ CORE DOCUMENTS ~

Selected and Introduced by

Jason W. Stevens

ASHBROOK PRESS

Library of Congress Cataloging-in-Publication Data
The Causes of the Civil War;
Selected and Introduced by Jason W. Stevens
p. cm.
Includes Index
1. United States - Politics and government.
ISBN 978-1-878802-47-7 (pbk.)

Cover images, above the title, left to right:
Charles King, *Henry Clay, Late Speaker of the United States House of Representatives . . .*, engraved by Peter Maverick, New York, 1822, Library of Congress Prints and Photographs Division, LC-DIG-pga-07465.
John C. Calhoun, published 1855–1865, Brady-Handy photograph collection, Library of Congress Prints and Photographs Division, LC-DIG-cwpbh-02605.
Samuel Montague Fassett, *Abraham Lincoln, half-length portrait, facing right*, October 4, 1859, Library of Congress Prints and Photographs Division, LC-USZ62-11492.
Portrait of Frederick Douglass as a Younger Man, engraved by J. C. Buttre from a daguerreotype, (Frontispiece: Frederick Douglass, *My Bondage and My Freedom* [New York and Auburn: Miller, Orton & Mulligan, 1855]), via Wikimedia Commons, https://commons.wikimedia.org/wiki/File:Frederick_Douglass_as_a_younger_man.jpg.
Jefferson Davis, between 1855 and 1865, Brady-Handy photograph collection, Library of Congress, Prints and Photographs Division, LC-DIG-cwpbh-00879.

Cover image, below the title:
Photo taken between December 2, 1861 and March 10, 1862, showing from left to right: William, Lucinda Hughes, Fannie (seated on Lucinda's lap), Mary (in cradle), Frances Hughes (standing), Martha, Julia (behind Martha), Harriet, and Charles or Marshall. The women and their children were enslaved at the time this photograph was taken on a plantation just west of Alexandria, Virginia, that belonged to Felix Richards. Frances and her children were enslaved by Felix, while Lucinda and her children were enslaved by his wife, Amelia McCrae Richards. Collection of the Smithsonian National Museum of African American History and Culture, 2014.174.8.

Interior design/composition: Brad Walrod/Kenoza Type, Inc.

Ashbrook Center at Ashland University
401 College Avenue
Ashland, Ohio 44805
www.ashbrook.org

ABOUT THE ASHBROOK CENTER

The Ashbrook Center restores and strengthens the capacities of the American people for constitutional self-government. Ashbrook teaches students and teachers across our country what America is and what she represents in the long history of the world. Offering a variety of resources and programs, Ashbrook is the largest university-based educator in the enduring principles and practice of free government. Dedicated in 1983 by President Ronald Reagan, the Ashbrook Center is governed by its own board and responsible for raising all of the funds necessary for its many programs.

BRING THE DOCUMENTS AND DEBATES OF THE NATION'S PAST INTO THE PRESENT

Readers of this volume may be particularly interested in Ashbrook's Teaching American History programs which provide an opportunity for secondary educators to explore themes in American history and self-government through the study of original historical documents. Designed especially for teachers, our seminar-style programs are offered online and on location, both on our campus and at sites around the country. We use discussions, not lectures and texts, not textbooks so that each seminar is a conversation among peers in which each attendee is an active participant in learning.

For more information, please visit us online at Ashbrook.org, TeachingAmericanHistory.org, and ReligionInAmerica.org.

Contents

General Editor's Introduction

This volume is another in the Ashbrook Center's collection of primary document volumes covering major periods, themes, and institutions in American history and government. It is the second of a planned trilogy on the conflict over slavery. *Reconstruction* has already appeared; *The Civil War* will follow. The documents in this volume explain the political, constitutional, moral, social, and economic causes of the Civil War. As the nation expanded, it had to face the question of whether new states and thus political power and ultimately the Union would be slave or free. Compromise, in 1820 and again in 1850, was the first resort, but the nation could not evade the moral question forever. Was slavery right or wrong, just or unjust? Politically, that question expressed itself in the different opinions Americans held of the Declaration of Independence and its assertion of human equality. Was the Declaration a mere political expression of the colonists' desire to control their own affairs, or did it express a moral truth which was the necessary foundation of self-government and which could not be denied without ultimately destroying self-government? The documents in this volume trace the struggle over this question.

When completed, the Ashbrook document collections will be a comprehensive and authoritative account of America's story, told in the words of those who wrote it-America's presidents, labor leaders, farmers, philosophers, industrialists, politicians, workers, explorers, religious leaders, judges, soldiers; its slaveholders and abolitionists; its expansionists and isolationists; its reformers and stand-patters; its strict and broad constructionists; its hard-eyed realists and visionary utopians-all united in their commitment to equality and liberty, yet all also divided often by their different understandings of these most fundamental American ideas. The documents are about all this-the still unfinished American experiment with self-government.

As this volume does, each of the volumes in the series will contain key documents on its period, theme, or institution, selected by an expert and reviewed by an editorial board. Each volume will have an introduction highlighting key documents and themes. In an appendix to each volume, there will also be a thematic table of contents, showing the connections between various documents. Another appendix will provide study questions for each document, as well as questions that refer to other documents in the collection, tying them together as the thematic table of contents does. Each document will be checked against an authoritative original source and have an introduction outlining its significance. We will provide notes to each document to identify people, events, movements, or ideas that may be unfamiliar to non-specialist readers and to improve understanding of the document's historical context. For the same reason, we have modernized spelling, punctuation and most capitalization.

In sum, our intent is that the documents and their supporting material provide reliable and unique access to the richness of the American story.

Jason Stevens, Visiting Assistant Professor of History and Political Science at Ashland University, selected the documents and wrote the introductions. David Tucker served as the General Editor. Joan Livingston was the copyeditor. Sarah Morgan Smith oversaw production. Ali Brosky and Ellen Tucker provided assistance with various aspects of the process.

David Tucker
General Editor and Senior Fellow
The Ashbrook Center

Introduction

This volume of primary documents on the causes of the Civil War presents the history of the American political order during its most tumultuous and challenging time. More than a century and a half after the crisis came to an end, Americans remain fascinated by it, as they should be. The Civil War is the defining event in American political development. It put to the test whether the "one people," as Thomas Jefferson wrote in the Declaration of Independence, would remain one.

The documents selected for inclusion in this volume range from a little-known 1819 Congressional speech by James Tallmadge Jr. on the future status of slavery in the territories (Document 1) to Abraham Lincoln's widely read First Inaugural Address in 1861 (Document 26), in which he tried to prevent civil war as Southern states seceded. In between, the reader will discover the central political, constitutional, moral, social, and economic themes that shaped the nation's history during its most critical period, as told by those who lived through it.

The documents trace these themes, from both the Northern and Southern points of view. In their famous debate in 1830, Senators Daniel Webster (Massachusetts) and Robert Y. Hayne (South Carolina) argued over two radically different understandings of the origin and nature of the American Union and the legality of secession (Document 4). William Lloyd Garrison (Document 5), John C. Calhoun (Document 6), and Abraham Lincoln (Document 24) discussed the proper relationship between the Constitution and the Union, and its effect on understanding secession and the dissolution of the government. George Fitzhugh (Document 13) and James Henry Hammond (Document 16) argued that the slave system of the South was superior to the free labor system of the North, while William H. Seward (Document 19) and Abraham Lincoln (Document 20) defended free labor. Speeches and resolutions before Congress (Documents 1, 2, 4, 6, 7, 8, 10, 11, 16); interpretations of executive power by Abraham Lincoln (Document 26); and arguments in the *Dred Scott* Supreme Court case (Documents 14 and 15) addressed the use and abuse of the legitimate powers under the Constitution of the three branches of government. Finally, and most important, Lincoln and Stephen A. Douglas argued over the limits of popular sovereignty, and thus over the connection between the Declaration of Independence and the Constitution (Documents 15, 18, and 24).

Despite these different perspectives, however, all of the documents in this collection revolve around one central idea that is at the heart of any attempt to understand the coming of the Civil War: slavery, or, perhaps more rightly, the extension of slavery into the territories. From out of the territories new states came into the Union, and with them the power either to protect or to destroy slavery forever by Constitutional amendment, depending on whether proslavery or antislavery forces dominated in the Congress and in the state legislatures. It was in the territories, therefore, that everyone at the time understood that the future of slavery, and with it, the future of the nation, would be decided.

No one can read these documents today without sensing the overwhelming significance the debate over slavery had in the minds of the people of that era, as it was the only serious issue that threatened to divide them and destroy their political existence. South Carolina's Declaration of the Causes of Secession (Document 23), like similar reports issued by every state that eventually left the Union, identified the protection of slavery as the primary justification for secession. From all points of view and all walks of life, the core argument always came back to slavery in one way or another, as these documents illustrate.

From these documents, the reader can come to understand and appreciate not only the history of the United States during the Civil War era, but also something about the challenges we have faced and the progress we have made as "one people." If we are to remain one and dedicated to our defining proposition-that all are created equal-every generation of Americans must understand the time and the reasons why we almost ceased to be.

Jason W. Stevens
Ashland University

Causes of the Civil War

CORE DOCUMENTS

DOCUMENT 1

Speech to Congress

James Tallmadge Jr.

February 15, 1819

During the early part of the nineteenth century, or the period known as "The Era of Good Feelings," a sectional crisis arose in the United States over the future status of slavery in the federal territory acquired with the purchase of the Louisiana Territory from France in 1803. Open and avowed threats to break up and dissolve the Union were freely made, especially after Representative James Tallmadge Jr., a Democratic-Republican from New York and a veteran of the War of 1812, attached a controversial anti-slavery amendment to the bill for Missouri statehood. Known as the "Tallmadge Amendment," it sought to prohibit the influx of any more slaves into Missouri and further required that all offspring born to slaves after statehood would be freed at twenty-five years of age. Tallmadge's floor speech in support of the amendment was widely circulated and republished by anti-slavery forces, who shared his abhorrence of slavery and his desire to provide for its future prohibition by Congressional legislation. The amendment narrowly passed the House of Representatives, but was promptly rejected by the U.S. Senate. Congress adjourned the next month, with no possible resolution to the Missouri crisis in sight.

It is worth noting Tallmadge's remark that it would be an insult to the House to assume that any member would argue that slavery was a good thing morally or politically. Tallmadge was here reflecting the generally held view among the Founders, from both the North and South, that slavery was an evil, but it was a view that the Missouri crisis called into question among southerners. In response to the arguments of those like Tallmadge opposed to slavery, southerners began to express the view that slavery was not an evil but a good thing (Documents 4 and 6).

SOURCE: *Annals of Congress*, House of Representatives, 15th Congress, 2nd Session, 1203–14, https://memory.loc.gov/cgi-bin/ampage?collId=llac&fileName=033/llac033.db&recNum=599.

Mr. Tallmadge, of New York, rose.-Sir, said he, it has been my desire and my intention to avoid any debate on the present painful and unpleasant subject. When I had the honor to submit to this House the amendment now under consideration, I accompanied it with a declaration, that it was intended to confine its operation to the newly acquired territory across the Mississippi; and I then expressly declared that I would in no manner intermeddle with the slaveholding states, nor attempt manumission in any one of the original states in the Union. Sir, I even went further, and stated that I was aware of the delicacy of the subject, and that I had learned from Southern gentlemen the difficulties and the dangers of having free blacks intermingling with slaves; and, on that account, and with view to the safety of the white population of the adjoining states, I would not even advocate the prohibition of slavery in the Alabama Territory;[1] because, surrounded as it was by slaveholding states, and with only imaginary lines of division, the intercourse between slaves and free blacks could not be prevented, and a servile war might be the result. While we deprecate and mourn over the evil of slavery, humanity and good morals require us to wish its abolition, under circumstances, consistent with the safety of the white population. Willingly, therefore, will I submit to an evil which we cannot safely remedy. I admitted all that had been said of the danger of having free blacks visible to slaves, and therefore did not hesitate to pledge myself that I would neither advise nor attempt coercive manumission. But, sir, all these reasons cease when we cross the banks of the Mississippi, a newly acquired territory, never contemplated in the formation of our government, not included within the compromise or mutual pledge in the adoption of our Constitution, a new territory acquired by our common fund, and ought justly to be subject to our common legislation....

Sir, the honorable gentleman from Missouri, (Mr. Scott,)[2] who has just resumed his seat, has told us of the Ides of March, and has cautioned us to "beware the fate of Caesar and of Rome." Another gentleman, (Mr. Cobb)[3] from Georgia, in addition to other expressions of great warmth, has said, "that, if we persist, the Union will be dissolved;" and, with a look fixed on me, has told us, "we have kindled a fire which all the waters of the ocean cannot put out, which seas of blood can only extinguish."...

Sir, if a dissolution of the Union must take place, let it be so! If civil war,

---

[1] The present state of Alabama was first a territory, from December 1817 to December 1819, when it was admitted to the Union as a state.

[2] John Scott (1785–1861) was a delegate from the Missouri Territory.

[3] Thomas W. Cobb (1784–1830) was a representative from Georgia.

which gentlemen so much threaten, must come, I can only say, let it come! My hold on life is probably as frail as that of any man who now hears me; but, while that hold lasts, it shall be devoted to the service of my country-to the freedom of man. If blood is necessary to extinguish any fire which I have assisted to kindle, I can assure gentlemen, while I regret the necessity, I shall not forbear to contribute my mite. Sir, the violence to which gentlemen have resorted on this subject will not move my purpose, nor drive me from my place. I have the fortune and the honor to stand here as the representative of freemen, who possess intelligence to know their rights, who have the spirit to maintain them. Whatever might be my own private sentiments on this subject, standing here as the representative of others, no choice is left me. I know the will of my constituents, and, regardless of consequence, I will avow it; as their representative, I will proclaim their hatred to slavery in every shape; as their representative, here will I hold my stand, until this floor, with the Constitution of my country which supports it, shall sink beneath me. If I am doomed to fall, I shall at least have the painful consolation to believe that I fall, as a fragment, in the ruins of my country. . . .

Sir, has it already come to this; that in the Congress of the United States . . . the subject of slavery has become a subject of so much feeling-of such delicacy-of such danger, that it cannot safely be discussed? . . . Are we to be told of the dissolution of the Union; of civil war, and of seas of blood? And yet, with such awful threatenings before us, do gentlemen, in the same breath, insist upon the encouragement of this evil; upon the extensions of this monstrous scourge of the human race? An evil so fraught with such dire calamities to us as individuals, and to our nation, and threatening, in its progress, to overwhelm the civil and religious institutions of the country, with the liberties of the nation, ought at once to be met, and to be controlled. If its power, its influence, and its impending dangers have already arrived at such a point that it is not safe to discuss it on this floor, and it cannot now pass under consideration as a proper subject for general legislation, what will be the result when it is spread through your widely extended domain? Its present threatening aspect, and the violence of its supporters so far from inducing me to yield to its progress, prompts me to resist its march. Now is the time. It must now be met, and the extension of the evil must now be prevented, or the occasion is irrecoverably lost, and the evil can never be contracted.

Sir, extend your view across the Mississippi, over your newly acquired territory;[4] . . . Behold this extended empire, inhabited by the hardy sons of

---

[4] territory acquired by the United States through the Louisiana Purchase

American freemen-knowing their rights, and inheriting the will to protect them-owners of the soil on which they live, and interested in the institutions which they labor to defend-with two oceans laving[5] your shores, and tributary to your purposes bearing on their bosoms the commerce of your people. Compared to yours, the governments of Europe dwindle into insignificance, and the whole world is without a parallel. But, sir, reverse this scene; people this fair dominion with the slaves of your planters; extend slavery-this bane of man, this abomination of heaven-over your extended empire, and you prepare its dissolution; you turn its accumulated strength into positive weakness; you cherish a canker in your breast; you put poison in your bosom; you place a vulture on your heart-nay, you whet the dagger and place it in the hands of a portion of your population, stimulated to use it, by every tie, human and divine. . . .

Sir, we have been told, with apparent confidence, that we have no right to annex conditions to a state on its admission into the Union; and it has been urged that the proposed amendment, prohibiting the further introduction of slavery is unconstitutional. This position, asserted with so much confidence, remains unsupported by any argument, or by any authority derived from the Constitution itself. The Constitution strongly indicates an opposite conclusion, and seems to contemplate a difference between the old and the new states. The practice of the government has sanctioned this difference in many respects.

The third section of the fourth article of the Constitution says, "new States may be admitted by the Congress into this Union," and it is silent as to the terms and conditions upon which the new states may be so admitted. The fair inference from this silence is, that the Congress which might admit, should prescribe the time and the terms of such admission. The tenth section of the first article of the Constitution says, "the migration or importation of such persons as any of the States now existing shall think proper to admit, shall not be prohibited by the Congress prior to the year 1808." The words "now existing" clearly show the distinction for which we contend. The word slaves is nowhere mentioned in the Constitution, but this section has always been considered as applicable to them, and unquestionably reserved the right to prohibit their importation into any new state before the year 1808.

Congress, therefore, have power over the subject, probably as a matter of legislation, but more certainly as a right, to prescribe the time and the condition upon which any new state may be admitted into the family of the

---

[5] washing

Union. Sir, the bill now before us proves the correctness of my argument. It is filled with conditions and limitations. The territory is required to take a census, and is to be admitted only on condition that it have forty thousand inhabitants. I have already submitted amendments preventing the state from taxing the lands of the United States, and declaring all navigable waters shall remain open to the other states, and be exempt from any tolls or duties. And my friend (Mr. Taylor)[6] has submitted amendments prohibiting the state from taxing soldiers' lands for the period of five years. And to all these amendments we have heard no objection; they have passed unanimously. But now, when an amendment prohibiting the further introduction of slavery is proposed, the whole House is put in agitation, and we are confidently told that it is unconstitutional to annex conditions on the admission of a new state into the Union. The result of all this is, that all amendments and conditions are proper, which suit a certain class of gentlemen, but whatever amendment is proposed, which does not comport with their interests or their views, is unconstitutional, and a flagrant violation of this sacred charter of our rights. In order to be consistent, gentlemen must go back and strike out the various amendments to which they have already agreed. The Constitution applies equally to all, or to none.

Sir, we have been told that this is a new principle for which we contend, never before adopted, or thought of. So far from this being correct, it is due to the memory of our ancestors to say, it is an old principle, adopted by them, as the policy of our country. Whenever the United States have had the right and the power, they have heretofore prevented the extension of slavery. The states of Kentucky and Tennessee were taken off from other states, and were admitted into the Union without condition, because their lands were never owned by the United States. The Territory Northwest of the Ohio is all the land which ever belonged to them. Shortly after the cession of those lands to the Union, Congress passed, in 1787, a compact[7] which was declared to be unalterable, the sixth article of which provides that "there shall be neither slavery nor involuntary servitude in the said territory, otherwise than in the punishment for crimes, whereof the party shall have been duly convicted." In pursuance of this compact, all the states formed from that territory have been admitted into the Union upon various considerations, and among which the sixth article of this compact is included as one....

Sir, we have been told that the proposed amendment cannot be received,

[6] Congressman John W. Taylor of New York
[7] The Northwest Ordinance

because it is contrary to the treaty and cession of Louisiana. "Article 3. The inhabitants of the ceded territory shall be incorporated in the Union of the United States, and admitted as soon as possible, according to the principles of the Federal Constitution, the enjoyment of all the rights, advantages, and immunities of citizens of the United States; and, in the meantime, they shall be maintained and protected in the free enjoyment of their liberty, property, and the religion which they profess." I find nothing in this article of the treaty, incompatible with the proposed amendment. The rights, advantages, and immunities of citizens of the United States are guaranteed to the inhabitants of Louisiana. If one of them should choose to remove into Virginia, he could take his slaves with him; but if he removes to Indiana, or any of the states northwest of the Ohio, he cannot take his slaves with him. If the proposed amendment prevails, the inhabitants of Louisiana or the citizens of the United States can neither of them take slaves into the State of Missouri. All, therefore, may enjoy equal privileges. . . .

Sir, in the course of the debate on this subject, we have been told that, from the long habit of the Southern and Western people, the possession of slaves has become necessary to them, and an essential requisite in their living. It has been urged, from the nature of the climate and soil of the Southern countries, that the lands cannot be occupied or cultivated without slaves. It has been said that the slaves prosper in those places, and that they are much better off there than in their own native country. We have even been told that, if we succeed, and prevent slavery across the Mississippi, we shall greatly lessen the value of property there, and shall retard, for a long series of years, the settlement of that country.

Sir, if the Western country cannot be settled without slaves, gladly would I prevent its settlement till time shall be no more. If this class of arguments is to prevail, it sets all morals at defiance, and we are called to legislate on the subject, as a matter of mere personal interest. If this is to be the case, repeal all your laws prohibiting the slave trade; throw open this traffic to the commercial states of the East; and, if it better the condition of these wretched beings, invite the dark population of benighted Africa to be translated to the shores of Republican America. But, sir, I will not cast upon this or upon that gentleman an imputation so ungracious as the conclusion to which their arguments would necessarily tend. I do not believe any gentleman on this floor could here advocate the slave trade, or maintain, in the abstract, the principles of slavery. I will not outrage the decorum, nor insult the dignity of this House, by attempting to argue in this place, as an abstract proposition, the moral right of slavery. How gladly would the "legitimates of Europe chuckle"[8] to find an American Congress in debate on such a question!

As an evil brought upon us without our own fault, before the formation of our government, and as one of the sins of that nation from which we have revolted, we must of necessity legislate upon this subject. It is our business so to legislate, as never to encourage, but always to control this evil; and, while we strive to eradicate it, we ought to fix its limits, and render it subordinate to the safety of the white population, and the good order of civil society.

Sir, on this subject the eyes of Europe are turned upon you. You boast of the freedom of your Constitution and your laws; you have proclaimed, in the Declaration of Independence, "That all men are created equal; that they are endowed by their Creator with certain inalienable rights; that amongst these are life, liberty, and the pursuit of happiness;" and yet you have slaves in your country. The enemies of your government, and the legitimates of Europe, point to your inconsistencies, and blazon your supposed defects. If you allow slavery to pass into territories where you have the lawful power to exclude it, you will justly take upon yourself all the charges of inconsistency; but, confine it to the original slaveholding states, where you found it at the formation of your government, and you stand acquitted of all imputation....

Sir, there is yet another, and an important point of view in which this subject ought to be considered. We have been told by those who advocate the extension of slavery into the Missouri, that any attempt to control this legislation is a violation of that faith and mutual confidence upon which our Union was formed and our Constitution adopted. This argument might be considered plausible, if the restriction was attempted to be enforced against any of the slaveholding states, which had been a party in the adoption of the Constitution. But it can have no reference or application to a new district of country recently acquired, and never contemplated in the formation of the government, and not embraced in the mutual concessions and declared faith upon which the Constitution was adopted. The Constitution provides that the Representatives of the several states to this House shall be according to their numbers, including three-fifths of the slaves in the respective states. This is an important benefit yielded to the slaveholding states, as one of the mutual sacrifices for the Union. On this subject, I consider the faith of the Union pledged, and I never would attempt coercive manumission in a slaveholding state.

But none of the causes which induced the sacrifice of this principle, and

---

[8] "Legitimates of Europe" refers to kings and other hereditary rulers.

which now produce such an unequal representation of the free population of the country, exist as between us and the newly acquired territory across the Mississippi. That portion of country has no claims to such an unequal representation, unjust in its results upon the other states. Are the numerous slaves in extensive countries, which we may acquire by purchase, and admit as states into the Union, at once to be represented on this floor, under a clause of the Constitution, granted as a compromise and a benefit to the Southern states which had borne part in the Revolution? Such an extension of that clause in the Constitution would be unjust in its operations, unequal in its results, and a violation of its original intention. Abstract from the moral effects of slavery, its political consequence in the representation under this clause of the Constitution demonstrate the importance of the proposed amendment.

Sir, I shall bow in silence to the will of the majority, on whichever side it shall be expressed; yet I confidently hope that majority will be found on the side of an amendment, so replete with moral consequences, so pregnant with important politic results.

DOCUMENT 2

Missouri Compromise Act

Henry Clay

March 6, 1820

Abraham Lincoln once called Henry Clay his "beau ideal of a statesman." The 1820 Missouri Compromise and the Compromise of 1850 (Document 8) help to explain why. Clay was the principal author and architect of the law that finally, after much deliberation and debate, succeeded in relieving tense sectional differences that threatened to break apart the Union over the future status of slavery in the Louisiana Purchase territory. With both sides yielding something to the other, a compromise was brokered between Northern free states and Southern slave states to resolve what was known as "the Missouri crisis." Maine was admitted into the Union as a free state (in separate legislation) and Missouri came in as a slave state, thus maintaining the delicate balance between free and slave state forces in the U.S. Senate. In addition, the remaining Louisiana Territory was split along a geographical line at 36 degrees and 30 minutes north latitude. Slavery was prohibited north of this line (with the exception of Missouri), but any future states organized out of the territory south of this line might come into the Union with or without slavery. Both sides were satisfied with the result, and President James Monroe signed the legislation into law on March 6, 1820.

Apart from its connection to slavery, the Missouri Compromise Act is notable for continuing the policy of admitting new states as equals with the old and for providing for educational institutions and infrastructure, such as roads through the sale of public land.

SOURCE: *Statutes at Large*, 16th Congress, 1st Session, 545–48. Available at https://memory.loc.gov/cgi-bin/ampage?collId=llsl&fileName=003/llsl003.db&recNum=586.

An act to authorize the people of the Missouri territory to form a constitution and state government, and for the admission of such state into the Union on an equal footing with the original states, and to prohibit slavery in certain territories.

Be it enacted by the Senate and House of Representatives of the United States of America, in Congress assembled, that the inhabitants of that portion of the Missouri territory included within the boundaries herein after designated, be, and they are hereby, authorized to form for themselves a constitution and state government, and to assume such name as they shall deem proper; and the said state, when formed, shall be admitted into the Union, upon an equal footing with the original states, in all respects whatsoever.

Sec. 2. And be it further enacted, that the said state shall consist of all the territory included within the following boundaries, . . . Provided, the said state shall ratify the boundaries aforesaid. And provided also, That the said state shall have concurrent jurisdiction on the river Mississippi, and every other river bordering on the said state so far as the said rivers shall form a common boundary to the said state; and any other state or states, now or hereafter to be formed and bounded by the same, such rivers to be common to both; and that the river Mississippi, and the navigable rivers and waters leading into the same, shall be common highways, and forever free, as well to the inhabitants of the said state as to other citizens of the United States, without any tax, duty impost, or toll, therefor, imposed by the said state.

Sec. 3. And be it further enacted, that all free white male citizens of the United States, who shall have arrived at the age of twenty-one years, and have resided in said territory: three months previous to the day of election, and all other persons qualified to vote for representatives to the general assembly of the said territory, shall be qualified to be elected and they are hereby qualified and authorized to vote, and choose representatives to form a convention, who shall be apportioned amongst the several counties. . . .

And the election for the representatives aforesaid shall be holden on the first Monday, and two succeeding days of May next, throughout the several counties aforesaid in the said territory, and shall be, in every respect, held and conducted in the same manner, and under the same regulations as is prescribed by the laws of the said territory regulating elections therein for members of the general assembly. . . .

Sec. 4. And be it further enacted, that the members of the convention thus duly elected, shall be, and they are hereby authorized to meet at the seat of government of said territory on the second Monday of the month of June next; and the said convention, when so assembled, shall have power and authority to adjourn to any other place in the said territory, which to them shall seem best for the convenient transaction of their business; and which convention, when so met, shall first determine by a majority of the whole number elected, whether it be, or be not, expedient at that time to form a constitution and state government for the people within the said territory, as included within the boundaries above designated; and if it be deemed expedient, the convention shall be, and hereby is, authorized to form a constitution and state government; or, if it be deemed more expedient, the said convention shall provide by ordinance for electing representatives to form a constitution or frame of government; which said representatives shall be chosen in such manner, and in such proportion as they shall designate; and shall meet at such time and place as shall be prescribed by the said ordinance; and shall then form for the people of said territory, within the boundaries aforesaid, a constitution and state government: Provided, that the same, whenever formed, shall be republican, and not repugnant to the constitution of the United States; and that the legislature of said state shall never interfere with the primary disposal of the soil by the United States, nor with any regulations Congress may find necessary for securing the title in such soil to the bona fide purchasers; and that no tax shall be imposed on lands the property of the United States; and in no case shall non-resident proprietors be taxed higher than residents.

Sec. 5. And be it further enacted, that until the next general census shall be taken, the said state shall be entitled to one representative in the House of Representatives of the United States.

Sec. 6. And be it further enacted, that the following propositions be, and the same are hereby, offered to the convention of the said territory of Missouri, when formed, for their free acceptance or rejection, which, if accepted by the convention, shall be obligatory upon the United States:

First. That section numbered sixteen in every township, and when such section has been sold, or otherwise disposed of, other lands equivalent thereto, and as contiguous as may be, shall be granted to the state for the use of the inhabitants of such township, for the use of schools.

Second. That all salt springs, not exceeding twelve in number, with six sections of land adjoining to each, shall be granted to the said state for the use of said state, the same to be selected by the legislature of the said state, on or before the first day of January, in the year one thousand eight hundred and twenty-five; and the same, when so selected, to be used under such terms, conditions, and regulations, as the legislature of said state shall direct: Provided, that no salt spring, the right whereof now is, or hereafter shall be, confirmed or adjudged to any individual or individuals, shall, by this section, be granted to the said state: And provided also, that the legislature shall never sell or lease the same, at any one time, for a longer period than ten years, without the consent of Congress.

Third. That five per cent of the net proceeds of the sale of lands lying within the said territory or state, and which shall be sold by Congress, from and after the first day of January next, after deducting all expenses incident to the same, shall be reserved for making public roads and canals, of which three fifths shall be applied to those objects within the state, under the direction of the legislature thereof; and the other two fifths in defraying, under the direction of Congress, the expenses to be incurred in making of a road or roads, canal or canals, leading to the said state.

Fourth. That four entire sections of land be, and the same are hereby, granted to the said state, for the purpose of fixing their seat of government thereon; which said sections shall, under the direction of the legislature of said state, be located, as near as may be, in one body, at any time, in such townships and ranges as the legislature aforesaid may select, on any of the public lands of the United States: Provided, that such locations shall be made prior to the public sale of the lands of the United States surrounding such location.

Fifth. That thirty-six sections, or one entire township, which shall be designated by the President of the United States, together with the other lands heretofore reserved for that purpose, shall be reserved for the use of a seminary of learning, and vested in the legislature of said state, to be appropriated solely to the use of such seminary by the said legislature: Provided, that the five foregoing propositions herein offered, are on the condition that the convention of the said state shall provide, by an ordinance, irrevocable without the consent or the United States, that every and each tract of land sold by the United States, from and after the first day of January next, shall remain exempt from any tax laid by order or under the authority of the state, whether for state, county, or township, or any other purpose whatever, for the term of five years from and after the day of sale; and further, that the bounty lands granted, or hereafter to be granted, for military services during the late war, shall, while they continue to be held by the patentees, or their heirs remain exempt as aforesaid from taxation for the term of three year; from and after the date of the patents respectively.

Sec. 7. And be it further enacted, That in case a constitution and state government shall be formed for the people of the said territory of Missouri, the said convention or representatives, as soon thereafter as may be, shall cause a true and attested copy of such constitution or frame of state government, as shall be formed or provided, to be transmitted to Congress.

Sec. 8. And be it further enacted, That in all that territory ceded by France to the United States, under the name of Louisiana, which lies north of thirty-six degrees and thirty minutes north latitude, not included within the limits of the state, contemplated by this act, slavery and involuntary servitude, otherwise than in the punishment of crimes, whereof the parties shall have been duly convicted, shall be, and is hereby, forever prohibited: Provided always, that any person escaping into the same, from whom labor or service is lawfully claimed, in any state or territory of the United States, such fugitive may be lawfully reclaimed and conveyed to the person claiming his or her labor or service as aforesaid.

DOCUMENT 3

Letter to John Holmes

Thomas Jefferson

April 22, 1820

John Holmes was a U.S. Representative from Massachusetts and one of the earliest supporters of the Missouri Compromise in Congress. Before moving to the U.S. Senate as one of the first two senators from the newly formed state of Maine, he mailed a letter to Thomas Jefferson with a copy of a pamphlet he had published to the citizens of Maine on the Missouri question. Jefferson, in retirement at Monticello, responded to Holmes's inquiry shortly after the passage of the Missouri Compromise. In his response, Jefferson congratulated Holmes on his defense of the measure, but worried about the effects of drawing a literal line of separation across the nation in regard to a moral and political principle. Jefferson, himself a slave-owner, makes clear in the rest of the letter not only his hatred of slavery, but his personal desire to see all men everywhere free.

The letter also notes in passing that expatriation of the slaves-removing them from the United States-should accompany their emancipation. This was a standard view in the period leading to the Civil War. Whites felt that the history of antagonism between whites and blacks would make it impossible for them to be fellow-citizens. Blacks who could express a view (Document 9) recognized the problem of embittered racial relations, but most often took the view that the United States was as much their country as it was the white man's. The letter also contains a brief statement of the so-called diffusion theory for ending slavery. This theory held that slavery was more likely to end if it was spread over the United States. As improbable as this may sound to us today, to some in the nineteenth century it seemed true because, as Jefferson explained, it would mean that the cost of emancipation and expatriation would not fall only on the Southern states. Jefferson's view of the limited power of the Federal government, as he made clear in this letter, persuaded him that it should not be the agent for emancipation and expatriation. Abraham Lincoln later argued that the federal government should play this role, supporting states in their efforts to emancipate and relocate slaves, although acknowledging that the U.S. Constitution gave the states the primary responsibility for dealing with slavery within their borders (Documents 15 and 26).

SOURCE: Thomas Jefferson to John Holmes. -04-22, 1820. Manuscript/Mixed Material. Library of Congress, https://www.loc.gov/item/mtjbib023795/.

I thank you, dear sir, for the copy you have been so kind as to send me of the letter to your constituents on the Missouri question. It is a perfect justification to them. I had for a long time ceased to read newspapers, or pay any attention to public affairs, confident they were in good hands, and content to be a passenger in our bark to the shore from which I am not distant. But this momentous question, like a fire bell in the night, awakened and filled me with terror. I considered it at once as the knell of the Union. It is hushed, indeed, for the moment. But this is a reprieve only, not a final sentence. A geographical line, coinciding with a marked principle, moral and political, once conceived and held up to the angry passions of men, will never be obliterated; and every new irritation will mark it deeper and deeper. I can say, with conscious truth, that there is not a man on earth who would sacrifice more than I would to relieve us from this heavy reproach, in any practicable way. The cession of that kind of property, for so it is misnamed, is a bagatelle[1] which would not cost me a second thought, if, in that way, a general emancipation and expatriation could be effected; and, gradually, and with due sacrifices, I think it might be. But as it is, we have the wolf by the ears, and we can neither hold him, nor safely let him go. Justice is in one scale, and self-preservation in the other. Of one thing I am certain, that as the passage of slaves from one state to another, would not make a slave of a single human being who would not be so without it, so their diffusion over a greater surface would make them individually happier, and proportionally facilitate the accomplishment of their emancipation, by dividing the burthen on a greater number of coadjutors.[2] An abstinence too, from this act of power, would remove the jealousy excited by the undertaking of Congress to regulate the condition of the different descriptions of men composing a state. This certainly is the exclusive right of every state, which nothing in the Constitution has taken from them and given to the general government. Could Congress, for example, say, that the non-freemen of Connecticut shall be freemen, or that they shall not emigrate into any other state?

---

[1] a small thing, a trifle

[2] Someone who works with someone or an assistant

I regret that I am now to die in the belief, that the useless sacrifice of themselves by the generation of 1776, to acquire self-government and happiness to their country, is to be thrown away by the unwise and unworthy passions of their sons, and that my only consolation is to be, that I live not to weep over it. If they would but dispassionately weigh the blessings they will throw away, against an abstract principle more likely to be effected by union than by scission, they would pause before they would perpetrate this act of suicide on themselves, and of treason against the hopes of the world. To yourself, as the faithful advocate of the Union, I tender the offering of my high esteem and respect.

DOCUMENT 4

The Webster-Hayne Debates

Daniel Webster and Robert Y. Hayne

January 1830

The Senate debates between Whig Senator Daniel Webster of Massachusetts and Democrat Senator Robert Y. Hayne of South Carolina in January 1830 started out as a disagreement over the sale of Western lands and turned into one of the most famous verbal contests in American history. During the course of the debates, the senators touched on pressing political issues of the day-the tariff, Western lands, internal improvements-because behind these and others were two very different understandings of the origin and nature of the American Union. Webster argued that the American people had created the Union to promote the good of the whole. Hayne argued that the sovereign and independent states had created the Union to promote their particular interests. Hayne maintained that the states retained the authority to nullify federal law, Webster that federal law expressed the will of the American people and could not be nullified by a minority of the people in a state. Nullification, Webster maintained, was a political absurdity. In this regard, Webster anticipated an argument that Abraham Lincoln made in his First Inaugural Address (Document 26). These irreconcilable views of national supremacy and state sovereignty framed the constitutional struggle that led to Civil War thirty years later. It is worth noting that in the course of the debate, on the very floor of the Senate, both Hayne and Webster raised the specter of civil war 30 years before it commenced.

SOURCE: Daniel Webster, *The Webster-Hayne Debate on the Nature of the Constitution: Selected Documents*, ed. Herman Belz (Indianapolis: Liberty Fund, 2000). https://oll.libertyfund.org/titles/1557.

Speech of Senator Robert Y. Hayne of South Carolina, January 19, 1830

In coming to the consideration of the next great question, what ought to be the future policy of the government in relation to the public lands? we find the most opposite and irreconcilable opinions between the two parties which

I have before described. On the one side it is contended that the public land ought to be reserved as a permanent fund for revenue, and future distribution among the states, while, on the other, it is insisted that the whole of these lands of right belong to, and ought to be relinquished to, the states in which they lie.... Will it promote the welfare of the United States to have at our disposal a permanent treasury, not drawn from the pockets of the people, but to be derived from a source independent of them? Would it be safe to confide such a treasure to the keeping of our national rulers? to expose them to the temptations inseparable from the direction and control of a fund which might be enlarged or diminished almost at pleasure, without imposing burthens upon the people? Sir, I may be singular-perhaps I stand alone here in the opinion, but it is one I have long entertained, that one of the greatest safeguards of liberty is a jealous watchfulness on the part of the people, over the collection and expenditure of the public money-a watchfulness that can only be secured where the money is drawn by taxation directly from the pockets of the people. Every scheme or contrivance by which rulers are able to procure the command of money by means unknown to, unseen or unfelt by, the people, destroys this security. Even the revenue system of this country, by which the whole of our pecuniary resources are derived from indirect taxation, from duties upon imports, has done much to weaken the responsibility of our federal rulers to the people, and has made them, in some measure, careless of their rights, and regardless of the high trust committed to their care. Can any man believe, sir, that, if twenty-three millions per annum was now levied by direct taxation, or by an apportionment of the same among the states, instead of being raised by an indirect tax, of the severe effect of which few are aware, that the waste and extravagance, the unauthorized imposition of duties, and appropriations of money for unconstitutional objects, would have been tolerated for a single year? My life upon it, sir, they would not. I distrust, therefore, sir, the policy of creating a great permanent national treasury, whether to be derived from public lands or from any other source. If I had, sir, the powers of a magician, and could, by a wave of my hand, convert this capital into gold for such a purpose, I would not do it. If I could, by a mere act of my will, put at the disposal of the federal government any amount of treasure which I might think proper to name, I should limit the amount to the means necessary for the legitimate purposes of the government. Sir, an immense national treasury would be a fund for corruption. It would enable Congress and the Executive to exercise a control over states, as well as over great interests in the country, nay, even over corporations and individuals-utterly destructive of the purity, and fatal to the duration of our institutions. It would be equally fatal to the sovereignty and independence of the states. Sir, I am one of those who believe that the very life of our system is the independence of the states, and that there is no evil more to be deprecated than the consolidation of this government. It is only by a strict adherence to the limitations imposed by the Constitution on the federal government, that this system works well, and can answer the great ends for which it was instituted. I am opposed, therefore, in any shape, to all unnecessary extension of the powers, or the influence of the Legislature or Executive of the Union over the states, or the people of the states; and, most of all, I am opposed to those partial distributions of favors, whether by legislation or appropriation, which has a direct and powerful tendency to spread corruption through the land; to create an abject spirit of dependence; to sow the seeds of dissolution; to produce jealousy among the different portions of the Union, and finally to sap the very foundations of the government itself. . . .

Speech of Senator Daniel Webster of Massachusetts, January 20, 1830

[O]pinions were expressed yesterday on the general subject of the public lands, and on some other subjects, by the gentleman from South Carolina [Senator Robert Hayne], so widely different from my own, that I am not willing to let the occasion pass without some reply. . . .

. . . Consolidation!-that perpetual cry, both of terror and delusion-consolidation! Sir, when gentlemen speak of the effects of a common fund, belonging to all the states, as having a tendency to consolidation, what do they mean? Do they mean, or can they mean, anything more than that the Union of the states will be strengthened, by whatever continues or furnishes inducements to the people of the states to hold together? If they mean merely this, then, no doubt, the public lands as well as everything else in which we have a common interest, tends to consolidation; and to this species of consolidation every true American ought to be attached; it is neither more nor less than strengthening the Union itself. This is the sense in which the Framers of the Constitution use the word consolidation; and in which sense I adopt and cherish it. They tell us, in the letter submitting the Constitution to the consideration of the country, that, "in all our deliberations on this subject, we kept steadily in our view that which appears to us the greatest interest of every true American-the consolidation of our Union-in which is involved our prosperity, felicity, safety; perhaps our national existence. This important consideration, seriously and deeply impressed on our minds, led each state in the Convention to be less rigid, on points of inferior magnitude, than might have been otherwise expected."

This, sir, is General Washington's consolidation. This is the true constitutional consolidation. I wish to see no new powers drawn to the general government; but I confess I rejoice in whatever tends to strengthen the bond that unites us, and encourages the hope that our Union may be perpetual. And, therefore, I cannot but feel regret at the expression of such opinions as the gentleman has avowed; because I think their obvious tendency is to weaken the bond of our connection. I know that there are some persons in the part of the country from which the honorable member comes, who habitually speak of the Union in terms of indifference, or even of disparagement. The honorable member himself is not, I trust, and can never be, one of these. They significantly declare, that it is time to calculate the value of the Union; and their aim seems to be to enumerate, and to magnify all the evils, real and imaginary, which the government under the Union produces.

The tendency of all these ideas and sentiments is obviously to bring the Union into discussion, as a mere question of present and temporary expediency; nothing more than a mere matter of profit and loss. The Union to be preserved, while it suits local and temporary purposes to preserve it; and to be sundered whenever it shall be found to thwart such purposes. Union, of itself, is considered by the disciples of this school as hardly a good. It is only regarded as a possible means of good; or on the other hand, as a possible means of evil. They cherish no deep and fixed regard for it, flowing from a thorough conviction of its absolute and vital necessity to our welfare. Sir, I deprecate and deplore this tone of thinking and acting. I deem far otherwise of the Union of the states; and so did the Framers of the Constitution themselves. What they said I believe; fully and sincerely believe, that the Union of the states is essential to the prosperity and safety of the states. I am a Unionist, and in this sense a national Republican. I would strengthen the ties that hold us together. Far, indeed, in my wishes, very far distant be the day, when our associated and fraternal stripes shall be severed asunder, and when that happy constellation under which we have risen to so much renown, shall be broken up, and be seen sinking, star after star, into obscurity and night!...

...I maintain that, from the day of the cession of the territories by the states to Congress, no portion of the country has acted, either with more liberality or more intelligence, on the subject of the Western lands in the new states, than New England. This statement, though strong, is no stronger than the strictest truth will warrant. Let us look at the historical facts. So soon as the cessions were obtained, it became necessary to make provision for the government and disposition of the territory....

At the foundation of the constitution of these new Northwestern states, ... [*was*] fixed, forever, the character of the population in the vast regions Northwest of the Ohio, by excluding from them involuntary servitude. It impressed on the soil itself, while it was yet a wilderness, an incapacity to bear up any other than free men. It laid the interdict against personal servitude, in original compact, not only deeper than all local law, but deeper, also, than all local constitutions. Under the circumstances then existing, I look upon this original and seasonable provision, as a real good attained. We see its consequences at this moment, and we shall never cease to see them, perhaps, while the Ohio shall flow. It was a great and salutary measure of prevention. Sir, I should fear the rebuke of no intelligent gentleman of Kentucky, were I to ask whether, if such an ordinance could have been applied to his own state, while it yet was a wilderness, and before Boone had passed the gap of the Alleghany, he does not suppose it would have contributed to the ultimate greatness of that commonwealth?...

Speech of Senator Robert Y. Hayne of South Carolina, January 25, 1830

... The honorable gentleman from Massachusetts [Senator Daniel Webster] has gone out of his way to pass a high eulogium on the state of Ohio.... To all this, sir, I was disposed most cordially to respond. When, however, the gentleman proceeded to contrast the state of Ohio with Kentucky, to the disadvantage of the latter, I listened to him with regret.... In contrasting the state of Ohio with Kentucky, for the purpose of pointing out the superiority of the former, and of attributing that superiority to the existence of slavery, in the one state, and its absence in the other, I thought I could discern the very spirit of the Missouri question[1] intruded into this debate, for objects best known to the gentleman himself....

... The impression which has gone abroad, of the weakness of the South, as connected with the slave question, exposes us to such constant attacks, has done us so much injury, and is calculated to produce such infinite mischiefs, that I embrace the occasion presented by the remarks of the gentleman from Massachusetts, to declare that we are ready to meet the question promptly

[1] See Document 2.

and fearlessly. It is one from which we are not disposed to shrink, in whatever form or under whatever circumstances it may be pressed upon us. We are ready to make up the issue with the gentleman, as to the influence of slavery on individual and national character-on the prosperity and greatness, either of the United States, or of particular states.

Sir, when arraigned before the bar of public opinion, on this charge of slavery, we can stand up with conscious rectitude, plead not guilty, and put ourselves upon God and our country. Sir, we will not stop to inquire whether the black man, as some philosophers have contended, is of an inferior race, nor whether his color and condition are the effects of a curse inflicted for the offences of his ancestors.[2] We deal in no abstractions. We will not look back to inquire whether our fathers were guiltless in introducing slaves into this country. If an inquiry should ever be instituted in these matters, however, it will be found that the profits of the slave trade were not confined to the South. Southern ships and Southern sailors were not the instruments of bringing slaves to the shores of America, nor did our merchants reap the profits of that "accursed traffic."

But, sir, we will pass over all this. If slavery, as it now exists in this country, be an evil, we of the present day found it ready made to our hands. Finding our lot cast among a people, whom God had manifestly committed to our care, we did not sit down to speculate on abstract questions of theoretical liberty. We met it as a practical question of obligation and duty. We resolved to make the best of the situation in which Providence had placed us, and to fulfil the high trust which had developed upon us as the owners of slaves, in the only way in which such a trust could be fulfilled, without spreading misery and ruin throughout the land. We found that we had to deal with a people whose physical, moral, and intellectual habits and character, totally disqualified them from the enjoyment of the blessings of freedom. We could not send them back to the shores from whence their fathers had been taken; their numbers forbade the thought, even if we did not know that their condition here is infinitely preferable to what it possibly could be among the barren sands and savage tribes of Africa; and it was wholly irreconcilable with all our notions of humanity to tear asunder the tender ties which they

[2] See Genesis 9:20–27. These verses recount the first occurrence of slavery. Noah grew a vineyard, got drunk on wine and lay naked. Ham, one of Noah's sons, saw him uncovered, for which Noah cursed him by making Ham's son, Canaan, a slave to Ham's brothers. This episode was used in nineteenth century America as a Biblical justification for slavery.

had formed among us, to gratify the feelings of a false philanthropy. What a commentary on the wisdom, justice, and humanity, of the Southern slave owner is presented by the example of certain benevolent associations and charitable individuals elsewhere. Shedding weak tears over sufferings which had existence only in their own sickly imaginations, these "friends of humanity" set themselves systematically to work to seduce the slaves of the South from their masters. By means of missionaries and political tracts, the scheme was in a great measure successful.

Thousands of these deluded victims of fanaticism were seduced into the enjoyment of freedom in our Northern cities. And what has been the consequence? Go to these cities now, and ask the question. Visit the dark and narrow lanes, and obscure recesses, which have been assigned by common consent as the abodes of those outcasts of the world-the free people of color. Sir, there does not exist, on the face of the whole earth, a population so poor, so wretched, so vile, so loathsome, so utterly destitute of all the comforts, conveniences, and decencies of life, as the unfortunate blacks of Philadelphia and New York, and Boston. Liberty has been to them the greatest of calamities, the heaviest of curses. Sir, I have had some opportunities of making comparisons between the condition of the free Negroes of the North and the slaves of the South, and the comparison has left not only an indelible impression of the superior advantages of the latter, but has gone far to reconcile me to slavery itself....

On this subject, as in all others, we ask nothing of our Northern brethren but to "let us alone;" leave us to the undisturbed management of our domestic concerns, and the direction of our own industry, and we will ask no more. Sir, all our difficulties on this subject have arisen from interference from abroad, which has disturbed, and may again disturb, our domestic tranquility, just so far as to bring down punishment upon the heads of the unfortunate victims of a fanatical and mistaken humanity....

In the course of my former remarks, I took occasion to deprecate, as one of the greatest of evils, the consolidation of this government. The gentleman takes alarm at the sound. "Consolidation," like the "tariff," grates upon his ear. He tells us, "we have heard much, of late, about consolidation; that it is the rallying word for all who are endeavoring to weaken the Union by adding to the power of the states." But consolidation, says the gentleman, was the very object for which the Union was formed; and in support of that opinion, he read a passage from the address of the president of the Convention[3] to

[3] George Washington

Congress (which he assumes to be authority on his side of the question.) But, sir, the gentleman is mistaken. The object of the Framers of the Constitution, as disclosed in that address, was not the consolidation of the government, but "the consolidation of the Union." It was not to draw power from the states, in order to transfer it to a great national government, but, in the language of the Constitution itself, "to form a more perfect union;" and by what means? By "establishing justice," "promoting domestic tranquility," and "securing the blessings of liberty to ourselves and our posterity." This is the true reading of the Constitution. But, according to the gentleman's reading, the object of the Constitution was to consolidate the government, and the means would seem to be, the promotion of injustice, causing domestic discord, and depriving the states and the people "of the blessings of liberty" forever....

The honorable gentleman from Massachusetts while he exonerates me personally from the charge, intimates that there is a party in the country who are looking to disunion.... Sir, when the gentleman provokes me to such a conflict, I meet him at the threshold. I will struggle while I have life, for our altars and our fire sides, and if God gives me strength, I will drive back the invader discomfited. Nor shall I stop there. If the gentleman provokes the war, he shall have war. Sir, I will not stop at the border; I will carry the war into the enemy's territory, and not consent to lay down my arms, until I shall have obtained "indemnity for the past, and security for the future."[4] It is with unfeigned reluctance that I enter upon the performance of this part of my duty. I shrink almost instinctively from a course, however necessary, which may have a tendency to excite sectional feelings, and sectional jealousies. But, sir, the task has been forced upon me, and I proceed right onward to the performance of my duty; be the consequences what they may, the responsibility is with those who have imposed upon me this necessity....

Who, then, Mr. President, are the true friends of the Union? Those who would confine the federal government strictly within the limits prescribed by the Constitution-who would preserve to the states and the people all powers not expressly delegated-who would make this a federal and not a national Union-and who, administering the government in a spirit of equal justice, would make it a blessing and not a curse. And who are its enemies? Those who are in favor of consolidation; who are constantly stealing power from the states and adding strength to the federal government; who, assuming

[4] Perhaps a quotation from a speech in Parliament in 1803 of Lord Castlereagh, Robert Stewart, 2nd Marquess of Londonderry (1769–1822) during a debate over the conduct of British officials in India.

an unwarrantable jurisdiction over the states and the people, undertake to regulate the whole industry and capital of the country....

The senator from Massachusetts, in denouncing what he is pleased to call the Carolina doctrine,[5] has attempted to throw ridicule upon the idea that a state has any constitutional remedy by the exercise of its sovereign authority against "a gross, palpable, and deliberate violation of the Constitution." He called it "an idle" or "a ridiculous notion," or something to that effect; and added, that it would make the Union "a mere rope of sand"....

Sir, as to the doctrine that the federal government is the exclusive judge of the extent as well as the limitations of its powers, it seems to be utterly subversive of the sovereignty and independence of the states. It makes but little difference, in my estimation, whether Congress or the Supreme Court, are invested with this power. If the federal government, in all or any of its departments, are to prescribe the limits of its own authority; and the states are bound to submit to the decision, and are not to be allowed to examine and decide for themselves, when the barriers of the Constitution shall be overleaped, this is practically "a government without limitation of powers;" the states are at once reduced to mere petty corporations, and the people are entirely at your mercy. I have but one word more to add. In all the efforts that have been made by South Carolina to resist the unconstitutional laws which Congress has extended over them, she has kept steadily in view the preservation of the Union, by the only means by which she believes it can be long preserved-a firm, manly, and steady resistance against usurpation. The measures of the federal government have, it is true, prostrated her interests, and will soon involve the whole South in irretrievable ruin....

Speech of Senator Daniel Webster of Massachusetts, January 26 and 27, 1830

When the honorable member rose, in his first speech, I paid him the respect of attentive listening; and when he sat down, though surprised, and I must say even astonished, at some of his opinions, nothing was farther from my intention than to commence any personal warfare: and through the whole of

[5] The idea that a state could nullify a federal law, associated with South Carolina, especially after the publication of John C. Calhoun's South Carolina Exposition and Protest (1828) in response to the tariff passed in that year. Several state governments or courts, some in the north, had espoused the idea of nullification prior to 1828. For Calhoun, see Documents 6 and 7.

the few remarks I made in answer, I avoided, studiously and carefully, everything which I thought possible to be construed into disrespect....

I spoke, sir, of the ordinance of 1787, which prohibited slavery, in all future times, northwest of the Ohio,[6] as a measure of great wisdom and foresight; and one which had been attended with highly beneficial and permanent consequences. I supposed, that on this point, no two gentlemen in the Senate could entertain different opinions. But, the simple expression of this sentiment has led the gentleman, not only into a labored defense of slavery, in the abstract, and on principle, but, also, into a warm accusation against me, as having attacked the system of domestic slavery, now existing in the Southern states. For all this, there was not the slightest foundation, in anything said or intimated by me. I did not utter a single word, which any ingenuity could torture into an attack on the slavery of the South. I said, only, that it was highly wise and useful in legislating for the northwestern country, while it was yet a wilderness, to prohibit the introduction of slaves: and added, that I presumed, in the neighboring state of Kentucky, there was no reflecting and intelligent gentleman, who would doubt, that if the same prohibition had been extended, at the same early period, over that commonwealth, her strength and population would, at this day, have been far greater than they are. If these opinions be thought doubtful, they are, nevertheless, I trust, neither extraordinary nor disrespectful. They attack nobody, and menace nobody....

I know, full well, that it is, and has been, the settled policy of some persons in the South, for years, to represent the people of the North as disposed to interfere with them, in their own exclusive and peculiar concerns. This is a delicate and sensitive point, in southern feeling; and of late years it has always been touched, and generally with effect, whenever the object has been to unite the whole South against northern men, or northern measures. This feeling, always carefully kept alive, and maintained at too intense a heat to admit discrimination or reflection, is a lever of great power in our political machine. It moves vast bodies, and gives to them one and the same direction. But the feeling is without all adequate cause, and the suspicion which exists wholly groundless. There is not, and never has been, a disposition in the North to interfere with these interests of the South. Such interference has never been supposed to be within the power of government; nor has

[6] The Northwest Ordinance. The following states came from the territory north and west of the Ohio river: Ohio (1803), Indiana (1816), Illinois (1818), Michigan (1837), Wisconsin (1848) and Minnesota (1858).

it been, in any way, attempted. It has always been regarded as a matter of domestic policy, left with the states themselves, and with which the federal government had nothing to do. Certainly, sir, I am, and ever have been of that opinion. The gentleman, indeed, argues that slavery, in the abstract, is no evil. Most assuredly, I need not say I differ with him, altogether and most widely, on that point. I regard domestic slavery as one of the greatest of evils, both moral and political....

This leads, sir, to the real and wide difference, in political opinion, between the honorable gentleman and myself.... "What interest," asks he, "has South Carolina in a canal in Ohio?" Sir, this very question is full of significance. It develops the gentleman's whole political system; and its answer expounds mine.... On that system, Ohio and Carolina are different governments, and different countries, connected here, it is true, by some slight and ill-defined bond of union, but, in all main respects, separate and diverse. On that system, Carolina has no more interest in a canal in Ohio than in Mexico. The gentleman, therefore, only follows out his own principles; he does no more than arrive at the natural conclusions of his own doctrines; he only announces the true results of that creed, which he has adopted himself, and would persuade others to adopt, when he thus declares that South Carolina has no interest in a public work in Ohio.

Sir, we narrow-minded people of New England do not reason thus. Our notion of things is entirely different. We look upon the states, not as separated, but as united. We love to dwell on that union, and on the mutual happiness which it has so much promoted, and the common renown which it has so greatly contributed to acquire. In our contemplation, Carolina and Ohio are parts of the same country; states, united under the same general government, having interests, common, associated, intermingled. In whatever is within the proper sphere of the constitutional power of this government, we look upon the states as one. We do not impose geographical limits to our patriotic feeling or regard; we do not follow rivers and mountains, and lines of latitude, to find boundaries, beyond which public improvements do not benefit us. We who come here, as agents and representatives of these narrow-minded and selfish men of New England, consider ourselves as bound to regard, with equal eye, the good of the whole, in whatever is within our power of legislation....

There yet remains to be performed, Mr. President, by far the most grave and important duty, which I feel to be devolved on me, by this occasion. It is to state, and to defend, what I conceive to be the true principles of the Constitution under which we are here assembled....

I understand the honorable gentleman from South Carolina to maintain, that it is a right of the state legislatures to interfere, whenever, in their judgment, this government transcends its constitutional limits, and to arrest the operation of its laws.

I understand him to maintain this right, as a right existing under the Constitution; not as a right to overthrow it, on the ground of extreme necessity, such as would justify violent revolution.

I understand him to maintain an authority, on the part of the states, thus to interfere, for the purpose of correcting the exercise of power by the general government, of checking it, and of compelling it to conform to their opinion of the extent of its powers.

I understand him to maintain, that the ultimate power of judging of the constitutional extent of its own authority, is not lodged exclusively in the general government, or any branch of it; but that, on the contrary, the states may lawfully decide for themselves, and each state for itself, whether, in a given case, the act of the general government transcends its power.

I understand him to insist, that if the exigency of the case, in the opinion of any state government, require it, such state government may, by its own sovereign authority, annul an act of the general government, which it deems plainly and palpably unconstitutional.

This is the sum of what I understand from him, to be the South Carolina doctrine; and the doctrine which he maintains. I propose to consider it, and to compare it with the Constitution. Allow me to say, as a preliminary remark, that I call this the South Carolina doctrine, only because the gentleman himself has so denominated it. . . .

We, sir, who oppose the Carolina doctrine, do not deny that the people may, if they choose, throw off any government, when it becomes oppressive and intolerable, and erect a better in its stead. We all know that civil institutions are established for the public benefit, and that when they cease to answer the ends of their existence, they may be changed. But I do not understand the doctrine now contended for to be that which, for the sake of distinctness, we may call the right of revolution. I understand the gentleman to maintain, that, without revolution, without civil commotion, without rebellion, a remedy for supposed abuse and transgression of the powers of the general government lies in a direct appeal to the interference of the state governments. . . .

. . . I say, the right of a state to annul a law of Congress, cannot be maintained, but on the ground of the unalienable right of man to resist oppression;

that is to say, upon the ground of revolution. I admit that there is an ultimate violent remedy, above the Constitution, and in defiance of the Constitution, which may be resorted to, when a revolution is to be justified. But I do not admit that, under the Constitution, and in conformity with it, there is any mode in which a state government, as a member of the Union, can interfere and stop the progress of the general government, by force of her own laws, under any circumstances whatever.

This leads us to inquire into the origin of this government, and the source of its power. Whose agent is it? Is it the creature of the state legislatures, or the creature of the people? If the government of the United States be the agent of the state governments, then they may control it, provided they can agree in the manner of controlling it; if it be the agent of the people, then the people alone can control it, restrain it, modify, or reform it. It is observable enough, that the doctrine for which the honorable gentleman contends, leads him to the necessity of maintaining, not only that this general government is the creature of the states, but that it is the creature of each of the states severally; so that each may assert the power, for itself, of determining whether it acts within the limits of its authority. It is the servant of four-and-twenty masters, of different wills and different purposes, and yet bound to obey all. This absurdity (for it seems no less) arises from a misconception as to the origin of this government and its true character. It is, sir, the people's Constitution, the people's government; made for the people; made by the people; and answerable to the people. The people of the United States have declared that this Constitution shall be the Supreme Law....

I must now beg to ask, sir, whence is this supposed right of the states derived?—where do they find the power to interfere with the laws of the Union? Sir, the opinion which the honorable gentleman maintains, is a notion, founded in a total misapprehension, in my judgment, of the origin of this government, and of the foundation on which it stands. I hold it to be a popular government, erected by the people; those who administer it responsible to the people; and itself capable of being amended and modified, just as the people may choose it should be.... This government, sir, is the independent offspring of the popular will. It is not the creature of state Legislatures; nay, more, if the whole truth must be told, the people brought it into existence, established it, and have hitherto supported it, for the very purpose, amongst others, of imposing certain salutary restraints on state sovereignties. The states cannot now make war; they cannot contract alliances; they cannot make, each for itself, separate regulations of commerce;

they cannot lay imposts; they cannot coin money. If this Constitution, sir, be the creature of state Legislatures, it must be admitted that it has obtained a strange control over the volitions of its creators. . . .

Sir, the very chief end, the main design, for which the whole Constitution was framed and adopted, was to establish a government that should not be obliged to act through state agency, or depend on state opinion and state discretion. The people had had quite enough of that kind of government, under the Confederacy. Under that system, the legal action-the application of law to individuals, belonged exclusively to the states. Congress could only recommend-their acts were not of binding force, till the states had adopted and sanctioned them. Are we in that condition still? Are we yet at the mercy of state discretion, and state construction? Sir, if we are, then vain will be our attempt to maintain the Constitution under which we sit. . . .

And now, Mr. President, let me run the honorable gentleman's doctrine a little into its practical application. Let us look at his probable *modus operandi*. . . . Now, I wish to be informed *how* this state interference is to be put in practice, without violence, bloodshed, and rebellion. . . . The militia of the state will be called out to sustain the nullifying act. . . . [Its leader] would have a knot before him, which he could not untie. He must cut it with his sword. He must say to his followers [members of the state militia], defend yourselves with your bayonets; and this is war-civil war. . . .

While the Union lasts, we have high, exciting, gratifying prospects spread out before us, for us and our children. Beyond that I seek not to penetrate the veil. God grant that, in my day, at least, that curtain may not rise. God grant that on my vision never may be opened what lies behind. When my eyes shall be turned to behold, for the last time, the sun in Heaven, may I not see him shining on the broken and dishonored fragments of a once glorious Union; on states dissevered, discordant, belligerent; on a land rent with civil feuds, or drenched, it may be, in fraternal blood! Let their last feeble and lingering glance, rather behold the gorgeous Ensign of the Republic, now known and honored throughout the earth, still full high advanced, its arms and trophies streaming in their original luster, not a stripe erased or polluted, nor a single star obscured-bearing for its motto, no such miserable interrogatory as, what is all this worth? Nor those other words of delusion and folly, liberty first, and union afterwards-but everywhere, spread all over in characters of living light, blazing on all its ample folds, as they float over the sea and over the land, and in every wind under the whole Heavens, that other sentiment, dear to every true American heart-liberty and union, now and forever, one and inseparable!

Mr. Hayne having rejoined to Mr. Webster, especially on the constitutional question-

Mr. Webster arose, and, in conclusion, said: A few words, Mr. President on this constitutional argument, which the honorable gentleman has labored to reconstruct....

When the gentleman says the Constitution is a compact between the states, he uses language exactly applicable to the old Confederation. He speaks as if he were in Congress before 1789. He describes fully that old state of things then existing. The Confederation was, in strictness, a compact; the states, as states, were parties to it. We had no other general government. But that was found insufficient, and inadequate to the public exigencies. The people were not satisfied with it, and undertook to establish a better. They undertook to form a general government, which should stand on a new basis-not a confederacy, not a league, not a compact between states, but a Constitution; a popular government, founded in popular election, directly responsible to the people themselves, and divided into branches, with prescribed limits of power, and prescribed duties. They ordained such a government; they gave it the name of a Constitution, and therein they established a distribution of powers between this, their general government, and their several state governments. When they shall become dissatisfied with this distribution, they can alter it. Their own power over their own instrument remains. But until they shall alter it, it must stand as their will, and is equally binding on the general government and on the states...

Finally, sir, the honorable gentleman says, that the states will only interfere, by their power, to preserve the Constitution. They will not destroy it, they will not impair it-they will only save, they will only preserve, they will only strengthen it! Ah! sir, this is but the old story. All regulated governments, all free governments, have been broken up by similar disinterested and well-disposed interference! It is the common pretense. But I take leave of the subject.

Speech of Senator Robert Y. Hayne of South Carolina, January 27, 1830

... The gentleman insists that the states have no right to decide whether the constitution has been violated by acts of Congress or not,-but that the federal government is the exclusive judge of the extent of its own powers; and that in case of a violation of the constitution, however "deliberate, palpable and dangerous," a state has no constitutional redress, except where the matter can be brought before the Supreme Court, whose decision must be final and conclusive on the subject. Having thus distinctly stated the points in dispute between the gentleman and myself, I proceed to examine them.

And here it will be necessary to go back to the origin of the federal government. It cannot be doubted, and is not denied, that before the formation of the constitution, each state was an independent sovereignty, possessing all the rights and powers appertaining to independent nations; nor can it be denied that, after the Constitution was formed, they remained equally sovereign and independent, as to all powers, not expressly delegated to the federal government. This would have been the case even if no positive provision to that effect had been inserted in that instrument. But to remove all doubt it is expressly declared, by the 10th article of the amendment of the Constitution, "that the powers not delegated to the states, by the Constitution, nor prohibited by it to the states, are reserved to the states respectively, or to the people."...

The whole form and structure of the federal government, the opinions of the Framers of the Constitution, and the organization of the state governments, demonstrate that though the states have surrendered certain specific powers, they have not surrendered their sovereignty....

No doubt can exist, that, before the states entered into the compact, they possessed the right to the fullest extent, of determining the limits of their own powers-it is incident to all sovereignty. Now, have they given away that right, or agreed to limit or restrict it in any respect? Assuredly not. They have agreed, that certain specific powers shall be exercised by the federal government; but the moment that government steps beyond the limits of its charter, the right of the states "to interpose for arresting the progress of the evil, and for maintaining within their respective limits the authorities, rights, and liberties, appertaining to them,"[7] is as full and complete as it was before the Constitution was formed. It was plenary then, and never having been surrendered, must be plenary now....

But the gentleman apprehends that this will "make the Union a rope of sand." Sir, I have shown that it is a power indispensably necessary to the preservation of the constitutional rights of the states, and of the people. I

[7] Hayne quotes from the Virginia Resolution (1798), authored by James Madison, to protest the Alien and Sedition Acts (1798). The Virginia Resolution asserted that when the federal government undertook the "deliberate, palpable, and dangerous exercise of" powers not granted to it in the constitution, states had the right and duty to interpose their authority to prevent this evil.

now proceed to show that it is perfectly safe, and will practically have no effect but to keep the federal government within the limits of the Constitution, and prevent those unwarrantable assumptions of power, which cannot fail to impair the rights of the states, and finally destroy the Union itself....

A state will be restrained by a sincere love of the Union. The people of the United States cherish a devotion to the Union, so pure, so ardent, that nothing short of intolerable oppression, can ever tempt them to do anything that may possibly endanger it. Sir, there exists, moreover, a deep and settled conviction of the benefits, which result from a close connection of all the states, for purposes of mutual protection and defense. This will co-operate with the feelings of patriotism to induce a state to avoid any measures calculated to endanger that connection....

The gentleman has made an eloquent appeal to our hearts in favor of union. Sir, I cordially respond to that appeal. I will yield to no gentleman here in sincere attachment to the Union,-but it is a Union founded on the Constitution, and not such a Union as that gentleman would give us, that is dear to my heart. If this is to become one great "consolidated government," swallowing up the rights of the states, and the liberties of the citizen, "riding and ruling over the plundered ploughman, and beggared yeomanry,"[8] the Union will not be worth preserving. Sir, it is because South Carolina loves the Union, and would preserve it forever, that she is opposing now, while there is hope, those usurpations of the federal government, which, once established, will, sooner or later, tear this Union into fragments....

[8] Hayne quotes from Thomas Jefferson to William Branch Giles, December 26, 1825, https://teachingamericanhistory.org/library/document/letter-to-william-branch-giles/?_sft_document_author=thomas-jefferson.

DOCUMENT 5

"On the Constitution and the Union"

William Lloyd Garrison

December 29, 1832

William Lloyd Garrison was a world-renowned abolitionist and founding editor of The Liberator, *a popular anti-slavery Boston newspaper. Begun in 1831,* The Liberator's *uncompromising stance in favor of immediate emancipation for all slaves quickly earned Garrison the reputation, especially in the South, as a dangerous fanatic and agitator. Using the newspaper as his personal soapbox, Garrison denounced not only slavery but everyone and everything that supported it, including the U.S. Constitution and the American Union. The Constitution, Garrison believed, was a pact with the devil that ought to be immediately discarded for its unjust and unnecessary compromises with slavery. The Union was similarly tainted by the presence of slavery in the South and was not worth saving, so long as slavery continued to exist. Garrison's firebrand abolitionism propelled him to the forefront of the anti-slavery movement thirty years before the Civil War, a position he would continue to occupy until the passage of the Thirteenth Amendment in 1865.*

SOURCE: William Lloyd Garrison, "The Great Crisis," *The Liberator*, 52, 2 (December 29, 1832), 206–207.

... There is much declamation about the sacredness of the compact which was formed between the free and slave states, on the adoption of the Constitution. A sacred compact, forsooth! We pronounce it the most bloody and heaven-daring arrangement ever made by men for the continuance and protection of a system of the most atrocious villainy ever exhibited on earth. Yes-we recognize the compact, but with feelings of shame and indignation; and it will be held in everlasting infamy by the friends of justice and humanity throughout the world. It was a compact formed at the sacrifice of the bodies and souls of millions of our race, for the sake of achieving a political object-an unblushing and monstrous coalition to do evil that good might come. Such a compact was, in the nature of things and according to the law of God, null and void from the beginning. No body of men ever had the right to guarantee the holding of human beings in bondage. Who or what were the framers of our government, that they should dare confirm and authorize such high-handed villainy-such a flagrant robbery of the inalienable rights of man-such a glaring violation of all the precepts and injunctions of the gospel-such a savage war upon a sixth part of our whole population? -They were men, like ourselves-as fallible, as sinful, as weak, as ourselves. By the infamous bargain which they made between themselves, they virtually dethroned the Most High God, and trampled beneath their feet their own solemn and heaven-attested Declaration, that all men are created equal, and endowed by their Creator with certain inalienable rights-among which are life, liberty, and the pursuit of happiness. They had no lawful power to bind themselves, or their posterity, for one hour-for one moment-by such an unholy alliance. It was not valid then-it is not valid now. Still they persisted in maintaining it-and still do their successors, the people of Massachusetts, of New England, and of the twelve free states, persist in maintaining it. A sacred compact! a sacred compact! What, then, is wicked and ignominious?

This, then, is the relation in which we of New England stand to the holders of slaves at the south, and this is virtually our language toward them-"Go on, most worthy associates, from day to day, from month to month, from year to year, from generation to generation, plundering two millions of human beings of their liberty and the fruits of their toil-driving them into the fields like cattle-starving and lacerating their bodies-selling the husband from his wife, the wife from her husband, and children from their parents-spilling their blood-withholding the Bible from their hands and all knowledge from their minds-and kidnapping annually sixty thousand infants, the offspring of pollution and shame! Go on, in these practices-we do not wish nor mean to interfere, for the rescue of your victims, even by expostulation or warning-we like your company too well to offend you by denouncing your conduct-although we know that by every principle of law which does not utterly disgrace us by assimilating us to pirates, that they have as good and as true a right to the equal protection of the law as we have; and although we ourselves stand prepared to die, rather than submit even to a fragment of the intolerable load of oppression to which we are subjecting them-yet, never mind-let that be-they have grown old in suffering and we in iniquity-and we have nothing to do now but to speak peace, peace, to one another in our sins. We are too wicked ever to love them as God commands us to do-we are so resolute in our wickedness as not even to desire to do so-and we are so proud in our iniquity that we will hate and revile whoever disturbs us in it. We want, like the devils of old, to be let alone in our sin. We are unalterably determined, and neither God nor man shall move us from this resolution, that our colored fellow subjects never shall be free or happy in their native land. Go on, from bad to worse iniquity-add link to link to the chains upon the bodies of your victims-add constantly to the intolerable burdens under which they groan-and if, goaded to desperation by your cruelties; they should rise to assert their rights and redress their wrongs, fear nothing-we are pledged, by a sacred compact, to shoot them like dogs and rescue you from their vengeance! Go on-we never will forsake you, for "there is honor among thieves"- our swords are ready to leap from their scabbards, and our muskets to pour forth deadly volleys, as soon as you are in danger. We pledge you our physical strength, by the sacredness of the national compact-a compact by which we have enabled you already to plunder, persecute and destroy two millions of slaves, who now lie beneath the sod; and by which we now give you the same piratical license to prey upon a much larger number of victims and all their posterity. Go on-and by this sacred instrument, the Constitution of the United States, dripping as it is with human blood, we solemnly pledge you our lives, our fortunes, and our sacred honor, that we will stand by you to the last."

People of New England, and of the free states! Is it true that slavery is no concern of yours? Have you no right even to protest against it, or to seek its removal? Are you not the main pillars of its support? How long do you mean to be answerable to God and the world, for spilling the blood of the poor innocents? Be not afraid to look the monster slavery boldly in the face. He is your implacable foe-the vampire who is sucking your life-blood-the ravager of a large portion of your country, and the enemy of God and man. Never hope to be a united, or happy, or prosperous people while he exists. He has an appetite like the grave-a spirit as malignant as that of the bottomless pit-and an influence as dreadful as the corruption of death. Awake to your danger! The struggle is a mighty one-it cannot be avoided-it should not be, if it could.

It is said that if you agitate this question, you will divide the Union. Believe it not; but should disunion follow, the fault will not be yours. You must perform your duty, faithfully, fearlessly and promptly, and leave the consequences to God: that duty clearly is, to cease from giving countenance and protection to southern kidnappers. Let them separate, if they can muster courage enough-and the liberation of their slaves is certain. Be assured that slavery will very speedily destroy this Union, if it be let alone; but even if the

Union can be preserved by treading upon the necks, spilling the blood, and destroying the souls of millions of your race, we say it is not worth a price like this, and that it is in the highest degree criminal for you to continue the present compact. Let the pillars thereof fall-let the superstructure crumble into dust-if it must be upheld by robbery and oppression.

DOCUMENT 6

Speech on Abolition Petitions

John C. Calhoun

February 6, 1837

Perhaps more than those of any other American political figure, the beliefs of John C. Calhoun (1782–1850) significantly influenced the South's secession from the Union. Although he spent most of his career as a Congressman and Senator from South Carolina, Calhoun also served as Secretary of State, Secretary of War, and Vice President of the United States. By the late-1830s, the American Founding generation was dead and gone. It was also a time when the U.S. Congress was inundated with a rush of anti-slavery petitions from many Northern abolitionist groups demanding the prohibition or restriction of slavery. There had been about 700,000 slaves in the United States in 1790. By 1830, there were over two million. Calhoun, one-third of the Senate's "Great Triumvirate" that also included Henry Clay and Daniel Webster, spoke out against what he believed to be unwarranted encroachments by the Congress on slavery, the regulation of which was a right belonging only to the states. It was in the course of this speech that Calhoun first expressed the idea that slavery was a "positive good," an unrecognizable thesis to the American Founders (Document 1), yet one that would come to characterize the moral and political opinion of the next generation of southerners.

SOURCE: John C. Calhoun, *Speeches of John C. Calhoun: delivered in the Congress of the United States from 1811 to the present time* (New York: Harper's and Brothers, 1843), 222–226, https://archive.org/stream/speechesofjohnccooincalh#page/222/mode/2up.

. . . I do not belong, said Mr. Calhoun, to the school which holds that aggression is to be met by concession. Mine is the opposite creed, which teaches that encroachments must be met at the beginning, and that those who act on the opposite principle are prepared to become slaves. In this case, in particular I hold concession or compromise to be fatal. If we concede an inch, concession would follow concession-compromise would follow compromise, until our ranks would be so broken that effectual resistance would be impossible. We must meet the enemy on the frontier, with a fixed determination of maintaining our position at every hazard. Consent to receive these insulting petitions, and the next demand will be that they be referred to a committee in order that they may be deliberated and acted upon. At the last session we were modestly asked to receive them, simply to lay them on the table, without any view to ulterior action. . . . I then said, that the next step would be to refer the petition to a committee, and I already see indications that such is now the intention. If we yield, that will be followed by another, and we will thus proceed, step by step, to the final consummation of the object of these petitions. We are now told that the most effectual mode of arresting the progress of abolition is to reason it down; and with this view it is urged that the petitions ought to be referred to a committee. That is the very ground which was taken at the last session in the other House, but instead of arresting its progress it has since advanced more rapidly than ever. The most unquestionable right may be rendered doubtful, if once admitted to be a subject of controversy, and that would be the case in the present instance. The subject is beyond the jurisdiction of Congress-they have no right to touch it in any shape or form, or to make it the subject of deliberation or discussion. . . .

As widely as this incendiary spirit has spread, it has not yet infected this body, or the great mass of the intelligent and business portion of the North; but unless it be speedily stopped, it will spread and work upwards till it brings the two great sections of the Union into deadly conflict. This is not a new impression with me. Several years since, in a discussion with one of the senators from Massachusetts (Mr. Webster),[1] before this fell spirit had showed itself, I then predicted that the doctrine of the proclamation and the Force Bill[2]-that this government had a right, in the last resort, to determine the extent of its own powers, and enforce its decision at the point of the bayonet, which was so warmly maintained by that senator, would at no distant day arouse the dormant spirit of abolitionism. I told him that the doctrine was tantamount to the assumption of unlimited power on the part of the government, and that such would be the impression on the public mind in a large portion of the Union. The consequence would be inevitable. A large portion of the Northern states believed slavery to be a sin, and would consider it as an obligation of conscience to abolish it if they should feel themselves in

[1] See Document 4.

[2] "An Act Further to Provide for the Collection of Duties on Imports" (1833), was a law passed by the U.S. Congress during the Nullification Crisis when in response to tariffs it found unfavorable to its interests, South Carolina declared its right to nullify a federal law.

any degree responsible for its continuance, and that this doctrine would necessarily lead to the belief of such responsibility. I then predicted that it would commence as it has with this fanatical portion of society, and that they would begin their operations on the ignorant, the weak, the young, and the thoughtless-and gradually extend upwards till they would become strong enough to obtain political control, when he and others holding the highest stations in society, would, however reluctant, be compelled to yield to their doctrines, or be driven into obscurity. But four years have since elapsed, and all this is already in a course of regular fulfilment.

Standing at the point of time at which we have now arrived, it will not be more difficult to trace the course of future events now than it was then. They who imagine that the spirit now abroad in the North, will die away of itself without a shock or convulsion, have formed a very inadequate conception of its real character; it will continue to rise and spread, unless prompt and efficient measures to stay its progress be adopted. Already it has taken possession of the pulpit, of the schools, and, to a considerable extent, of the press; those great instruments by which the mind of the rising generation will be formed.

However sound the great body of the non-slaveholding states are at present, in the course of a few years they will be succeeded by those who will have been taught to hate the people and institutions of nearly one-half of this Union, with a hatred deadlier than one hostile nation ever entertained towards another. It is easy to see the end. By the necessary course of events, if left to themselves, we must become, finally, two people. It is impossible under the deadly hatred which must spring up between the two great nations, if the present causes are permitted to operate unchecked, that we should continue under the same political system. The conflicting elements would burst the Union asunder, powerful as are the links which hold it together. Abolition and the Union cannot coexist. As the friend of the Union I openly proclaim it-and the sooner it is known the better. The former may now be controlled, but in a short time it will be beyond the power of man to arrest the course of events. We of the South will not, cannot, surrender our institutions. To maintain the existing relations between the two races, inhabiting that section of the Union, is indispensable to the peace and happiness of both. It cannot be subverted without drenching the country in blood, and extirpating one or the other of the races. Be it good or bad, [slavery] has grown up with our society and institutions, and is so interwoven with them that to destroy it would be to destroy us as a people. But let me not be understood as admitting, even by implication, that the existing relations between the two races in the slaveholding states is an evil: far otherwise; I hold it to be a good, as it has thus far proved itself to be to both, and will continue to prove so if not disturbed by the fell spirit of abolition. I appeal to facts. Never before has the black race of central Africa, from the dawn of history to the present day, attained a condition so civilized and so improved, not only physically, but morally and intellectually. . . .

In the meantime, the white or European race, has not degenerated. It has kept pace with its brethren in other sections of the Union where slavery does not exist. It is odious to make comparison; but I appeal to all sides whether the South is not equal in virtue, intelligence, patriotism, courage, disinterestedness, and all the high qualities which adorn our nature. . . .

But I take higher ground. I hold that in the present state of civilization, where two races of different origin, and distinguished by color, and other physical differences, as well as intellectual, are brought together, the relation now existing in the slaveholding states between the two, is, instead of an evil, a good-a positive good. I feel myself called upon to speak freely upon the subject where the honor and interests of those I represent are involved. I hold then, that there never has yet existed a wealthy and civilized society in which one portion of the community did not, in point of fact, live on the labor of the other. . . . I may say with truth, that in few countries so much is left to the share of the laborer, and so little exacted from him, or where there is more kind attention paid to him in sickness or infirmities of age. Compare his condition with the tenants of the poor houses in the more civilized portions of Europe-look at the sick, and the old and infirm slave, on one hand, in the midst of his family and friends, under the kind superintending care of his master and mistress, and compare it with the forlorn and wretched condition of the pauper in the poorhouse. But I will not dwell on this aspect of the question; I turn to the political; and here I fearlessly assert that the existing relation between the two races in the South, against which these blind fanatics are waging war, forms the most solid and durable foundation on which to rear free and stable political institutions. It is useless to disguise the fact. There is and always has been in an advanced stage of wealth and civilization, a conflict between labor and capital. The condition of society in the South exempts us from the disorders and dangers resulting from this conflict; and which explains why it is that the political condition of the slaveholding states has been so much more stable and quieter than that of the North. . . .

Surrounded as the slaveholding states are with such imminent perils, I rejoice to think that our means of defense are ample, if we shall prove to have the intelligence and spirit to see and apply them before it is too late. All we want is concert,[3] to lay aside all party differences and unite with zeal and energy in repelling approaching dangers. Let there be concert of action, and we shall find ample means of security without resorting to secession or disunion. I speak with full knowledge and a thorough examination of the subject, and for one see my way clearly. . . . I dare not hope that anything I can say will arouse the South to a due sense of danger; I fear it is beyond the power of mortal voice to awaken it in time from the fatal security into which it has fallen.

[3] agreement or harmony

DOCUMENT 7

Speech on the Oregon Bill

John C. Calhoun

June 27, 1848

Shortly before his death in 1850, John C. Calhoun (b.1782) delivered what was to be one of his last major speeches in the U.S. Senate. The subject was the Oregon Bill, which organized the territory of Oregon on anti-slavery principles. Calhoun argued against the bill on the grounds that, because the territories are the property of all the states, any attempt by a Northern majority to deprive the Southern minority of the right to emigrate, with their slaves, into the territory violated the doctrine of states' rights. The argument was consistent with Calhoun's longstanding view that states were equal in sovereignty to the federal government and therefore had the right to nullify federal laws and leave the Union, if a majority of states sought to deprive a state of any of its rights. In this speech, Calhoun made clear that the basis of his states rights' position was a rejection of the claim in the Declaration of Independence that all men are equal. Less than a decade after Calhoun's Oregon Bill speech, the Supreme Court in the 1857 Dred Scott case (Document 14) essentially endorsed Calhoun's thesis that the right of property in a slave is affirmed in the Constitution and that Congress cannot lawfully prohibit slavery in the territories.

SOURCE: *Speech of Mr. Calhoun, of South Carolina, on the Oregon Bill, Delivered in the Senate of the United States, June 27, 1848,* (Washington, D.C.: Towers printer, 1848), https://babel.hathitrust.org/cgi/pt?id=yale.39002087601150;view=1up;seq=1.

... The first question which offers itself for consideration is: Have the Northern states the power which they claim, to prevent the Southern people from emigrating freely, with their property, into territories belonging to the United States, and to monopolize them for their exclusive benefit? ...

Now, I put the question solemnly to the senators from the North: Can you rightly and justly exclude the South from territories of the United States, and monopolize them for yourselves, even if, in your opinion, you should have the power? It is this question I wish to press on your attention with all due solemnity and decorum. The North and the South stand in the relation of partners in a common Union, with equal dignity and equal rights. We of the South have contributed our full share of funds, and shed our full share of blood for the acquisition of our territories. Can you, then, on any principle of equity and justice, deprive us of our full share in their benefit and advantage? Are you ready to affirm that a majority of the partners in a joint concern have the right to monopolize its benefits to the exclusion of the minority, even in cases where they have contributed their full share to the concern? . . .

I turn now to my friends of the South, and ask: What are you prepared to do? If neither the barriers of the Constitution nor the high sense of right and justice should prove sufficient to protect you, are you prepared to sink down into a state of acknowledged inferiority; to be stripped of your dignity of equals among equals, and be deprived of your equality of rights in this federal partnership of states? If so, you are woefully degenerated from your sires, and will well deserve to change condition with your slaves; but if not, prepare to meet the issue. The time is at hand, if the question should not be speedily settled, when the South must rise up, and bravely defend herself, or sink down into base and acknowledged inferiority. . . . At no other period could the two great parties into which the country is divided be made to see and feel so clearly and intensely the embarrassment and danger caused by the question. Indeed, they must be blind not to perceive that there is a power in action that must burst asunder the ties that bind them together, strong as they are, unless it should be speedily settled. Now is the time, if ever. Cast your eyes to the North, and mark what is going on there; reflect on the tendency of events for the last three years in reference to this the most vital of all questions, and you must see that no time should be lost. . . .

. . . I have believed, from the beginning, that this was the only question sufficiently potent to dissolve the Union, and subvert our system of government; and that the sooner it was met and settled, the safer and better for all. I have never doubted but that, if permitted to progress beyond a certain point, its settlement would become impossible, and am under deep conviction that it is now rapidly approaching it-and that if it is ever to be averted, it must be done speedily. In uttering these opinions I look to the whole. If I speak earnestly, it is to save and protect all. As deep as is the stake of the South in the Union and our political institutions, it is not deeper than that of the North. We shall be as well prepared and as capable of meeting whatever may come, as you.

Now, let me say, senators, if our Union and system of government are doomed to perish, and we to share the fate of so many great people who have gone before us, the historian, who, in some future day, may record the events ending in so calamitous a result, will devote his first chapter to the ordinance of 1787,[1] lauded as it and its authors have been, as the first of that series which led to it. His next chapter will be devoted to the Missouri Compromise,[2] and the next to the present agitation. Whether there will be another beyond, I know not. It will depend on what we may do.

If he should possess a philosophical turn of mind, and be disposed to look to more remote and recondite causes, he will trace it to a proposition which originated in a hypothetical truism, but which, as now expressed and now understood, is the most false and dangerous of all political errors. The proposition to which I allude, has become an axiom in the minds of a vast majority on both sides of the Atlantic, and is repeated daily from tongue to tongue, as an established and incontrovertible truth; it is, that "all men are born free and equal."[3] I am not afraid to attack error, however deeply it may be entrenched, or however widely extended, whenever it becomes my duty to do so, as I believe it to be on this subject and occasion.

Taking the proposition literally (it is in that sense it is understood), there is not a word of truth in it. It begins with "all men are born," which is utterly untrue. Men are not born. Infants are born. They grow to be men. And concludes with asserting that they are born "free and equal," which is not less false. They are not born free. While infants they are incapable of freedom, being destitute alike of the capacity of thinking and acting, without which there can be no freedom. Besides, they are necessarily born subject to their parents, and remain so among all people, savage and civilized, until the development of their intellect and physical capacity enables them to take care of themselves. They grow to all the freedom of which the condition in which they were born permits, by growing to be men. Nor is it less false that they are born "equal." They are not so in any sense in which it can be regarded; and thus, as I have asserted, there is not a word of truth in the whole proposition, as expressed and generally understood.

If we trace it back, we shall find the proposition differently expressed in the Declaration of Independence. That asserts that "all men are created equal." The form of expression, though less dangerous, is not less erroneous. All men

---

[1] The Northwest Ordinance, which prohibited slavery in the territory north and west of the Ohio River. The following states came from this territory: Ohio (1803), Indiana (1816), Illinois (1818), Michigan (1837), Wisconsin (1848), and Minnesota (1858).

[2] Documents 1–3

[3] Quoted from the Massachusetts Declaration of Rights (1780).

are not created. According to the Bible, only two, a man and a woman, ever were, and of these one was pronounced subordinate to the other. All others have come into the world by being born, and in no sense, as I have shown, either free or equal. But this form of expression being less striking and popular, has given way to the present, and under the authority of a document put forth on so great an occasion, and leading to such important consequences, has spread far and wide, and fixed itself deeply in the public mind. It was inserted in our Declaration of Independence without any necessity. It made no necessary part of our justification in separating from the parent country, and declaring ourselves independent. Breach of our chartered privileges, and lawless encroachment on our acknowledged and well-established rights by the parent country, were the real causes, and of themselves sufficient, without resorting to any other, to justify the step. Nor had it any weight in constructing the governments which were substituted in the place of the colonial. They were formed of the old materials and on practical and well-established principles, borrowed for the most part from our own experience and that of the country from which we sprang.

If the proposition be traced still further back, it will be found to have been adopted from certain writers on government who had attained much celebrity in the early settlement of these states, and with whose writings all the prominent actors in our revolution were familiar. Among these, [John] Locke and [Algernon] Sydney[4] were prominent. But they expressed it very differently. According to their expression, "all men in the state of nature were free and equal." . . .

. . . But it is equally clear, that man cannot exist in such a state; that he is by nature social, and that society is necessary, not only to the proper development of all his faculties, moral and intellectual, but to the very existence of his race. Such being the case, the state is a purely hypothetical one; and when we say all men are free and equal in it, we announce a mere hypothetical truism; that is, a truism resting on a mere supposition that cannot exist, and of course one of little or no practical value.

But to call it a state of nature was a great misnomer, and has led to

---

[4] John Locke (1632–1704) was a philosopher. Algernon Sydney (1623–1683) was a politician and political writer, who defended republicanism. Jefferson cited Locke and Sydney, as well as Aristotle and Cicero, as authors who expressed "the harmonizing sentiments" that he had captured in the Declaration of Independence. Jefferson to Henry Lee, May 8, 1825, https://teachingamericanhistory.org/library/document/letter-to-henry-lee/.

dangerous errors; for that cannot justly be called a state of nature which is so opposed to the constitution of man as to be inconsistent with the existence of his race and the development of the high faculties, mental and moral, with which he is endowed by his Creator.

Nor is the social state of itself his natural state; for society can no more exist without government, in one form or another, than man without society. It is the political, then, which includes the social, that is his natural state. It is the one for which his Creator formed him, into which he is impelled irresistibly, and in which only his race can exist and all its faculties be fully developed.

Such being the case, it follows that any, the worst form of government, is better than anarchy; and that individual liberty, or freedom, must be subordinate to whatever power may be necessary to protect society against anarchy within or destruction from without; for the safety and well-being of society is as paramount to individual liberty, as the safety and well-being of the race is to that of individuals; and in the same proportion, the power necessary for the safety of society is paramount to individual liberty. On the contrary, government has no right to control individual liberty beyond what is necessary to the safety and well-being of society. Such is the boundary which separates the power of government and the liberty of the citizen or subject in the political state, which, as I have shown, is the natural state of man-the only one in which his race can exist, and the one in which he is born, lives, and dies.

It follows from all this that the quantum of power on the part of the government, and of liberty on that of individuals, instead of being equal in all cases, must necessarily be very unequal among different people, according to their different conditions. For just in proportion as a people are ignorant, stupid, debased, corrupt, exposed to violence within and danger from without, the power necessary for government to possess, in order to preserve society against anarchy and destruction becomes greater and greater, and individual liberty less and less, until the lowest condition is reached, when absolute and despotic power becomes necessary on the part of the government, and individual liberty extinct. So, on the contrary, just as a people rise in the scale of intelligence, virtue, and patriotism, and the more perfectly they become acquainted with the nature of government, the ends for which it was ordered, and how it ought to be administered, and the less the tendency to violence and disorder within, and danger from abroad, the power necessary for government becomes less and less, and individual liberty greater and greater. Instead, then, of all men having the same right to liberty and equality, as is claimed by those who hold that they are all born free and equal, liberty is the noble and highest reward bestowed on mental and moral development, combined with favorable circumstances. Instead, then, of liberty and equality being born with man; instead of all men and all classes and descriptions being equally entitled to them, they are high prizes to be won, and are in their most perfect state, not only the highest reward that can be bestowed on our race, but the most difficult to be won-and when won, the most difficult to be preserved.

They have been made vastly more so by the dangerous error I have attempted to expose, that all men are born free and equal, as if those high qualities belonged to man without effort to acquire them, and to all equally alike, regardless of their intellectual and moral condition. The attempt to carry into practice this, the most dangerous of all political error, and to bestow on all, without regard to their fitness either to acquire or maintain liberty, that unbounded and individual liberty supposed to belong to man in the hypothetical and misnamed state of nature, has done more to retard the cause of liberty and civilization, and is doing more at present, than all other causes combined. While it is powerful to pull down governments, it is still more powerful to prevent their construction on proper principles. It is the leading cause among those which have placed Europe in its present anarchical condition, and which mainly stands in the way of reconstructing good governments in the place of those which have been overthrown, threatening thereby the quarter of the globe most advanced in progress and civilization with hopeless anarchy, to be followed by military despotism. Nor are we exempt from its disorganizing effects. We now begin to experience the danger of admitting so great an error to have a place in the declaration of our independence. For a long time it lay dormant; but in the process of time it began to germinate, and produce its poisonous fruits. It had strong hold on the mind of Mr. Jefferson, the author of that document, which caused him to take an utterly false view of the subordinate relation of the black to the white race in the South; and to hold, in consequence, that the former, though utterly unqualified to possess liberty, were as fully entitled to both liberty and equality as the latter; and that to deprive them of it was unjust and immoral. To this error, his proposition to exclude slavery from the territory northwest of the Ohio may be traced, and to that the ordinance of '87, and through it the deep and dangerous agitation which now threatens to engulf, and will certainly engulf, if not speedily settled, our political institutions, and involve the country in countless woes.

DOCUMENT 8

Compromise of 1850

Henry Clay

January 29, 1850

As a consequence of the war with Mexico (1846–1848), the United States gained a large territory in the Southwest, now comprising the states of California, Nevada, Arizona, Utah, and parts of Wyoming, New Mexico, and Colorado. The question immediately arose as to whether the organization of this territory would permit slavery. In addition, the discovery of gold in California (1848) led to a rush of people to the gold fields and its subsequent request to enter the Union as a free state. At the same time, southerners complained that Northern states were interfering, in violation of the Constitution (Article IV, section 2) and federal law, with the recovery of slaves who escaped to their jurisdiction. Finally, those opposed to slavery were particularly disturbed by its existence in the nation's capital and campaigned for its abolition there. And, of course, the slave population had continued to grow. In 1830, there had been just over 2 million. In 1850, there were over 3 million. By 1850, these various conflicts created by the presence and continued growth of slavery threatened the existence of the Union.

Faced with this crisis, Whig Senator Henry Clay (1777–1852) proposed a compromise, as he had done 30 years before during the Missouri Crisis (Documents 1 and 2). On January 29, 1850, Clay rose in the Senate to offer a series of resolutions, reproduced here, addressing the issues dividing the country. The resolutions became a set of five laws passed by Congress in 1850, with the assistance of first-term Democrat Senator Stephen A. Douglas of Illinois (Documents 11 and 18). Together, the laws are referred to as the Compromise of 1850. The Compromise succeeded in quelling sectional conflict. Both pro- and anti-slavery factions yielded something to the other. California was admitted as a free state while Congress remained silent on the question of slavery in the Utah and New Mexico territories. Texas was reorganized with its present boundaries, and the slave trade (but not slavery itself) was abolished in the District of Columbia. The South also got a stricter fugitive slave law. Clay-always "the man for a crisis," as Abraham Lincoln called him-died two years after the Compromise of 1850, before sectional conflict ignited again one final time.

SOURCE: *Congressional Globe*, 31st Congress, 1st Session, 244–47, https://memory.loc.gov/cgi-bin/ampage?collId=llcg&fileName=022/llcg022.db&recNum=331. Clay presented his resolutions in a speech. We reprint here only the text of the resolutions.

It being desirable, for the peace, concord, and harmony of the Union of these states, to settle and adjust amicably all existing questions of controversy between them arising out of the institution of slavery upon a fair, equitable and just basis: therefore,

Resolved, that California, with suitable boundaries, ought, upon her application to be admitted as one of the states of this Union, without the imposition by Congress of any restriction in respect to the exclusion or introduction of slavery within those boundaries.

Resolved, that as slavery does not exist by law, and is not likely to be introduced into any of the territory acquired by the United States from the republic of Mexico, it is inexpedient for Congress to provide by law either for its introduction into, or exclusion from, any part of the said territory; and that appropriate territorial governments ought to be established by Congress in all of the said territory, not assigned as the boundaries of the proposed state of California, without the adoption of any restriction or condition on the subject of slavery.

Resolved, that the western boundary of the state of Texas[1] ought to be fixed on the Rio del Norte, commencing one marine league from its mouth, and running up that river to the southern line of New Mexico; thence with that line eastwardly, and so continuing in the same direction to the line as established between the United States and Spain, excluding any portion of New Mexico, whether lying on the east or west of that river.

Resolved, that it be proposed to the state of Texas, that the United States

---

[1] The two resolutions dealing with the state of Texas were only indirectly related to slavery. Texas had claims to territory to its west that the United States won from Mexico in 1848. Organizing that territory did have a direct connection to the slavery issue, but the territory could not be organized without settling the claims of Texas, which joined the Union in 1845, after seceding from Mexico. Clay's resolutions addressed the Texas border issue, resolving it with a compromise within the broader compromise: Texas gave up its claims on the western territory in exchange for some help paying the debts it had incurred freeing itself from Mexico. To support this compromise, Clay argued that in accepting Texas into the Union, the United States had accepted responsibility for its debts.

will provide for the payment of all that portion of the legitimate and bona fide public debt of that state contracted prior to its annexation to the United States, and for which the duties on foreign imports were pledged by the said state to its creditors, not exceeding the sum of ______ dollars, in consideration of the said duties so pledged having been no longer applicable to that object after the said annexation, but having thenceforward become payable to the United States; and upon the condition, also, that the said state of Texas shall, by some solemn and authentic act of her legislature or of a convention, relinquish to the United States any claim which it has to any part of New Mexico.

Resolved, that it is inexpedient to abolish slavery in the District of Columbia whilst that institution continues to exist in the state of Maryland, without the consent of that state, without the consent of the people of the District, and without just compensation to the owners of slaves within the District.

But, resolved, that it is expedient to prohibit, within the District, the slave trade in slaves brought into it from states or places beyond the limits of the District, either to be sold therein as merchandise, or to be transported to other markets without the District of Columbia.

Resolved, that more effectual provision ought to be made by law, according to the requirement of the Constitution, for the restitution and delivery of persons bound to service or labor in any state, who may escape into any other state or territory in the Union. And,

Resolved, that Congress has no power to promote or obstruct the trade in slaves between the slaveholding states; but that the admission or exclusion of slaves brought from one into another of them, depends exclusively upon their own particular laws.

DOCUMENT 9

"What to the Slave Is the Fourth of July?"

Frederick Douglass

July 5, 1852

Frederick Douglass (c. 1818–1895) was born a slave. As a child, he received some instruction, but largely taught himself to read. After escaping to freedom in the North, Douglass quickly became a renowned orator and fierce critic of slavery in abolitionist circles. Douglass delivered this speech to the Ladies' Anti-Slavery Society of Rochester, New York on the meaning and significance of the Fourth of July to the slave. Speaking on July 5, the day after Independence Day (something Douglass had insisted upon), and before a predominantly white audience, Douglass eloquently explained why the Fourth of July was not a holiday celebrated by slaves, former slaves, or their descendants. Instead, Douglass explained that the day was a time of mourning to the slave who was constantly reminded of the unfulfilled promises of liberty and equality from the Declaration of Independence.

The speech shows the moral outrage that powered the abolition movement and made it so threatening to Southern slave holders, but also to anyone willing to tolerate or ignore slavery. (In this speech, for example, Douglass excoriated America's churches.) Of course, others besides abolitionists considered slavery a great moral and political evil (Documents 12, 19, 21). Unlike some other abolitionists (Document 5), however, Douglass did not see the Constitution as a pro-slavery document, as he made clear in this speech.

SOURCE: *Frederick Douglass: Selected Speeches and Writings*, ed. Philip S. Foner (Chicago: Lawrence Hill, 1999), 188–206. http://rbscp.lib.rochester.edu/2945

My subject, then fellow-citizens, is American slavery. I shall see, this day, and its popular characteristics, from the slave's point of view. Standing, there, identified with the American bondman, making his wrongs mine, I do not hesitate to declare, with all my soul, that the character and conduct of this nation never looked blacker to me than on this 4th of July! Whether we turn to the declarations of the past, or to the professions of the present, the conduct of the nation seems equally hideous and revolting. America is false to the past, false to the present, and solemnly binds herself to be false to the future. Standing with God and the crushed and bleeding slave on this occasion, I will, in the name of humanity which is outraged, in the name of liberty which is fettered, in the name of the constitution and the Bible, which are disregarded and trampled upon, dare to call in question and to denounce, with all the emphasis I can command, everything that serves to perpetuate slavery-the great sin and shame of America! "I will not equivocate; I will not excuse;"[1] I will use the severest language I can command; and yet not one word shall escape me that any man, whose judgment is not blinded by prejudice, or who is not at heart a slaveholder, shall not confess to be right and just.

But I fancy I hear some one of my audience say, it is just in this circumstance that you and your brother abolitionists fail to make a favorable impression on the public mind. Would you argue more, and denounce less, would you persuade more, and rebuke less, your cause would be much more likely to succeed. But, I submit, where all is plain there is nothing to be argued. What point in the anti-slavery creed would you have me argue? On what branch of the subject do the people of this country need light? Must I undertake to prove that the slave is a man? That point is conceded already. Nobody doubts it. The slaveholders themselves acknowledge it in the enactment of laws for their government. They acknowledge it when they punish disobedience on the part of the slave. There are seventy-two crimes in the state of Virginia, which, if committed by a black man, (no matter how ignorant he be), subject him to the punishment of death; while only two of the same crimes will subject a white man to the like punishment. What is this but the acknowledgement that the slave is a moral, intellectual and responsible being? The manhood of the slave is conceded. It is admitted in the fact that Southern statute books are covered with enactments forbidding, under severe fines and penalties, the teaching of the slave to read or to write. When you can point to any such laws, in reference to the beasts of the field, then I may consent to argue the manhood of the slave. When the dogs in your streets, when the fowls of the air, when the cattle on your hills, when the fish of the sea, and the reptiles that crawl, shall be unable to distinguish the slave from a brute, then will I argue with you that the slave is a man!

For the present, it is enough to affirm the equal manhood of the Negro race. Is it not astonishing that, while we are ploughing, planting and reaping, using all kinds of mechanical tools, erecting houses, constructing bridges,

---

[1] The words of William Lloyd Garrison (Document 5) in the first issue of the *Liberator*, January 1, 1831.

building ships, working in metals of brass, iron, copper, silver and gold; that, while we are reading, writing and cyphering, acting as clerks, merchants and secretaries, having among us lawyers, doctors, ministers, poets, authors, editors, orators and teachers; that, while we are engaged in all manner of enterprises common to other men, digging gold in California, capturing the whale in the Pacific, feeding sheep and cattle on the hill-side, living, moving, acting, thinking, planning, living in families as husbands, wives and children, and, above all, confessing and worshipping the Christian's God, and looking hopefully for life and immortality beyond the grave, we are called upon to prove that we are men!

Would you have me argue that man is entitled to liberty? that he is the rightful owner of his own body? You have already declared it. Must I argue the wrongfulness of slavery? Is that a question for Republicans? Is it to be settled by the rules of logic and argumentation, as a matter beset with great difficulty, involving a doubtful application of the principle of justice, hard to be understood? How should I look to-day, in the presence of Americans, dividing, and subdividing a discourse, to show that men have a natural right to freedom? speaking of it relatively, and positively, negatively, and affirmatively. To do so, would be to make myself ridiculous, and to offer an insult to your understanding. There is not a man beneath the canopy of heaven, that does not know that slavery is wrong for him.

What, am I to argue that it is wrong to make men brutes, to rob them of their liberty, to work them without wages, to keep them ignorant of their relations to their fellow men, to beat them with sticks, to flay their flesh with the lash, to load their limbs with irons, to hunt them with dogs, to sell them at auction, to sunder their families, to knock out their teeth, to burn their flesh, to starve them into obedience and submission to their masters? Must I argue that a system thus marked with blood, and stained with pollution, is wrong? No! I will not. I have better employments for my time and strength than such arguments would imply.

What, then, remains to be argued? Is it that slavery is not divine; that God did not establish it; that our doctors of divinity are mistaken? There is blasphemy in the thought. That which is inhuman, cannot be divine! Who can reason on such a proposition? They that can, may; I cannot. The time for such argument is passed.

At a time like this, scorching irony, not convincing argument, is needed. O! had I the ability, and could I reach the nation's ear, I would, today, pour out a fiery stream of biting ridicule, blasting reproach, withering sarcasm, and stern rebuke. For it is not light that is needed, but fire; it is not the gentle shower, but thunder. We need the storm, the whirlwind, and the earthquake. The feeling of the nation must be quickened; the conscience of the nation must be roused; the propriety of the nation must be startled; the hypocrisy of the nation must be exposed; and its crimes against God and man must be proclaimed and denounced.

What, to the American slave, is your 4th of July? I answer: a day that reveals to him, more than all other days in the year, the gross injustice and cruelty to which he is the constant victim. To him, your celebration is a sham; your boasted liberty, an unholy license; your national greatness, swelling vanity; your sounds of rejoicing are empty and heartless; your denunciations of tyrants, brass fronted impudence; your shouts of liberty and equality, hollow mockery; your prayers and hymns, your sermons and thanksgivings, with all your religious parade, and solemnity, are, to him, mere bombast, fraud, deception, impiety, and hypocrisy-a thin veil to cover up crimes which would disgrace a nation of savages. There is not a nation on the earth guilty of practices, more shocking and bloody, than are the people of these United States, at this very hour. . . .

Take the American slave trade, which, we are told by the papers, is especially prosperous just now. . . . That trade has long since been denounced by this government, as piracy. It has been denounced with burning words, from the high places of the nation, as an execrable traffic. To arrest it, to put an end to it, this nation keeps a squadron, at immense cost, on the coast of Africa. Everywhere, in this country, it is safe to speak of this foreign slave trade, as a most inhuman traffic, opposed alike to the laws of God and of man. . . . It is, however, a notable fact that, while so much execration is poured out by Americans upon those engaged in the foreign slave trade, the men engaged in the slave trade between the states pass without condemnation, and their business is deemed honorable. . . .

But a still more inhuman, disgraceful, and scandalous state of things remains to be presented. By an act of the American Congress,[2] not yet two years old, slavery has been nationalized in its most horrible and revolting form. By that act, Mason and Dixon's line has been obliterated; New York has become as Virginia; and the power to hold, hunt, and sell men, women, and children as slaves remains no longer a mere state institution, but is now an institution of the whole United States. The power is co-extensive with the Star-Spangled Banner and American Christianity. Where these go, may also go the merciless slave-hunter. . . . For black men there are neither law, justice,

[2] The Fugitive Slave Law passed as part of the Compromise of 1850 (Document 8).

humanity, nor religion. The Fugitive Slave Law makes mercy to them a crime; and bribes the judge who tries them. An American judge gets ten dollars for every victim he consigns to slavery, and five, when he fails to do so. The oath of any two villains is sufficient, under this hell-black enactment, to send the most pious and exemplary black man into the remorseless jaws of slavery! His own testimony is nothing. He can bring no witnesses for himself. The minister of American justice is bound by the law to hear but one side; and that side, is the side of the oppressor. Let this damning fact be perpetually told. Let it be thundered around the world, that, in tyrant-killing, king-hating, people-loving, democratic, Christian America, the seats of justice are filled with judges, who hold their offices under an open and palpable bribe, and are bound, in deciding in the case of a man's liberty, hear only his accusers!...

[T]he church of this country is not only indifferent to the wrongs of the slave, it actually takes sides with the oppressors. It has made itself the bulwark of American slavery, and the shield of American slave-hunters. Many of its most eloquent Divines, who stand as the very lights of the church, have shamelessly given the sanction of religion and the Bible to the whole slave system. They have taught that man may, properly, be a slave; that the relation of master and slave is ordained of God; that to send back an escaped bondman to his master is clearly the duty of all the followers of the Lord Jesus Christ; and this horrible blasphemy is palmed off upon the world for Christianity....

Let the religious press, the pulpit, the Sunday school, the conference meeting, the great ecclesiastical, missionary, Bible and tract associations of the land array their immense powers against slavery and slaveholding; and the whole system of crime and blood would be scattered to the winds; and that they do not do this involves them in the most awful responsibility of which the mind can conceive....

Fellow-citizens! I will not enlarge further on your national inconsistencies. The existence of slavery in this country brands your republicanism as a sham, your humanity as a base pretense, and your Christianity as a lie. It destroys your moral power abroad; it corrupts your politicians at home. It saps the foundation of religion; it makes your name a hissing, and a bye-word to a mocking earth. It is the antagonistic force in your government, the only thing that seriously disturbs and endangers your Union. It fetters your progress; it is the enemy of improvement, the deadly foe of education; it fosters pride; it breeds insolence; it promotes vice; it shelters crime; it is a curse to the earth that supports it; and yet, you cling to it, as if it were the sheet anchor of all your hopes. Oh! be warned! be warned! a horrible reptile is coiled up in your nation's bosom; the venomous creature is nursing at the tender breast of your youthful republic; for the love of God, tear away, and fling from you the hideous monster, and let the weight of twenty millions crush and destroy it forever!

But it is answered in reply to all this, that precisely what I have now denounced is, in fact, guaranteed and sanctioned by the Constitution of the United States; that the right to hold and to hunt slaves is a part of that Constitution framed by the illustrious Fathers of this Republic. . . .

. . . But I differ from those who charge this baseness on the framers of the Constitution of the United States. It is a slander upon their memory, at least, so I believe. . . .

Fellow-citizens! there is no matter in respect to which, the people of the North have allowed themselves to be so ruinously imposed upon, as that of the pro-slavery character of the Constitution. In that instrument I hold there is neither warrant, license, nor sanction of the hateful thing; but, interpreted as it ought to be interpreted, the Constitution is a glorious liberty document. Read its preamble, consider its purposes. Is slavery among them? Is it at the gateway? or is it in the temple? It is neither. While I do not intend to argue this question on the present occasion, let me ask, if it be not somewhat singular that, if the Constitution were intended to be, by its framers and adopters, a slave-holding instrument, why neither slavery, slave-holding, nor slave can anywhere be found in it. What would be thought of an instrument, drawn up, legally drawn up, for the purpose of entitling the city of Rochester to a track of land, in which no mention of land was made? . . .

Now, take the Constitution according to its plain reading, and I defy the presentation of a single pro-slavery clause in it. On the other hand it will be found to contain principles and purposes, entirely hostile to the existence of slavery. . . .

. . . Allow me to say, in conclusion, notwithstanding the dark picture I have this day presented of the state of the nation, I do not despair of this country. There are forces in operation, which must inevitably work the downfall of slavery. "The arm of the Lord is not shortened,"[3] and the doom of slavery is certain. I, therefore, leave off where I began, with hope. While drawing encouragement from the Declaration of Independence, the great principles it contains, and the genius of American Institutions, my spirit is also cheered by the obvious tendencies of the age. Nations do not now stand in the same relation to each other that they did ages ago. No nation can now shut itself up from the surrounding world, and trot round in the same old path of its

---

[3] Numbers 11:23, Isaiah 59:1.

fathers without interference. The time was when such could be done. Long established customs of hurtful character could formerly fence themselves in, and do their evil work with social impunity. Knowledge was then confined and enjoyed by the privileged few, and the multitude walked on in mental darkness. But a change has now come over the affairs of mankind. Walled cities and empires have become unfashionable. The arm of commerce has borne away the gates of the strong city. Intelligence is penetrating the darkest corners of the globe. It makes its pathway over and under the sea, as well as on the earth. Wind, steam, and lightning are its chartered agents. Oceans no longer divide, but link nations together. From Boston to London is now a holiday excursion. Space is comparatively annihilated. Thoughts expressed on one side of the Atlantic, are distinctly heard on the other. The far off and almost fabulous Pacific rolls in grandeur at our feet. The Celestial Empire, the mystery of ages, is being solved. The fiat of the Almighty, "Let there be Light," has not yet spent its force. No abuse, no outrage whether in taste, sport or avarice, can now hide itself from the all-pervading light. The iron shoe, and crippled foot of China must be seen, in contrast with nature. Africa must rise and put on her yet unwoven garment. "Ethiopia shall stretch out her hand unto God."[4] In the fervent aspirations of William Lloyd Garrison, I say, and let every heart join in saying it:

God speed the year of jubilee
The wide world o'er
When from their galling chains set free,
Th' oppress'd shall vilely bend the knee,
And wear the yoke of tyranny
Like brutes no more.
That year will come, and freedom's reign,
To man his plundered rights again
Restore. . . .[5]

[4] Psalm 68:31
[5] William Lloyd Garrison, *The Signal of Liberty*, Vol. 4, No. 47, March 17, 1845, 1.

Free and Slave-Holding States and Territories

[London: John Murray; Edinburgh: W. & A.K. Johnston, 1857]

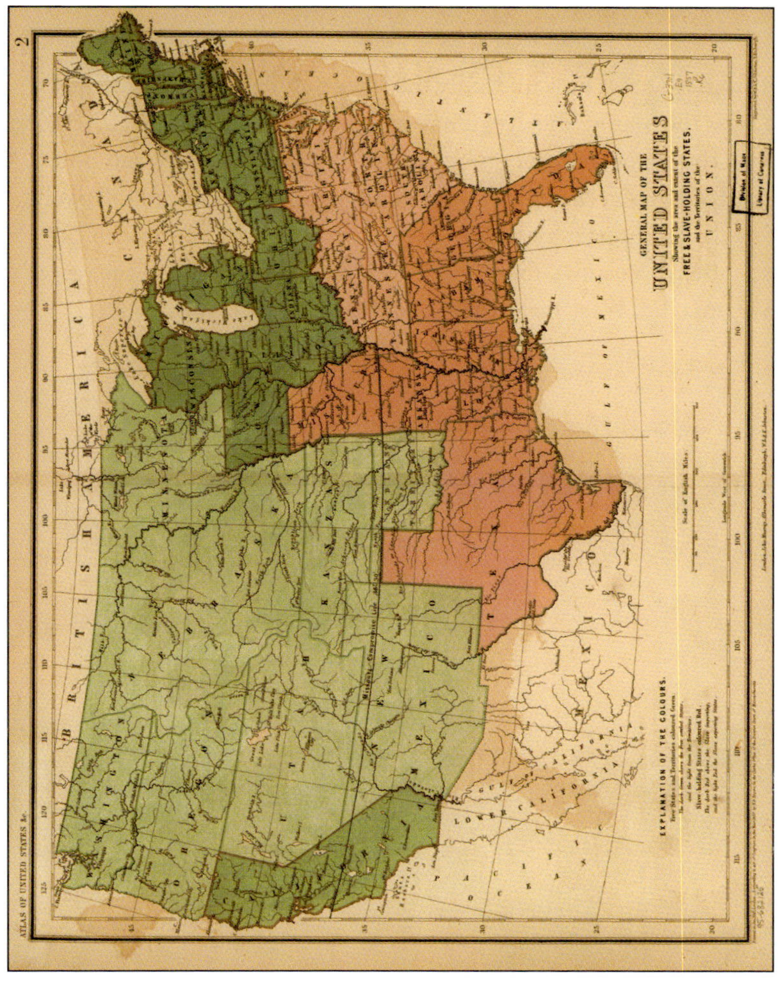

SOURCE: Library of Congress, https://www.loc.gov/item/95682125/.

Distribution of the Slave Population by State

Compiled from the US Census of 1860

This map shows how unevenly the slave population was distributed across the South. The distribution of slaves did have some correlation with the support for secession. In the large upland area stretching southwest from the border with Pennsylvania, which had relatively few slaves, support for the Union was significant. The western counties of Virginia, for example, refused to secede when the rest of Virginia did. West Virginia was admitted to the Union in 1863.

SOURCE: Henry S. Graham Washington, 1861. Library of Congress, https://www.loc.gov/item/99447026/.

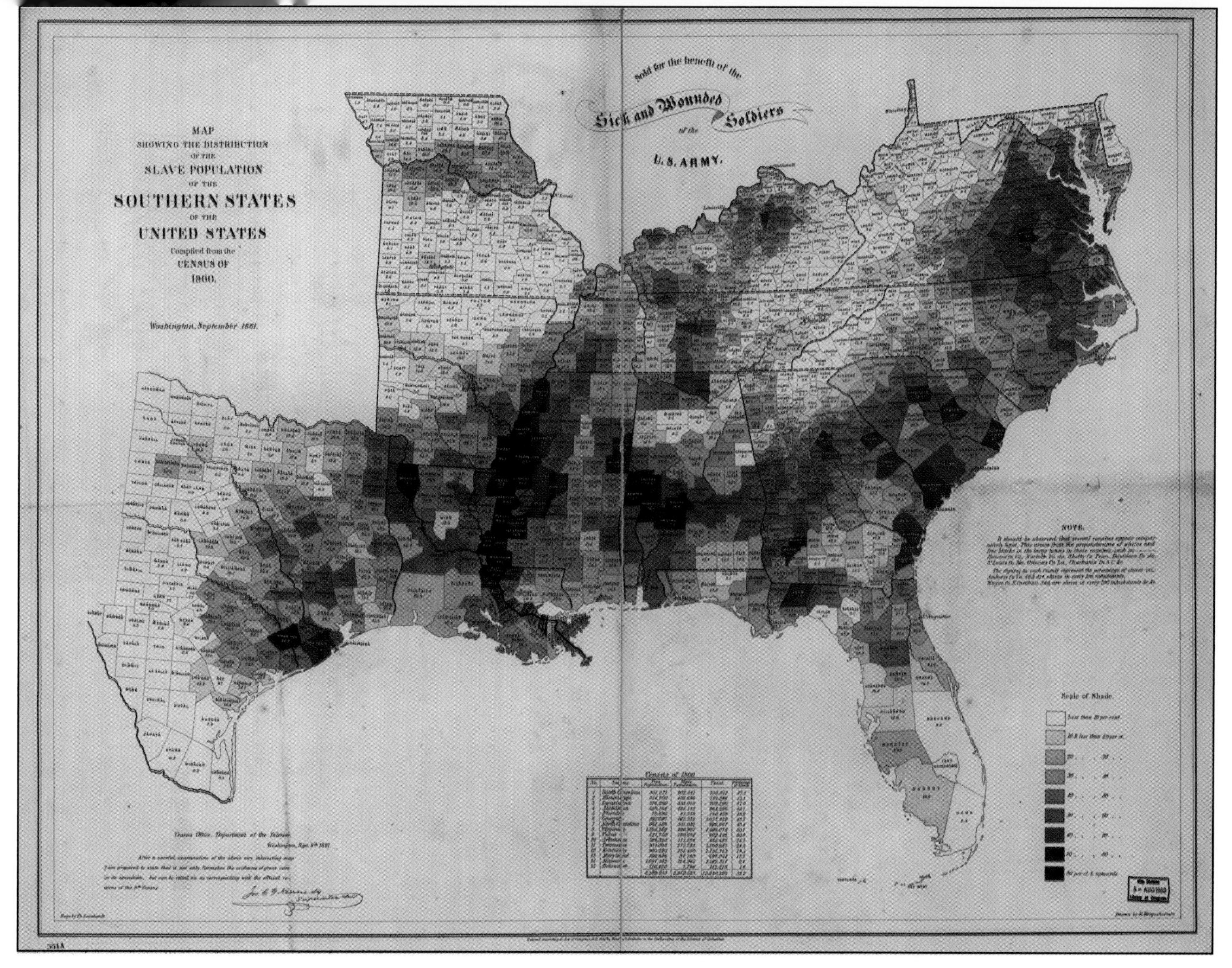

Sold for the benefit of the
Sick and Wounded Soldiers
of the
U.S. ARMY.
MAP
SHOWING THE DISTRIBUTION
OF THE
SLAVE POPULATION
OF THE
SOUTHERN STATES
OF THE
UNITED STATES
Compiled from the
CENSUS OF
1860.
Washington, September 1861.
NOTE.
Scale of Shade.
Census of 1860

Political Cartoon: Slavery Expansion and Free Soil

John L. Magee, Philadelphia, 1856.

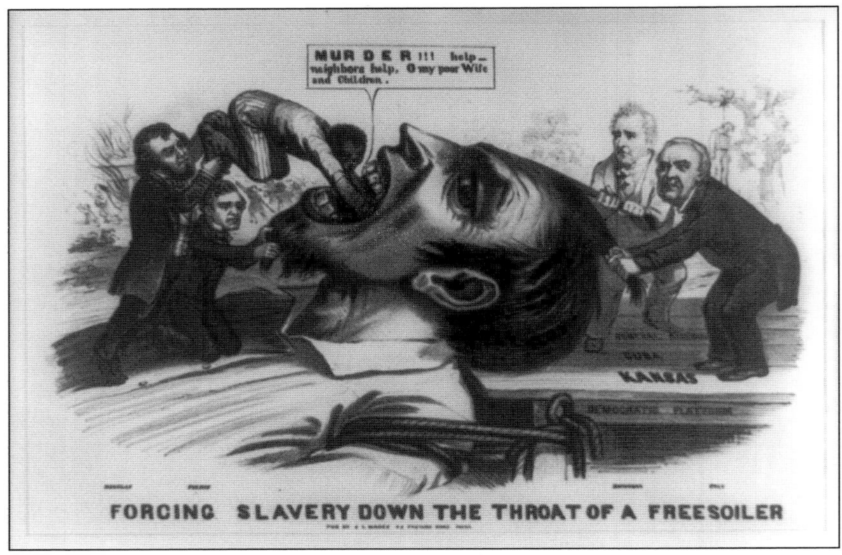

SOURCE: Library of Congress, LC-USZ62-92043

The artist lays on the Democrats the major blame for violence perpetrated against antislavery settlers in Kansas in the wake of the Kansas-Nebraska Act. Here a bearded "freesoiler" has been bound to the "Democratic Platform" and is restrained by two Lilliputian figures, presidential nominee James Buchanan and Democratic senator Lewis Cass. Democratic senator Stephen A. Douglas and president Franklin Pierce, also shown as tiny figures, force a black man into the giant's gaping mouth. The freesoiler's head rests on a platform marked "Kansas," "Cuba," and "Central America," probably referring to Democratic ambitions for the extension of slavery. In the background left is a scene of burning and pillage; on the right a dead man hangs from a tree.

SOURCE: Library of Congress, https://www.loc.gov/pictures/item/2008661578/

Kansas Broadside

Worcester, MA: November 22, 1854.

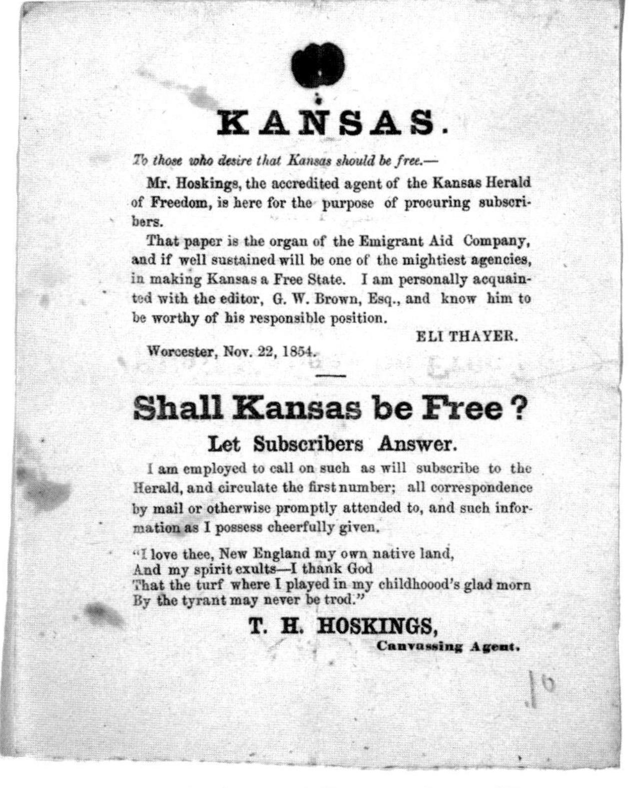

KANSAS.

To those who desire that Kansas should be free.—

Mr. Hoskings, the accredited agent of the Kansas Herald of Freedom, is here for the purpose of procuring subscribers.

That paper is the organ of the Emigrant Aid Company, and if well sustained will be one of the mightiest agencies, in making Kansas a Free State. I am personally acquainted with the editor, G. W. Brown, Esq., and know him to be worthy of his responsible position.

ELI THAYER.

Worcester, Nov. 22, 1854.

—

Shall Kansas be Free?

Let Subscribers Answer.

I am employed to call on such as will subscribe to the Herald, and circulate the first number; all correspondence by mail or otherwise promptly attended to, and such information as I possess cheerfully given.

"I love thee, New England my own native land,
And my spirit exults—I thank God
That the turf where I played in my childhoood's glad morn
By the tyrant may never be trod."

T. H. HOSKINGS,
Canvassing Agent.

SOURCE: Printed Ephemera Collection, Library of Congress, https://www.loc.gov/item/rbpe.02000100/

A broadside was a large piece of printed paper used for public announcements. This broadside encourages people to subscribe to the Kansas Herald of Freedom, the newspaper of the Emigrant Aid Society. The purpose of the Society, which Eli Thayer, along with other businessmen, helped found was to support the settlement in Kansas of people who opposed slavery. Founded just before the passage of the Kansas- Nebraska Act (Documents 11 and 12), the Society was both a political and business activity. It never made money for its stockholders and settled about 2,000 people in the territory. In 1860, just before its admission to the Union, Kansas had a population of about 100,000.

Broadside Advertising for a Runaway Slave

Culpeper County, Virginia, Stevensburg, 1854

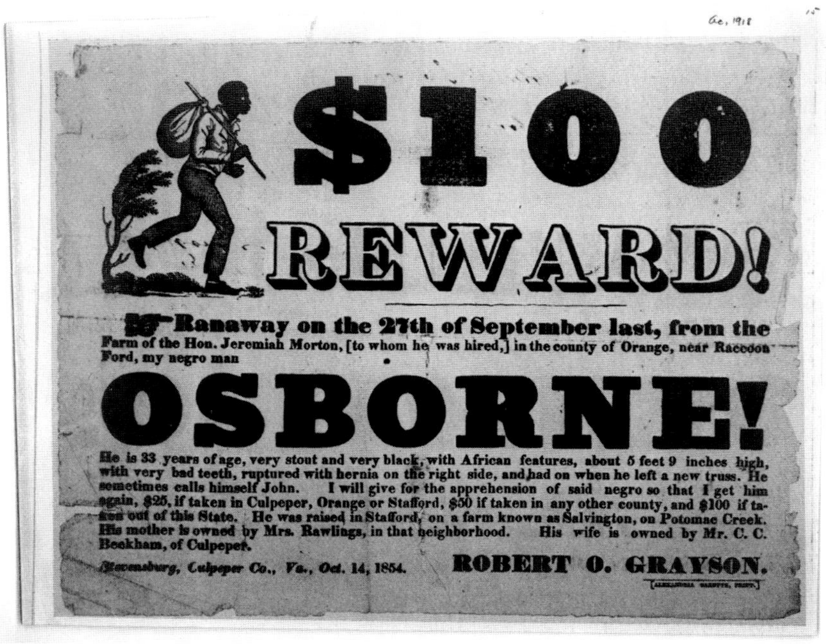

SOURCE: Library of Congress, https://www.loc.gov/item/rbpe.18604300/.

Warning to the Colored People of Boston

Boston, 1851

CAUTION!!

COLORED PEOPLE

OF BOSTON, ONE & ALL,

You are hereby respectfully CAUTIONED and advised, to avoid conversing with the

Watchmen and Police Officers of Boston,

For since the recent ORDER OF THE MAYOR & ALDERMEN, they are empowered to act as

KIDNAPPERS

AND

Slave Catchers,

And they have already been actually employed in KIDNAPPING, CATCHING, AND KEEPING SLAVES. Therefore, if you value your LIBERTY, and the *Welfare of the Fugitives* among you, *Shun* them in every possible manner, as so many *HOUNDS* on the track of the most unfortunate of your race.

Keep a Sharp Look Out for KIDNAPPERS, and have TOP EYE open.

APRIL 24, 1851.

SOURCE: Library of Congress, http://hdl.loc.gov/loc.rbc/rbpe.06002200/.

The fugitive slave law, part of the Compromise of 1850 (Document 8), required that law enforcement in the North help recover African Americans who had escaped from slavery. In response, citizens organized to warn African Americans that watchmen and policemen might be a danger to their freedom.

Advertisement for the Sale of Young Negroes

New Orleans, 1840

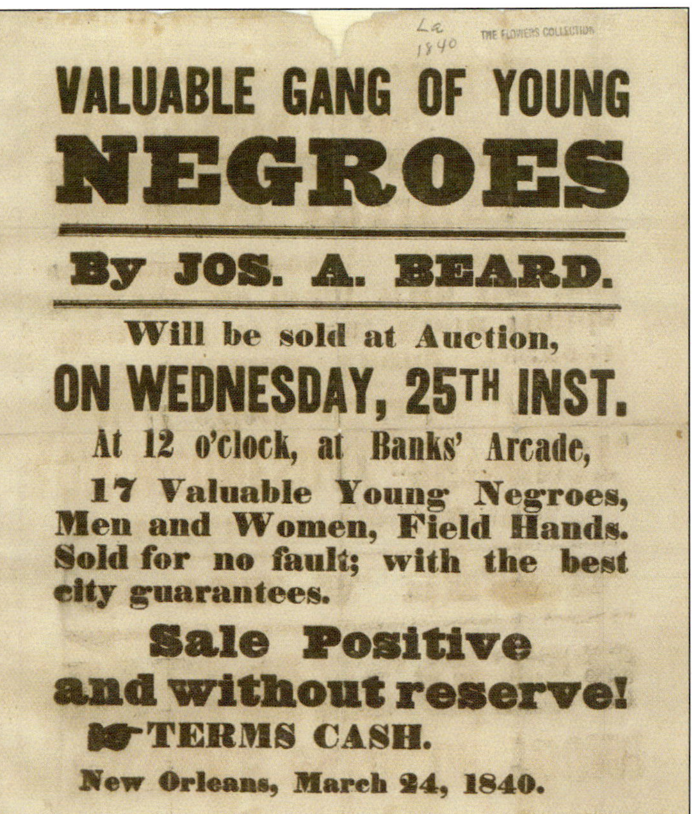

SOURCE: Duke University Libraries Digital Collections, https://repository.duke.edu/dc/broadsides/bdsla10566.

An example of an advertisement for a sale of slaves. The phrase "city guarantees" refers to the New Orleans city buyer protection laws governing the sale of slaves.

DOCUMENT 10

Appeal of the Independent Democrats in Congress to the American People

January 19, 1854

The Compromise of 1850 (Document 8) did not resolve the slavery issue. It merely postponed the reckoning. The reckoning came closer to beginning in the early 1850s with the effort to organize a central portion of the Louisiana Purchase territory. The critical issue again was whether slavery would be allowed in the territory, complicated by the issue of whether a transcontinental railroad would take a Northern or Southern route. In an effort to resolve these issues, Stephen A. Douglas (1813–1861), Democrat Senator from Illinois, after consulting with President Franklin Pierce (1804–1869), a Democrat from New Hampshire, eventually proposed a law to organize two territories, Kansas and Nebraska, whose inhabitants would decide for themselves whether the territories would permit slavery. This was the principle of popular sovereignty that Douglas claimed was a solution to the slavery question in accord with the fundamental principles of American government (Document 11). In making this claim, Douglas hoped to increase the chances that his bill would become law. By apparently transferring the political fight over slavery from Congress to the territorial conventions that would adopt constitutions and apply for statehood, it might make it easier for some members of Congress or senators to vote for the bill. Basing territorial organization on popular sovereignty, however, also meant repealing the Missouri Compromise that had prohibited slavery north of 36 degrees, 30 minutes north latitude in the Louisiana Purchase territory (Document 2). Debate over the law was bitter, especially in the House of Representatives, where violence almost occurred. The law passed by a large margin in the Senate, but only by three votes in the House. President Pierce signed the bill into law May 30, 1854.

The Kansas-Nebraska Act had several consequences. It led to actual not just political warfare in Kansas, which bordered Missouri, a slave state, as pro- and anti-slavery forces battled for control. It caused the Whig Party to cease to exist as a national party, since Northern Whigs voted against the law, finally breaking the party into Northern and Southern wings. Northern Whigs joined with Free-Soil party members to form the Republican Party. This left only the Democrats as a national party, but as this appeal makes clear, the law strained the party to the breaking point. That point came in 1860 (Document 22). Finally, instead of decreasing division over slavery, the Kansas-Nebraska Act increased it, since those opposed to slavery saw the repeal of the Missouri Compromise line as a breach of faith and an opportunity for slavery to spread across the western lands.

The Appeal of the Independent Democrats shows how strong was opposition to Douglas's bill, even among some Northern Democrats. Douglas, who aspired to be president, had to answer this criticism, which he did in a speech on the Senate floor eleven days after the appeal appeared (Document 11).

SOURCE: *Congressional Globe*, Senate, 33rd Congress, First Session, 281–282, https://memory.loc.gov/cgi-bin/ampage.

As senators and representatives in the Congress of the United States it is our duty to warn our constituents, whenever imminent danger menaces the freedom of our institutions or the permanency of the Union.

Such danger, as we firmly believe, now impends, and we earnestly solicit your prompt attention to it.

At the last session of Congress a bill for the organization of the Territory of Nebraska passed the House of Representatives by an overwhelming majority. That bill was based on the principle of excluding slavery from the new Territory. It was not taken up for consideration in the Senate and consequently failed to become a law.

At the present session a new Nebraska bill has been reported by the Senate Committee on Territories, which, should it unhappily receive the sanction of Congress, will open all the unorganized territories of the Union to the ingress of slavery.

We arraign this bill as a gross violation of a sacred pledge; as a criminal betrayal of precious rights; as part and parcel of an atrocious plot to exclude from a vast unoccupied region immigrants from the Old World and free laborers from our own states, and convert it into a dreary region of despotism, inhabited by masters and slaves.

Take your maps, fellow citizens, we entreat you, and see what country it is which this bill gratuitously and recklessly proposes to open to slavery....

This immense region, occupying the very heart of the North American Continent, and larger, by thirty-three thousand square miles, than all the existing free states including California... the bill now before the Senate, without reason and without excuse, but in flagrant disregard of sound policy and sacred faith, purposes to open to slavery.

We beg your attention, fellow-citizens, to a few historical facts:

The original settled policy of the United States, clearly indicated by the Jefferson proviso of 1784 and the Ordinance of 1787, was non-extension of slavery. In 1803 Louisiana was acquired by purchase from France.... Congress, instead of providing for the abolition of slavery in this new territory, permitted its continuance. In 1812, the state of Louisiana was organized and admitted into the Union with slavery.

In 1818, six years later, the inhabitants of the territory of Missouri applied to Congress for authority to form a state constitution, and for admission into the Union. There were, at that time, in the whole territory acquired from France, outside of the state of Louisiana, not three thousand slaves.

There was no apology, in the circumstances of the country, for the continuance of slavery. The original national policy was against it, and not less the plain language of the treaty under which the territory had been acquired from France.

It was proposed, therefore, to incorporate in the bill authorizing the formation of a state government, a provision requiring that the constitution of the new state should contain an article providing for the abolition of existing slavery, and prohibiting the further introduction of slaves.

This provision was vehemently and pertinaciously opposed, but finally prevailed in the House of Representatives by a decided vote. In the Senate it was rejected, and in consequence of the disagreement between the two Houses the bill was lost.

At the next session of Congress, the controversy was renewed with increased violence. It was terminated at length by a compromise. Missouri was allowed to come into the Union with slavery; but a section was inserted in the act authorizing her admission, excluding slavery forever from all the territory acquired from France, not included in the new state, lying north of 36° 30'....

The question of the constitutionality of this prohibition was submitted by President Monroe to his cabinet. John Quincy Adams was then Secretary of State; John C. Calhoun was Secretary of War; William H. Crawford was Secretary of the Treasury; and William Wirt was Attorney-General. Each of these eminent men, three of them being from the slave states, gave a written opinion, affirming its constitutionality, and thereupon the act received the sanction of the president himself, also from a slave state.

Nothing is more certain in history than the fact that Missouri could not have been admitted as a slave state had not certain members from the free states been reconciled to the measure by the incorporation of this prohibition into the act of admission. Nothing is more certain than that this prohibition has been regarded and accepted by the whole country as a solemn compact against the extension of slavery into any part of the territory acquired from France lying north of 36° 30′, and not included in the new state of Missouri. The same act-let it be ever remembered-which authorized the formation of a constitution by the state, without a clause forbidding slavery, consecrated, beyond question and beyond honest recall, the whole remainder of the territory to freedom and free institutions forever. For more than thirty years during more than half our national existence under our present Constitution-this compact has been universally regarded and acted upon as inviolable American law. In conformity with it, Iowa was admitted as a free state and Minnesota has been organized as a free territory.

It is a strange and ominous fact, well calculated to awaken the worst apprehensions and the most fearful forebodings of future calamities, that it is now deliberately proposed to repeal this prohibition, by implication or directly-the latter certainly the manlier way-and thus to subvert the compact, and allow slavery in all the yet unorganized territory. We cannot, in this address, review the various pretenses under which it is attempted to cloak this monstrous wrong, but we must not altogether omit to notice one.

It is said that Nebraska sustains the same relations to slavery as did the territory acquired from Mexico prior to 1850, and that the pro-slavery clauses of the bill are necessary to carry into effect the compromise of that year.

No assertion could be more groundless....

The compromise acts themselves refute this pretension. In the third article of the second section of the joint resolution for annexing Texas to the United States, it is expressly declared that "in such state or states as shall be formed out of said territory north of said Missouri compromise line, slavery or involuntary servitude, except for crime, shall be prohibited;" and in the act for organizing New Mexico and settling the boundary of Texas, a proviso was incorporated,... which distinctly preserves this prohibition, and flouts the barefaced pretension that all the territory of the United States, whether south or north of the Missouri compromise line, is to be open to slavery.

...These pretenses, therefore, that the territory covered by the positive prohibition of 1820, sustains a similar relation to slavery with that acquired from Mexico, covered by no prohibition except that of disputed constitutional or Mexican law, and that the Compromises of 1850 require the incorporation of the pro-slavery clauses of the Utah and New Mexico Bill in the Nebraska act, are mere inventions, designed to cover from public reprehension meditated bad faith. Were he living now, no one would be more forward, more eloquent, or more indignant in his denunciation of that bad faith, than Henry Clay, the foremost champion of both compromises....

We confess our total inability properly to delineate the character or describe the consequences of this measure. Language fails to express the sentiments of indignation and abhorrence which it inspires; and no vision less penetrating and comprehensive than that of the All-Seeing can reach its evil issues....

We appeal to the people. We warn you that the dearest interests of freedom and the Union are in imminent peril. Demagogues may tell you that the Union can be maintained only by submitting to the demands of slavery. We tell you that the Union can only be maintained by the full recognition of the just claims of freedom and man. The Union was formed to establish justice and secure the blessings of liberty. When it fails to accomplish these ends it will be worthless, and when it becomes worthless it cannot long endure.

We entreat you to be mindful of that fundamental maxim of Democracy, equal rights and exact justice for all men. Do not submit to become agents in extending legalized oppression and systematized injustice over a vast territory yet exempt from these terrible evils.

We implore Christians and Christian ministers to interpose. Their divine religion requires them to behold in every man a brother, and to labor for the advancement and regeneration of the human race.

Whatever apologies may be offered for the toleration of slavery in the states, none can be offered for its extension into territories where it does not exist, and where that extension involves the repeal of ancient law and the violation of solemn compact. Let all protest, earnestly and emphatically, by correspondence, through the press, by memorials, by resolutions of public meetings and legislative bodies, and in whatever other mode may seem expedient, against this enormous crime.

For ourselves, we shall resist it by speech and vote, and with all the abilities which God has given us. Even if overcome in the impending struggle, we shall not submit. We shall go home to our constituents, erect anew the standard of freedom, and call on the people to come to the rescue of the country from the domination of slavery. We will not despair; for the cause of human freedom is the cause of God.

S. P. Chase[1]
Charles Sumner
J. R. Giddings
Edward Wade
Gerritt Smith
Alexander De Witt

[1] Salmon P. Chase (1808–1873) was a senator from Ohio. He later served in Lincoln's cabinet as Secretary of the Treasury. Charles Sumner (1811–1874) was a senator from Massachusetts. Joshua R. Giddings (1795–1864) was a representative from Ohio. Edward Wade (1802–1866) was a representative from Ohio. Gerritt Smith (1797–1874) was a representative from New York. Alexander De Witt (1798–1879) was a representative from Massachusetts.

DOCUMENT 11

Nebraska Territory

Stephen A. Douglas

January 30, 1854

In an effort to organize more western territory despite the growing conflict over slavery, Stephen A. Douglas (1813–1861), Democrat Senator from Illinois, offered a bill to create two new territories, Kansas and Nebraska. He dealt with slavery by giving the people in the two territories the authority to prohibit or allow it. Douglas defended this provision in the law by arguing that it was the basis of all government in America. It was just another form of popular sovereignty. The provision also increased the chances that the legislation to organize the territories would pass, since by appearing to transfer the political fight over slavery from Congress to the territorial conventions that would adopt constitutions and apply for statehood, popular sovereignty might make it easier for some members of Congress and senators to vote for the legislation. Douglas's Kansas-Nebraska Act passed (by only three votes in the House) but raised a storm of protest, especially over its repeal of the Missouri Compromise line (Documents 2, 10, 12), since this created new opportunities for the spread of slavery. Douglas answered his critics with this speech on the Senate floor.

SOURCE: *Congressional Globe,* Senate, 33rd Congress, 1st Session, 275–180, http://memory.loc.gov/cgi-bin/ampage80.

. . . Upon the other point-that pertaining to the question of slavery in the territories-it was the intention of the committee[1] to be equally explicit. We took the principles established by the Compromise Act of 1850[2] as our guide, and intended to make each and every provision of the bill accord with those principles. Those measures established and rest upon the great principle of self-government-that the people should be allowed to decide the questions of their domestic institutions for themselves, subject only to such limitations

[1] Douglas was chairman of the Senate Committee on Territories.

[2] Document 8

and restrictions as are imposed by the Constitution of the United States, instead of having them determined by an arbitrary or geographical line....

The leading feature of the compromise of 1850 was congressional non-intervention as to slavery in the territories; that the people of the territories, and of all the states, were to be allowed to do as they pleased upon the subject of slavery, subject only to the provisions of the Constitution of the United States.

That, sir, was the leading feature of the compromise measures of 1850. Those measures therefore, abandoned the idea of a geographical line as the boundary between free states and slave states; abandoned it because compelled to do it from an inability to maintain it; and in lieu of that substituted a great principle of self-government, which would allow the people to do as they thought proper. Now, the question is, when that new compromise, resting upon that great fundamental principle of freedom, was established, was it not an abandonment of the old one-the geographical line?[3] Was it not a supersedure of the old one within the very language of the substitute for the bill which is now under consideration?...

Mr. President, I repeat, that so far as the question of slavery is concerned, there is nothing in the bill under consideration which does not carry out the principle of the compromise measures of 1850, by leaving the people to do as they please, subject only to the provisions of the Constitution of the United States. If that principle is wrong, the bill is wrong. If that principle is right, the bill is right. It is unnecessary to quibble about phraseology or words; it is not the mere words, the mere phraseology that our constituents wish to judge by. They wish to know the legal effect of our legislation.

The legal effect of this bill, if it be passed as reported by the Committee on Territories, is neither to legislate slavery into these territories nor out of them, but to leave the people do as they please, under the provisions and subject to the limitations of the Constitution of the United States. Why should not this principle prevail? Why should any man, North or South, object to it? I will especially address the argument to my own section of country, and ask why should any Northern man object to this principle? If you will review the history of the slavery question in the United States, you will see that all the great results in behalf of free institutions which have been worked out, have been accomplished by the operation of this principle, and by it alone.

---

[3] the geographical line of the Missouri Compromise, 36 degrees and 30 minutes north latitude (Document 2)

When these states were colonies of Great Britain, every one of them was a slave-holding province. When the Constitution of the United States was formed, twelve out of the thirteen were slave-holding states. Since that time six of those states have become free. How has this been effected? Was it by virtue of abolition agitation in Congress? Was it in obedience to the dictates of the federal government? Not at all; but they have become free states under the silent but sure and irresistible working of that great principle of self-government which teaches every people to do that which the interests of themselves and their posterity morally and pecuniarily may require.

Under the operation of this principle New Hampshire became free, while South Carolina continued to hold slaves; Connecticut abolished slavery, while Georgia held on to it; Rhode Island abandoned the institution, while Maryland preserved it; New York, New Jersey, and Pennsylvania abolished slavery, while Virginia, North Carolina, and Kentucky retained it. Did they do it at your bidding? Did they do it at the dictation of the federal government? Did they do it in obedience to any of your Wilmot provisoes[4] or ordinances of '87?[5] Not at all; they did it by virtue of their right as freemen under the Constitution of the United States, to establish and abolish such institutions as they thought their own good required.

Let me ask you where have you succeeded in excluding slavery by an act of Congress from one inch of the American soil? You may tell me that you did it in the northwest territory, by the ordinance of 1787. I will show you by the history of the country that you did not accomplish any such thing. You prohibited slavery there by law, but you did not exclude it in fact. Illinois was a part of the northwest territory. With the exception of a few French and white settlements, it was a vast wilderness, filled with hostile savages, when the ordinance of 1787 was adopted. Yet, sir, when Illinois was organized into a territorial government it established and protected slavery, and maintained it in spite of your ordinance, and in defiance of its express prohibition. . . .

I do not like, I never did like, the system of legislation on our part, by which a geographical line, in violation of the laws of nature, and climate, and soil, and the laws of God, should be run to establish institutions for a people; yet, out of a regard for the peace and quiet of the country, out of respect for

---

[4] The Wilmot Proviso, authored by Representative David Wilmot, (D-PA), proposed in 1846 at the beginning of the War with Mexico that slavery be prohibited in any territory gained by the United States as a consequence of the war.

[5] The Northwest Ordinance (1787), which prohibited slavery in territory north and west of the Ohio River.

past pledges, and out of a desire to adhere faithfully to all compromises, I sustained the Missouri compromise so long as it was in force, and advocated its extension to the Pacific. Now, when that has been abandoned, when it has been superseded, when a great principle of self-government has been substituted for it, I choose to cling to that principle, and abide in good faith, not only by the letter, but by the spirit of the last compromise . . .

DOCUMENT 12

Speech on the Repeal of the Missouri Compromise

Abraham Lincoln

October 16, 1854

The first of several speeches from Abraham Lincoln (1809–1865) in this collection, this address at Peoria, Illinois on the subject of the repeal of the Missouri Compromise represents his return to politics after a short-lived retirement. Following his single two-year term in the U.S. House of Representatives from 1847–1849, Lincoln returned to his law practice and settled down, leaving public service behind. But the passage of the Kansas-Nebraska Act in 1854 (Documents 10 and 11), which allowed the people of the territories to decide for themselves whether they wanted slavery or not, roused Lincoln like nothing had before. The author of the law, Illinois Senator Stephen A. Douglas (1813–1861), insisted on the principle of popular sovereignty, that the people had a right to choose slavery or freedom by the vote with or without the permission of Congress. This meant the end for the Missouri Compromise of 1820 (Documents 2 and 11), which had affirmed Congress's right to prohibit the extension of slavery into the territories. It also meant, according to Lincoln, the end of the moral question surrounding slavery, since claims of right and wrong, good and bad, just and unjust, were now to be left to simple majority rule and settled by the advantage of the stronger. Lincoln's speech brought together with vigor and clarity the historical, political, and practical arguments against the expansion of slavery into the territories made since the Missouri Compromise of 1820. In responding to Douglas's argument about popular sovereignty, however, Lincoln went beyond historical and constitutional issues to examine the fundamental issue of American democracy. The American people are the sovereign, the ruling element, but are the people all-powerful? Lincoln argued that there is only one thing more powerful than the people, only one thing to which they must bow, the principle of eternal right.

We have excerpted and placed in Appendix E the historical argument that Lincoln made against the repeal of the Missouri Compromise, since this history provides useful background for all of the documents in this collection. We have also removed many of the practical arguments from this version of Lincoln's speech to focus on his political and moral argument.

SOURCE: *Life and Works of Abraham Lincoln*, Centenary Edition, Volume II, Marion Mills Miller, ed., (New York: The Current Literature Publishing Company, 1907), 218–275, https://archive.org/details/lifeworks02lincuoft/page/274.

The repeal of the Missouri Compromise, and the propriety of its restoration, constitute the subject of what I am about to say. . . .

I wish further to say, that I do not propose to question the patriotism, or to assail the motives of any man, or class of men; but rather to strictly confine myself to the naked merits of the question.

I also wish to be no less than national in all the positions I may take; and whenever I take ground which others have thought, or may think, narrow, sectional, and dangerous to the Union, I hope to give a reason, which will appear sufficient, at least to some, why I think differently.

And, as this subject is no other, than part and parcel of the larger general question of domestic slavery, I wish to make and to keep the distinction between the existing institution, and the extension of it, so broad, and so clear, that no honest man can misunderstand me, and no dishonest one, successfully misrepresent me. . . .

The foregoing history may not be precisely accurate in every particular; but I am sure it is sufficiently so, for all the uses I shall attempt to make of it, and in it, we have before us, the chief material enabling us to correctly judge whether the repeal of the Missouri Compromise is right or wrong.

I think, and shall try to show, that it is wrong; wrong in its direct effect, letting slavery into Kansas and Nebraska-and wrong in its prospective principle, allowing it to spread to every other part of the wide world, where men can be found inclined to take it.

This declared indifference, but as I must think, covert real zeal for the spread of slavery, I cannot but hate. I hate it because of the monstrous injustice of slavery itself. I hate it because it deprives our republican example of its just influence in the world-enables the enemies of free institutions, with plausibility, to taunt us as hypocrites-causes the real friends of freedom to doubt our sincerity, and especially because it forces so many really good men amongst ourselves into an open war with the very fundamental principles of civil liberty-criticizing the Declaration of Independence, and insisting that there is no right principle of action but self-interest.

Before proceeding, let me say I think I have no prejudice against the Southern people. They are just what we would be in their situation. If slavery did not now exist amongst them, they would not introduce it. If it did now exist amongst us, we should not instantly give it up. This I believe of the masses north and south. Doubtless there are individuals on both sides, who would not hold slaves under any circumstances; and others who would gladly introduce slavery anew, if it were out of existence. We know that some Southern men do free their slaves, go north, and become tip-top abolitionists; while some Northern ones go south, and become most cruel slave masters.

When Southern people tell us they are no more responsible for the origin of slavery, than we; I acknowledge the fact. When it is said that the institution exists; and that it is very difficult to get rid of it, in any satisfactory way, I can understand and appreciate the saying. I surely will not blame them for not doing what I should not know how to do myself. If all earthly power were given me, I should not know what to do, as to the existing institution. My first impulse would be to free all the slaves, and send them to Liberia,-to their own native land. But a moment's reflection would convince me, that whatever of high hope, (as I think there is) there may be in this, in the long run, its sudden execution is impossible. If they were all landed there in a day, they would all perish in the next ten days; and there are not surplus shipping and surplus money enough in the world to carry them there in many times ten days. What then? Free them all, and keep them among us as underlings? Is it quite certain that this betters their condition? I think I would not hold one in slavery, at any rate; yet the point is not clear enough for me to denounce people upon. What next? Free them, and make them politically and socially, our equals? My own feelings will not admit of this; and if mine would, we well know that those of the great mass of white people will not. Whether this feeling accords with justice and sound judgment, is not the sole question, if indeed, it is any part of it. A universal feeling, whether well or ill-founded, cannot be safely disregarded. We cannot, then, make them equals. It does seem to me that systems of gradual emancipation might be adopted; but for their tardiness in this, I will not undertake to judge our brethren of the South.

When they remind us of their constitutional rights, I acknowledge them, not grudgingly, but fully, and fairly; and I would give them any legislation for the reclaiming of their fugitives, which should not, in its stringency, be more likely to carry a free man into slavery, than our ordinary criminal laws are to hang an innocent one.

But all this, to my judgment, furnishes no more excuse for permitting slavery to go into our own free territory, than it would for reviving the African slave trade by law. The law which forbids the bringing of slaves from Africa; and that which has so long forbid the taking them to Nebraska, can hardly be distinguished on any moral principle; and the repeal of the former could find quite as plausible excuses as that of the latter.

The arguments by which the repeal of the Missouri Compromise is sought to be justified, are these:

First, that the Nebraska country needed a territorial government.

Second, that in various ways, the public had repudiated it, and demanded the repeal; and therefore should not now complain of it.

And lastly, that the repeal establishes a principle, which is intrinsically right. I will attempt an answer to each of them in its turn.

First, then, if that country was in need of a territorial organization, could it not have had it as well without as with the repeal? Iowa and Minnesota, to both of which the Missouri restriction applied, had, without its repeal, each in succession, territorial organizations. And even, the year before, a bill for Nebraska itself, was within an ace of passing, without the repealing clause; and this in the hands of the same men who are now the champions of repeal. Why no necessity then for the repeal? But still later, when this very bill was first brought in, it contained no repeal. But, say they, because the public had demanded, or rather commanded the repeal, the repeal was to accompany the organization, whenever that should occur.

Now I deny that the public ever demanded any such thing-ever repudiated the Missouri Compromise-ever commanded its repeal. I deny it, and call for the proof....

I now come to consider whether the repeal, with its avowed principle, is intrinsically right. I insist that it is not. Take the particular case. A controversy had arisen between the advocates and opponents of slavery, in relation to its establishment within the country we had purchased of France. The southern, and then best part of the purchase, was already in as a slave state. The controversy was settled by also letting Missouri in as a slave state; but with the agreement that within all the remaining part of the purchase, north of a certain line, there should never be slavery. As to what was to be done with the remaining part south of the line, nothing was said; but perhaps the fair implication was, that it should come in with slavery if it should so choose. The southern part, except a portion heretofore mentioned, afterwards did come in with slavery, as the state of Arkansas. All these many years since 1820, the northern part had remained a wilderness. At length settlements began in it also. In due course, Iowa, came in as a free state, and Minnesota was given a territorial government, without removing the slavery restriction. Finally the sole remaining part, north of the line, Kansas and Nebraska, was to be organized; and it is proposed, and carried, to blot out the old dividing line of thirty-four years standing, and to open the whole of that country to the introduction of slavery. Now, this, to my mind, is manifestly unjust. After an angry and dangerous controversy, the parties made friends by dividing the bone of contention. The one party first appropriates her own share, beyond all power to be disturbed in the possession of it; and then seizes the share of the other party. It is as if two starving men had divided their only loaf; the one had hastily swallowed his half, and then grabbed the other half just as he was putting it to his mouth....

Equal justice to the South, it is said, requires us to consent to the extending of slavery to new countries. That is to say, inasmuch as you do not object to my taking my hog to Nebraska, therefore I must not object to you taking your slave. Now, I admit this is perfectly logical, if there is no difference between hogs and Negroes. But while you thus require me to deny the humanity of the Negro, I wish to ask whether you of the South yourselves, have ever been willing to do as much? It is kindly provided that of all those who come into the world, only a small percentage are natural tyrants. That percentage is no larger in the slave states than in the free. The great majority, South as well as North, have human sympathies, of which they can no more divest themselves than they can of their sensibility to physical pain. These sympathies in the bosoms of the Southern people, manifest in many ways, their sense of the wrong of slavery, and their consciousness that, after all, there is humanity in the Negro. If they deny this, let me address them a few plain questions. In 1820 you joined the North, almost unanimously, in declaring the African slave trade piracy, and in annexing to it the punishment of death. Why did you do this? If you did not feel that it was wrong, why did you join in providing that men should be hung for it? The practice was no more than bringing wild Negroes from Africa, to sell to such as would buy them. But you never thought of hanging men for catching and selling wild horses, wild buffaloes or wild bears.

Again, you have amongst you, a sneaking individual, of the class of native tyrants, known as the "slave dealer." He watches your necessities, and crawls up to buy your slave, at a speculating price. If you cannot help it, you sell to him; but if you can help it, you drive him from your door. You despise him utterly. You do not recognize him as a friend, or even as an honest man. Your children must not play with his; they may rollick freely with the little Negroes, but not with the "slave dealers" children. If you are obliged to deal with him, you try to get through the job without so much as touching him.

It is common with you to join hands with the men you meet; but with the slave dealer you avoid the ceremony-instinctively shrinking from the snaky contact. If he grows rich and retires from business, you still remember him, and still keep up the ban of non-intercourse upon him and his family. Now why is this? You do not so treat the man who deals in corn, cattle or tobacco.

And yet again; there are in the United States and territories, including the District of Columbia, 433,643 free blacks. At $500 per head they are worth over two hundred millions of dollars. How comes this vast amount of property to be running about without owners? We do not see free horses or free cattle running at large. How is this? All these free blacks are the descendants of slaves, or have been slaves themselves, and they would be slaves now, but for something which has operated on their white owners, inducing them, at vast pecuniary sacrifices, to liberate them. What is that something? Is there any mistaking it? In all these cases it is your sense of justice, and human sympathy, continually telling you, that the poor Negro has some natural right to himself-that those who deny it, and make mere merchandise of him, deserve kickings, contempt and death.

And now, why will you ask us to deny the humanity of the slave and estimate him only as the equal of the hog? Why ask us to do what you will not do yourselves? Why ask us to do for nothing, what two hundred million dollars could not induce you to do?

But one great argument in the support of the repeal of the Missouri Compromise, is still to come. That argument is "the sacred right of self-government." It seems our distinguished senator[1] has found great difficulty in getting his antagonists, even in the Senate to meet him fairly on this argument. Some poet has said:

"Fools rush in where angels fear to tread."[2]

At the hazard of being thought one of the fools of this quotation, I meet that argument-I rush in, I take that bull by the horns.

I trust I understand, and truly estimate the right of self-government. My faith in the proposition that each man should do precisely as he pleases with all which is exclusively his own, lies at the foundation of the sense of justice there is in me. I extend the principles to communities of men, as well as to individuals. I so extend it, because it is politically wise, as well as naturally just; politically wise, in saving us from broils about matters which do not

[1] Stephen A. Douglas, Document 11.

[2] Alexander Pope, *An Essay on Criticism* (1711)

concern us. Here, or at Washington, I would not trouble myself with the oyster laws of Virginia, or the cranberry laws of Indiana.

The doctrine of self-government is right-absolutely and eternally right-but it has no just application, as here attempted. Or perhaps I should rather say that whether it has such just application depends upon whether a Negro is not or is a man. If he is not a man, why in that case, he who is a man may, as a matter of self-government, do just as he pleases with him. But if the Negro is a man, is it not to that extent, a total destruction of self-government, to say that he too shall not govern himself? When the white man governs himself that is self-government; but when he governs himself, and also governs another man, that is more than self-government-that is despotism. If the Negro is a man, why then my ancient faith teaches me that "all men are created equal;" and that there can be no moral right in connection with one man's making a slave of another. Judge Douglas frequently, with bitter irony and sarcasm, paraphrases our argument by saying "The white people of Nebraska are good enough to govern themselves, but they are not good enough to govern a few miserable Negroes!!"

Well I doubt not that the people of Nebraska are, and will continue to be as good as the average of people elsewhere. I do not say the contrary. What I do say is, that no man is good enough to govern another man, without that other's consent. I say this is the leading principle-the sheet anchor of American republicanism. Our Declaration of Independence says:

> "We hold these truths to be self-evident: that all men are created equal; that they are endowed by their Creator with certain inalienable rights; that among these are life, liberty and the pursuit of happiness. That to secure these rights, governments are instituted among men, deriving their just powers from the consent of the governed."

I have quoted so much at this time merely to show that according to our ancient faith, the just powers of governments are derived from the consent of the governed. Now the relation of masters and slaves is, pro tanto,[3] a total violation of this principle. The master not only governs the slave without his consent; but he governs him by a set of rules altogether different from those which he prescribes for himself. Allow ALL the governed an equal voice in the government, and that, and that only, is self-government.

---

[3] to that extent

Let it not be said I am contending for the establishment of political and social equality between the whites and blacks. I have already said the contrary. I am not now combating the argument of necessity, arising from the fact that the blacks are already amongst us; but I am combating what is set up as moral argument for allowing them to be taken where they have never yet been-arguing against the extension of a bad thing, which where it already exists we must of necessity, manage as we best can.

In support of his application of the doctrine of self-government, Senator Douglas has sought to bring to his aid the opinions and examples of our revolutionary fathers. I am glad he has done this. I love the sentiments of those old-time men; and shall be most happy to abide by their opinions. He shows us that when it was in contemplation for the colonies to break off from Great Britain, and set up a new government for themselves, several of the states instructed their delegates to go for the measure provided each state should be allowed to regulate its domestic concerts in its own way. I do not quote; but this in substance. This was right. I see nothing objectionable in it. I also think it probable that it had some reference to the existence of slavery amongst them. I will not deny that it had. But had it, in any reference to the carrying of slavery into new countries? That is the question; and we will let the fathers themselves answer it.

This same generation of men, and mostly the same individuals of the generation, who declared this principle-who declared independence-who fought the war of the revolution through-who afterwards made the Constitution under which we still live-these same men passed the ordinance of '87, declaring that slavery should never go to the north-west territory. I have no doubt Judge Douglas thinks they were very inconsistent in this. It is a question of discrimination between them and him. But there is not an inch of ground left for his claiming that their opinions-their example-their authority-are on his side in this controversy....

But you say this question should be left to the people of Nebraska, because they are more particularly interested. If this be the rule, you must leave it to each individual to say for himself whether he will have slaves. What better moral right have thirty-one citizens of Nebraska to say, that the thirty-second shall not hold slaves, than the people of the thirty-one states have to say that slavery shall not go into the thirty-second state at all?

But if it is a sacred right for the people of Nebraska to take and hold slaves there, it is equally their sacred right to buy them where they can buy them cheapest; and that undoubtedly will be on the coast of Africa; provided you will consent to not hang them for going there to buy them. You must remove this restriction too, from the sacred right of self-government. I am aware you say that taking slaves from the states of [to?] Nebraska, does not make slaves of freemen; but the African slave trader can say just as much. He does not catch free Negroes and bring them here. He finds them already slaves in the hands of their black captors, and he honestly buys them at the rate of about a red cotton handkerchief a head. This is very cheap, and it is a great abridgement of the sacred right of self-government to hang men for engaging in this profitable trade!

Another important objection to this application of the right of self-government, is that it enables the first few, to deprive the succeeding many, of a free exercise of the right of self-government. The first few may get slavery in, and the subsequent many cannot easily get it out. How common is the remark now in the slave states-"If we were only clear of our slaves, how much better it would be for us." They are actually deprived of the privilege of governing themselves as they would, by the action of a very few, in the beginning. The same thing was true of the whole nation at the time our Constitution was formed.

Whether slavery shall go into Nebraska, or other new territories, is not a matter of exclusive concern to the people who may go there. The whole nation is interested that the best use shall be made of these territories. We want them for the homes of free white people. This they cannot be, to any considerable extent, if slavery shall be planted within them. Slave states are places for poor white people to remove from; not to remove to. New free states are the places for poor people to go to and better their condition. For this use, the nation needs these territories.

Still further; there are constitutional relations between the slave and free states, which are degrading to the latter. We are under legal obligations to catch and return their runaway slaves to them-a sort of dirty, disagreeable job, which I believe, as a general rule the slaveholders will not perform for one another. Then again, in the control of the government-the management of the partnership affairs-they have greatly the advantage of us. By the Constitution, each state has two senators-each has a number of representatives, in proportion to the number of its people-and each has a number of presidential electors, equal to the whole number of its senators and representatives together. But in ascertaining the number of the people, for this purpose, five slaves are counted as being equal to three whites. The slaves do not vote; they are only counted and so used, as to swell the influence of the white people's votes. The practical effect of this is more aptly shown by a comparison of the states of South Carolina and Maine. South Carolina has six representatives, and so has Maine; South Carolina has eight presidential electors, and so has Maine. This is precise equality so far; and, of course they are equal in senators, each having two. Thus in the control of the government, the two states are equals precisely. But how are they in the number of their white people? Maine has 581,813-while South Carolina has 274,567. Maine has twice as many as South Carolina, and 32,679 over. Thus each white man in South Carolina is more than the double of any man in Maine. This is all because South Carolina, besides her free people, has 384,984 slaves. The South Carolinian has precisely the same advantage over the white man in every other free state, as well as in Maine. He is more than the double of any one of us in this crowd. The same advantage, but not to the same extent, is held by all the citizens of the slave states, over those of the free; and it is an absolute truth, without an exception, that there is no voter in any slave state, but who has more legal power in the government, than any voter in any free state. There is no instance of exact equality; and the disadvantage is against us the whole chapter through. This principle, in the aggregate, gives the slave states, in the present Congress, twenty additional representatives-being seven more than the whole majority by which they passed the Nebraska bill.

Now all this is manifestly unfair; yet I do not mention it to complain of it, in so far as it is already settled. It is in the Constitution; and I do not, for that cause, or any other cause, propose to destroy, or alter, or disregard the Constitution. I stand to it, fairly, fully, and firmly.

But when I am told I must leave it altogether to other people to say whether new partners are to be bred up and brought into the firm, on the same degrading terms against me, I respectfully demur. I insist, that whether I shall be a whole man, or only, the half of one, in comparison with others, is a question in which I am somewhat concerned; and one which no other man can have a sacred right of deciding for me. If I am wrong in this-if it really be a sacred right of self-government, in the man who shall go to Nebraska, to decide whether he will be the equal of me or the double of me, then after he shall have exercised that right, and thereby shall have reduced me to a still smaller fraction of a man than I already am, I should like for some gentleman deeply skilled in the mysteries of sacred rights, to provide himself with a microscope, and peep about, and find out, if he can, what has become of my sacred rights! They will surely be too small for detection with the naked eye.

Finally, I insist that if there is anything which it is the duty of the whole people to never entrust to any hands but their own, that thing is the preservation and perpetuity, of their own liberties, and institutions. And if they shall think, as I do, that the extension of slavery endangers them, more than any, or all other causes, how recreant to themselves, if they submit the question, and with it, the fate of their country, to a mere hand-full of men, bent only on temporary self-interest. If this question of slavery extension were an insignificant one-one having no power to do harm-it might be shuffled aside in this way. But being, as it is, the great Behemoth of danger, shall the strong gripe [grip?] of the nation be loosened upon him, to entrust him to the hands of such feeble keepers?

I have done with this mighty argument, of self-government. Go, sacred thing! Go in peace.

But Nebraska is urged as a great Union-saving measure. Well I too, go for saving the Union. Much as I hate slavery, I would consent to the extension of it rather than see the Union dissolved, just as I would consent to any great evil, to avoid a greater one. But when I go to Union saving, I must believe, at least, that the means I employ has some adaptation to the end. To my mind, Nebraska has no such adaptation.

"It hath no relish of salvation in it."[4]

It is an aggravation, rather, of the only one thing which ever endangers the Union. When it came upon us, all was peace and quiet. The nation was looking to the forming of new bonds of Union; and a long course of peace and prosperity seemed to lie before us. In the whole range of possibility, there scarcely appears to me to have been anything, out of which the slavery agitation could have been revived, except the very project of repealing the Missouri compromise. Every inch of territory we owned, already had a definite settlement of the slavery question, and by which, all parties were pledged to abide. Indeed, there was no uninhabited country on the continent, which we could acquire; if we except some extreme northern regions, which are wholly out of the question. In this state of case, the genius of discord himself, could scarcely have invented a way of again getting [setting?] us by the ears, but by turning back and destroying the peace measures of the past. The councils of that genius seem to have prevailed, the Missouri compromise was repealed; and here we are, in the midst of a new slavery agitation, such, I think, as we have never seen before. Who is responsible for this? Is it those who resist the measure; or those who, causelessly, brought it forward, and pressed it through, having reason to know, and, in fact, knowing it must and would be so resisted? It could not but be expected by its author, that it would be looked upon as a measure for the extension of slavery, aggravated by a gross breach of faith. Argue as you will, and long as you will, this is the naked

---

[4] William Shakespeare, *Hamlet* Act, 3, Scene 3

front and aspect, of the measure. And in this aspect, it could not but produce agitation. Slavery is founded in the selfishness of man's nature-opposition to it, in his love of justice. These principles are an eternal antagonism; and when brought into collision so fiercely, as slavery extension brings them, shocks, and throes, and convulsions must ceaselessly follow. Repeal the Missouri compromise-repeal all compromises-repeal the declaration of independence-repeal all past history, you still cannot repeal human nature. It still will be the abundance of man's heart, that slavery extension is wrong; and out of the abundance of his heart, his mouth will continue to speak.[5]...

The Missouri Compromise ought to be restored. For the sake of the Union, it ought to be restored. We ought to elect a House of Representatives which will vote its restoration. If by any means, we omit to do this, what follows! Slavery may or may not be established in Nebraska. But whether it be or not, we shall have repudiated-discarded from the councils of the Nation -the spirit of compromise; for who after this will ever trust in a national compromise? The spirit of mutual concession-that spirit which first gave us the Constitution, and which has thrice saved the Union-we shall have strangled and cast from us forever. And what shall we have in lieu of it? The South flushed with triumph and tempted to excesses; the North, betrayed, as they believe, brooding on wrong and burning for revenge. One side will provoke; the other resent. The one will taunt, the other defy; one agrees [aggresses?], the other retaliates. Already a few in the North, defy all constitutional restraints, resist the execution of the fugitive slave law, and even menace the institution of slavery in the states where it exists.

Already a few in the South, claim the constitutional right to take to and hold slaves in the free states-demand the revival of the slave trade; and demand a treaty with Great Britain by which fugitive slaves may be reclaimed from Canada. As yet they are but few on either side. It is a grave question for the lovers of the Union, whether the final destruction of the Missouri Compromise, and with it the spirit of all compromise will or will not embolden and embitter each of these, and fatally increase the numbers of both.

But restore the compromise, and what then? We thereby restore the national faith, the national confidence, the national feeling of brotherhood. We thereby reinstate the spirit of concession and compromise-that spirit which has never failed us in past perils, and which may be safely trusted for all the future. The South ought to join in doing this. The peace of the nation is as dear to them as to us. In memories of the past and hopes of the future,

---

[5] Lincoln paraphrases Mathew 12:34 and Luke 6:45.

they share as largely as we. It would be on their part, a great act-great in its spirit, and great in its effect. It would be worth to the nation a hundred years' purchase of peace and prosperity. And what of sacrifice would they make? They only surrender to us, what they gave us for a consideration long, long ago; what they have not now, asked for, struggled or cared for; what has been thrust upon them, not less to their own astonishment than to ours....

But even if we fail to technically restore the compromise, it is still a great point to carry a popular vote in favor of the restoration. The moral weight of such a vote cannot be estimated too highly. The authors of Nebraska are not at all satisfied with the destruction of the compromise-an endorsement of this principle they proclaim to be the great object. With them, Nebraska alone is a small matter-to establish a principle, for future use, is what they particularly desire.

That future use is to be the planting of slavery wherever in the wide world, local and unorganized opposition cannot prevent it. Now if you wish to give them this endorsement-if you wish to establish this principle-do so. I shall regret it; but it is your right. On the contrary if you are opposed to the principle-intend to give it no such endorsement-let no wheedling, no sophistry, divert you from throwing a direct vote against it.

Some men, mostly Whigs, who condemn the repeal of the Missouri Compromise, nevertheless hesitate to go for its restoration, lest they be thrown in company with the abolitionist. Will they allow me as an old Whig to tell them good humoredly, that I think this is very silly? Stand with anybody that stands right. Stand with him while he is right and part with him when he goes wrong. Stand with the abolitionist in restoring the Missouri Compromise; and stand against him when he attempts to repeal the fugitive slave law. In the latter case you stand with the Southern disunionist. What of that? you are still right. In both cases you are right. In both cases you oppose [expose?] the dangerous extremes. In both you stand on middle ground and hold the ship level and steady. In both you are national and nothing less than national. This is good old Whig ground. To desert such ground, because of any company, is to be less than a Whig-less than a man-less than an American.

I particularly object to the new position which the avowed principle of this Nebraska law gives to slavery in the body politic. I object to it because it assumes that there can be moral right in the enslaving of one man by another. I object to it as a dangerous dalliance for a free people-a sad evidence that, feeling prosperity we forget right-that liberty, as a principle, we have ceased to revere. I object to it because the fathers of the republic eschewed, and rejected it. The argument of "Necessity" was the only argument they ever admitted in favor of slavery; and so far, and so far only as it carried them, did they ever go. They found the institution existing among us, which they could not help; and they cast blame upon the British King for having permitted its introduction. Before the Constitution, they prohibited its introduction into the north-western Territory-the only country we owned, then free from it. At the framing and adoption of the Constitution, they forbore to so much as mention the word "slave" or "slavery" in the whole instrument. In the provision for the recovery of fugitives, the slave is spoken of as a "person held to serive or labor."[6] In that prohibiting the abolition of the African slave trade for twenty years, that trade is spoken of as "The migration or importation of such persons as any of the states now existing, shall think proper to admit," &c.[7] These are the only provisions alluding to slavery. Thus, the thing is hid away, in the Constitution, just as an afflicted man hides away a wen or a cancer, which he dares not cut out at once, lest he bleed to death; with the promise, nevertheless, that the cutting may begin at the end of a given time. Less than this our fathers could not do; and more they would not do. Necessity drove them so far, and farther, they would not go. But this is not all....

Thus we see, the plain unmistakable spirit of that age, towards slavery, was hostility to the principle, and toleration, only by necessity.

But now it is to be transformed into a "sacred right." Nebraska brings it forth, places it on the high road to extension and perpetuity; and, with a pat on its back, says to it, "Go, and God speed you." Henceforth it is to be the chief jewel of the nation-the very figure-head of the ship of state. Little by little, but steadily as man's march to the grave, we have been giving up the old for the new faith. Near eighty years ago we began by declaring that all men are created equal; but now from that beginning we have run down to the other declaration, that for some men to enslave others is a "sacred right of self- government." These principles cannot stand together. They are as opposite as God and mammon; and whoever holds to the one, must despise the other. When Pettit,[8] in connection with his support of the Nebraska bill, called the Declaration of Independence "a self-evident lie" he only did what consistency and candor require all other Nebraska men to do. Of the forty odd Nebraska senators who sat present and heard him, no one rebuked him. Nor am I apprized that any Nebraska newspaper, or any Nebraska orator, in the whole nation, has ever yet rebuked him. If this had been said among

[6] Article 4, section 2 of the Constitution
[7] Article 1, section 9 of the Constitution
[8] John Pettit (1807–1877) was a senator from Indiana.

Marion's men,[9] Southerners though they were, what would have become of the man who said it? If this had been said to the men who captured André, the man who said it, would probably have been hung sooner than Andre was.[10] If it had been said in old Independence Hall, seventy-eight years ago, the very door-keeper would have throttled the man, and thrust him into the street.

Let no one be deceived. The spirit of seventy-six and the spirit of Nebraska, are utter antagonisms; and the former is being rapidly displaced by the latter.

Fellow countrymen-Americans south, as well as north, shall we make no effort to arrest this? Already the liberal party throughout the world, express the apprehension "that the one retrograde institution in America, is undermining the principles of progress, and fatally violating the noblest political system the world ever saw."[11] This is not the taunt of enemies, but the warning of friends. Is it quite safe to disregard it-to despise it? Is there no danger to liberty itself, in discarding the earliest practice, and first precept of our ancient faith? In our greedy chase to make profit of the Negro, let us beware, lest we "cancel and tear to pieces"[12] even the white man's charter of freedom.

Our republican robe is soiled, and trailed in the dust. Let us repurify it. Let us turn and wash it white, in the spirit, if not the blood, of the Revolution. Let us turn slavery from its claims of "moral right," back upon its existing legal rights, and its arguments of "necessity." Let us return it to the position our fathers gave it; and there let it rest in peace. Let us re-adopt the Declaration of Independence, and with it, the practices, and policy, which harmonize with it. Let north and south-let all Americans-let all lovers of liberty everywhere-join in the great and good work. If we do this, we shall not only have saved the Union; but we shall have so saved it, as to make, and to keep it, forever worthy of the saving. We shall have so saved it, that the succeeding millions of free happy people, the world over, shall rise up, and call us blessed, to the latest generations.

---

[9] Francis Marion (c. 1732–1795) was a famous commander of rebel forces in the Carolinas in the Revolutionary War. His nickname was the Swamp Fox.

[10] John André (1750–1780) was a British officer hung as a spy during the Revolutionary War.

[11] Apparently a paraphrase of a quotation from a newspaper article. See W. Caleb McDaniel, "New light on a Lincoln quote," https://wcm1.web.rice.edu/new-light-on-lincoln-quote.html.

[12] *Macbeth*, Act III, Scene 2

DOCUMENT 13

Sociology for the South, or The Failure of Free Society

George Fitzhugh

1854

In the year that the Kansas-Nebraska Act roiled American politics, George Fitzhugh (1806–1881) published Sociology for the South. *Fitzhugh was a prominent American social theorist who popularized a political and social justification for Southern slavery. Fitzhugh's groundbreaking writing on the subject of slavery and its contributions to antebellum class structure was widely accepted throughout much of the South and even found its way into the North, as his social theories resonated with the poor working classes there. His first major work,* Sociology for the South, or The Failure of Free Society, *proclaimed that the free labor society of Northern industrialism was fundamentally flawed because, adhering to the principles of liberty and equality, it sought only the betterment of the strong while oppressing the weak. Southern slavery, with its emphasis on compassion and the material uplift of the less fortunate, promised a permanent escape from the competition, war, and class struggle that plagued Northern industrial society. These social theories were greatly admired by many for their simplicity and directness in defense of the Southern way of life. Fitzhugh's book supported the claim that slavery was a positive good (Documents 6, 16). Fitzhugh, of course, glossed over the many cruelties inflicted on the slaves and slave families. We should also note how easily Fitzhugh assimilated other relationships, such as those between a husband and wife, to the relationship between a master and his slave. For a defense of the Northern labor system, see Documents 19 and 20.*

SOURCE: George Fitzhugh, *Sociology for the South, or the Failure of Free Society* (Richmond, VA: A. Morris, Publisher, 1854), 245–249, 253–255, 257–258, https://docsouth.unc.edu/southlit/fitzhughsoc/fitzhugh.html.

The thing that has been, it is that which shall be; and that which is done is that which shall be done; and there is no new thing under the sun. Ecclesiastes 1:9.
Naturam expellas furca, tamen usque recurret. Horace.[1]

. . . But the chief and far most important enquiry is, how does slavery affect the condition of the slave? One of the wildest sects of Communists in France proposes not only to hold all property in common, but to divide the profits, not according to each man's in-put and labor, but according to each man's wants. Now this is precisely the system of domestic slavery with us. We provide for each slave, in old age and in infancy, in sickness and in health, not according to his labor, but according to his wants. The master's wants are costlier and more refined, and he therefore gets a larger share of the profits. A Southern farm is the beau ideal of Communism; it is a joint concern, in which the slave consumes more than the master, of the coarse products, and is far happier, because although the concern may fail, he is always sure of a support; he is only transferred to another master to participate in the profits of another concern; he marries when he pleases, because he knows he will have to work no more with a family than without one, and whether he live or die, that family will be taken care of; he exhibits all the pride of ownership, despises a partner in a smaller concern, "a poor man's Negro," boasts of "our crops, horses, fields and cattle;" and is as happy as a human being can be. And why should he not?—he enjoys as much of the fruits of the farm as he is capable of doing, and the wealthiest can do no more. Great wealth brings many additional cares, but few additional enjoyments. Our stomachs do not increase in capacity with our fortunes. We want no more clothing to keep us warm. We may create new wants, but we cannot create new pleasures. The intellectual enjoyments which wealth affords are probably balanced by the new cares it brings along with it.

There is no rivalry, no competition to get employment among slaves, as among free laborers. Nor is there a war between master and slave. The master's interest prevents his reducing the slave's allowance or wages in infancy or sickness, for he might lose the slave by so doing. His feeling for his slave never permits him to stint him in old age. The slaves are all well fed, well clad, have plenty of fuel, and are happy. They have no dread of the future—no

[1] Fitzhugh included these epigraphs on the cover of his book. The Latin reads, "You may expel nature with a pitchfork, but it will always return."

fear of want. A state of dependence is the only condition in which reciprocal affection can exist among human beings—the only situation in which the war of competition ceases, and peace, amity and good will arise. A state of independence always begets more or less of jealous rivalry and hostility. A man loves his children because they are weak, helpless and dependent; he loves his wife for similar reasons. When his children grow up and assert their independence, he is apt to transfer his affection to his grand-children. He ceases to love his wife when she becomes masculine or rebellious; but slaves are always dependent, never the rivals of their master. Hence, though men are often found at variance with wife or children, we never saw one who did not like his slaves, and rarely a slave who was not devoted to his master. "I am thy servant!" disarms me of the power of master. Every man feels the beauty, force and truth of this sentiment of Sterne.[2] But he who acknowledges its truth, tacitly admits that dependence is a tie of affection, that the relation of master and slave is one of mutual good will. Volumes written on the subject would not prove as much as this single sentiment. It has found its way to the heart of every reader, and carried conviction along with it. The slaveholder is like other men; he will not tread on the worm nor break the bruised reed. The ready submission of the slave, nine times out of ten, disarms his wrath even when the slave has offended. The habit of command may make him imperious and fit him for rule; but he is only imperious when thwarted or ordered by his equals; he would scorn to put on airs of command among blacks, whether slaves or free; he always speaks to them in a kind and subdued tone. We go farther, and say the slaveholder is better than others—because he has greater occasion for the exercise of the affection. His whole life is spent in providing for the minutest wants of others, in taking care of them in sickness and in health. Hence he is the least selfish of men. Is not the old bachelor who retires to seclusion, always selfish? Is not the head of a large family almost always kind and benevolent? And is not the slaveholder the head of the largest family? Nature compels master and slave to be friends; nature makes employers and free laborers enemies.

The institution of slavery gives full development and full play to the affections. Free society chills, stints and eradicates them. In a homely way the farm will support all, and we are not in a hurry to send our children into the world, to push their way and make their fortunes, with a capital of knavish maxims. We are better husbands, better fathers, better friends, and better

[2] Probably Laurence Sterne (1713-1768), a British writer and clergyman.

neighbors than our Northern brethren. The tie of kindred to the fifth degree is often a tie of affection with us. First cousins are scarcely acknowledged at the North, and even children are prematurely pushed off into the world. Love for others is the organic law of our society, as self-love is of theirs.

Every social structure must have its substratum. In free society this substratum, the weak, poor and ignorant, is borne down upon and oppressed with continually increasing weight by all above. We have solved the problem of relieving this substratum from the pressure from above. The slaves are the substratum, and the master's feelings and interests alike prevent him from bearing down upon and oppressing them. With us the pressure on society is like that of air or water, so equally diffused as not anywhere to be felt. With them it is the pressure of the enormous screw, never yielding, continually increasing. Free laborers are little better than trespassers on this earth given by God to all mankind. The birds of the air have nests, and the foxes have holes, but they have not where to lay their heads. They are driven to cities to dwell in damp and crowded cellars, and thousands are even forced to lie in the open air. This accounts for the rapid growth of Northern cities. The feudal barons were more generous and hospitable and less tyrannical than the petty landholders of modern times. Besides, each inhabitant of the barony was considered as having some right of residence, some claim to protection from the Lord of the Manor. A few of them escaped to the municipalities for purposes of trade, and to enjoy a larger liberty. Now penury and the want of a home drive thousands to towns. The slave always has a home, always an interest in the proceeds of the soil....

At the slaveholding South all is peace, quiet, plenty and contentment. We have no mobs, no trades unions, no strikes for higher wages, no armed resistance to the law, but little jealousy of the rich by the poor. We have but few in our jails, and fewer in our poor houses. We produce enough of the comforts and necessaries of life for a population three or four times as numerous as ours. We are wholly exempt from the torrent of pauperism, crime, agrarianism, and infidelity which Europe is pouring from her jails and alms houses on the already crowded North. Population increases slowly, wealth rapidly. In the tide water region of Eastern Virginia, as far as our experience extends, the crops have doubled in fifteen years, whilst the population has been almost stationary. In the same period the lands, owing to improvements of the soil and the many fine houses erected in the country, have nearly doubled in value. This ratio of improvement has been approximated or exceeded wherever in the South slaves are numerous. We have enough for the present, and no Malthusian specters frightening us for the future.[3] Wealth is more equally distributed than at the North, where a few millionaires own most of the property of the country. (These millionaires are men of cold hearts and weak minds; they know how to make money, but not how to use it, either for the benefit of themselves or of others.) High intellectual and moral attainments, refinement of head and heart, give standing to a man in the South, however poor he may be. Money is, with few exceptions, the only thing that ennobles at the North. We have poor among us, but none who are over-worked and underfed. We do not crowd cities because lands are abundant and their owners, kind, merciful and hospitable. The poor are as hospitable as the rich, the Negro as the white man. Nobody dreams of turning a friend, a relative, or a stranger from his door. The very Negro who deems it no crime to steal, would scorn to sell his hospitality. We have no loafers, because the poor relative or friend who borrows our horse, or spends a week under our roof, is a welcome guest. The loose economy, the wasteful mode of living at the South, is a blessing when rightly considered; it keeps want, scarcity and famine at a distance, because it leaves room for retrenchment. The nice, accurate economy of France, England and New England, keeps society always on the verge of famine, because it leaves no room to retrench, that is to live on a part only of what they now consume. Our society exhibits no appearance of precocity, no symptoms of decay. A long course of continuing improvement is in prospect before us, with no limits which human foresight can descry. Actual liberty and equality with our white population has been approached much nearer than in the free states. Few of our whites ever work as day laborers, none as cooks, scullions, ostlers, body servants, or in other menial capacities. One free citizen does not lord it over another; hence that feeling of independence and equality that distinguishes us; hence that pride of character, that self-respect, that gives us ascendancy when we come in contact with Northerners. It is a distinction to be a Southerner, as it was once to be a Roman citizen....

In conclusion, we will repeat the propositions, in somewhat different phraseology, with which we set out. First—that liberty and equality, with their concomitant free competition, beget a war in society that is as destructive to its weaker members as the custom of exposing the deformed and

[3] Thomas Robert Malthus (1766–1834) was a political economist who argued that an increase in the supply of food was likely to produce only a temporary benefit because it would lead to an increase in population, which would make food scarcer again. He also argued that population growth would outpace food production.

crippled children. Secondly—that slavery protects the weaker members of society just as do the relations of parent, guardian and husband, and is as necessary, as natural, and almost as universal as those relations. Is our demonstration imperfect? Does universal experience sustain our theory? Should the conclusions to which we have arrived appear strange and startling, let them therefore not be rejected without examination. The world has had but little opportunity to contrast the working of liberty and equality with the old order of things, which always partook more or less of the character of domestic slavery. The strong prepossession in the public mind in favor of the new system, makes it reluctant to attribute the evil phenomena which it exhibits, to defects inherent in the system itself. That these defects should not have been foreseen and pointed out by any process of a priori reasoning, is but another proof of the fallibility of human sagacity and foresight when attempting to foretell the operation of new institutions. It is as much as human reason can do, when examining the complex frame of society, to trace effects back to their causes—much more than it can do, to foresee what effects new causes will produce. We invite investigation.

DOCUMENT 14

Dred Scott v. Sandford

Roger Taney

March 6, 1857

Dred Scott v. Sandford *remains one of the most infamous Supreme Court cases ever decided. Dred Scott, a slave, sued for his freedom after his former master took him to live where slavery was outlawed, first, in the free state of Illinois and, later, in the free territory of what would become Minnesota. In a landmark 7–2 decision, Chief Justice Roger Taney (pronounced TAW-nee) declared that Dred Scott lacked standing (or the legal right to initiate a lawsuit) in the case because members of his race were not, and never could be, citizens of the United States; they had "no rights which the white man was bound to respect." Taney also concluded that Congress could not prohibit slavery in the territories, since the right to hold property in slaves is "distinctly and expressly affirmed in the Constitution." Taney was able to come to both of these conclusions in part because he believed that the American Founders did not mean to include African slaves or their descendants in the provision of the Declaration of Independence that asserts "all men are created equal."*

The two dissenting opinions, by Justices John McLean and Benjamin R. Curtis, short excerpts of which are included below, criticized Taney's contention that "persons of color" were not citizens when the Constitution was adopted, pointing out that at that time five states allowed African Americans to vote. This made them citizens of those states and thus of the United States. Both Curtis and McLean also argued that slavery was unjust and against nature. Curtis cited evidence to show that slavery had legal standing only in state law. Abraham Lincoln, who accused Judge Taney of being the first person to ever claim that the Founders did not mean to include the black man in the Declaration of Independence, also criticized the Supreme Court's ruling (Documents 15, 17, and Appendix E).

SOURCE: 60 U.S. 393, https://www.law.cornell.edu/supremecourt/text/60/393.

Mr. Chief Justice Taney delivered the opinion of the court....

The question is simply this: can a Negro whose ancestors were imported into this country and sold as slaves become a member of the political community formed and brought into existence by the Constitution of the United States, and as such become entitled to all the rights, and privileges, and immunities, guaranteed by that instrument to the citizen, one of which rights is the privilege of suing in a court of the United States in the cases specified in the Constitution?

It will be observed that the plea applies to that class of persons only whose ancestors were Negroes of the African race, and imported into this country and sold and held as slaves. The only matter in issue before the court, therefore, is, whether the descendants of such slaves, when they shall be emancipated, or who are born of parents who had become free before their birth, are citizens of a state in the sense in which the word "citizen" is used in the Constitution of the United States. And this being the only matter in dispute on the pleadings, the court must be understood as speaking in this opinion of that class only, that is, of those persons who are the descendants of Africans who were imported into this country and sold as slaves....

...The question before us is whether the class of persons described in the plea in abatement compose a portion of this people, and are constituent members of this sovereignty? We think they are not, and that they are not included, and were not intended to be included, under the word "citizens" in the Constitution, and can therefore claim none of the rights and privileges which that instrument provides for and secures to citizens of the United States. On the contrary, they were at that time considered as a subordinate and inferior class of beings who had been subjugated by the dominant race, and, whether emancipated or not, yet remained subject to their authority, and had no rights or privileges but such as those who held the power and the government might choose to grant them. It is not the province of the court to decide upon the justice or injustice, the policy or impolicy, of these laws. The decision of that question belonged to the political or lawmaking power, to those who formed the sovereignty and framed the Constitution. The duty of the court is to interpret the instrument they have framed with the best lights we can obtain on the subject, and to administer it as we find it, according to its true intent and meaning when it was adopted....

The question then arises, whether the provisions of the Constitution, in relation to the personal rights and privileges to which the citizen of a state should be entitled, embraced the Negro African race, at that time in this country, or who might afterwards be imported, who had then or should afterwards be made free in any state, and to put it in the power of a single state to make him a citizen of the United States and endue him with the full rights of citizenship in every other state without their consent? Does the Constitution of the United States act upon him whenever he shall be made free under the laws of a state, and raised there to the rank of a citizen, and immediately clothe him with all the privileges of a citizen in every other state, and in its own courts?

The court think the affirmative of these propositions cannot be maintained. And if it cannot, the plaintiff in error could not be a citizen of the state of Missouri within the meaning of the Constitution of the United States, and, consequently, was not entitled to sue in its courts....

It becomes necessary, therefore, to determine who were citizens of the several states when the Constitution was adopted. And in order to do this, we must recur to the governments and institutions of the thirteen colonies when they separated from Great Britain and formed new sovereignties, and took their places in the family of independent nations. We must inquire who, at that time, were recognized as the people or citizens of a state whose rights and liberties had been outraged by the English government, and who declared their independence and assumed the powers of government to defend their rights by force of arms.

In the opinion of the court, the legislation and histories of the times, and the language used in the Declaration of Independence, show that neither the class of persons who had been imported as slaves nor their descendants, whether they had become free or not, were then acknowledged as a part of the people, nor intended to be included in the general words used in that memorable instrument.

It is difficult at this day to realize the state of public opinion in relation to that unfortunate race which prevailed in the civilized and enlightened portions of the world at the time of the Declaration of Independence and when the Constitution of the United States was framed and adopted. But the public history of every European nation displays it in a manner too plain to be mistaken.

They had for more than a century before been regarded as beings of an inferior order, and altogether unfit to associate with the white race either in social or political relations, and so far inferior that they had no rights which the white man was bound to respect, and that the Negro might justly and lawfully be reduced to slavery for his benefit. He was bought and sold, and treated as an ordinary article of merchandise and traffic whenever a profit could be made by it. This opinion was at that time fixed and universal in the civilized portion of the white race. It was regarded as an axiom in morals as well as in politics which no one thought of disputing or supposed to be open to dispute, and men in every grade and position in society daily and habitually acted upon it in their private pursuits, as well as in matters of public concern, without doubting for a moment the correctness of this opinion. . . .

[Taney described two laws, one from Maryland, "a large slaveholding state," the other from Massachusetts, "the first state in which slavery ceased to exist." Both laws concerned marriage between whites and Negroes and mullatos.]

We give both of these laws in the words used by the respective legislative bodies because the language in which they are framed, as well as the provisions contained in them, show, too plainly to be misunderstood the degraded condition of this unhappy race. They were still in force when the Revolution began, and are a faithful index to the state of feeling towards the class of persons of whom they speak, and of the position they occupied throughout the thirteen colonies, in the eyes and thoughts of the men who framed the Declaration of Independence and established the state constitutions and governments. They show that a perpetual and impassable barrier was intended to be erected between the white race and the one which they had reduced to slavery, and governed as subjects with absolute and despotic power, and which they then looked upon as so far below them in the scale of created beings, that intermarriages between white persons and Negroes or mulattoes were regarded as unnatural and immoral, and punished as crimes, not only in the parties, but in the person who joined them in marriage. And no distinction in this respect was made between the free Negro or mulatto and the slave, but this stigma of the deepest degradation was fixed upon the whole race.

We refer to these historical facts for the purpose of showing the fixed opinions concerning that race upon which the statesmen of that day spoke and acted. It is necessary to do this in order to determine whether the general terms used in the Constitution of the United States as to the rights of man and the rights of the people was intended to include them, or to give to them or their posterity the benefit of any of its provisions.

The language of the Declaration of Independence is equally conclusive:

It begins by declaring that, "[w]hen in the course of human events it becomes necessary for one people to dissolve the political bands which have connected them with another, and to assume among the powers of the earth the separate and equal station to which the laws of nature and nature's God entitle them, a decent respect for the opinions of mankind requires that they should declare the causes which impel them to the separation."

It then proceeds to say:

"We hold these truths to be self-evident: that all men are created equal; that they are endowed by their Creator with certain unalienable rights; that among them is [sic] life, liberty, and the pursuit of happiness; that to secure these rights, governments are instituted, deriving their just powers from the consent of the governed."

The general words above quoted would seem to embrace the whole human family, and if they were used in a similar instrument at this day would be so understood. But it is too clear for dispute that the enslaved African race were not intended to be included, and formed no part of the people who framed and adopted this declaration, for if the language, as understood in that day, would embrace them, the conduct of the distinguished men who framed the Declaration of Independence would have been utterly and flagrantly inconsistent with the principles they asserted, and instead of the sympathy of mankind to which they so confidently appealed, they would have deserved and received universal rebuke and reprobation.

Yet the men who framed this declaration were great men—high in literary acquirements, high in their sense of honor, and incapable of asserting principles inconsistent with those on which they were acting. They perfectly understood the meaning of the language they used, and how it would be understood by others, and they knew that it would not in any part of the civilized world be supposed to embrace the Negro race, which, by common consent, had been excluded from civilized governments and the family of nations, and doomed to slavery. They spoke and acted according to the then established doctrines and principles, and in the ordinary language of the day, and no one misunderstood them. The unhappy black race were separated from the white by indelible marks, and laws long before established, and were never thought of or spoken of except as property, and when the claims of the owner or the profit of the trader were supposed to need protection.

This state of public opinion had undergone no change when the Constitution was adopted, as is equally evident from its provisions and language.

The brief preamble sets forth by whom it was formed, for what purposes, and for whose benefit and protection. It declares that it is formed by the people of the United States—that is to say, by those who were members of the different political communities in the several states—and its great object is declared to be to secure the blessings of liberty to themselves and their posterity. It speaks in general terms of the people of the United States, and of citizens of the several states, when it is providing for the exercise of the powers granted or the privileges secured to the citizen. It does not define what description of persons are intended to be included under these terms, or who shall be regarded as a citizen and one of the people. It uses them as terms so well understood that no further description or definition was necessary.

But there are two clauses in the Constitution which point directly and specifically to the Negro race as a separate class of persons, and show clearly that they were not regarded as a portion of the people or citizens of the government then formed.

One of these clauses reserves to each of the thirteen states the right to import slaves until the year 1808 if it thinks proper. And the importation which it thus sanctions was unquestionably of persons of the race of which we are speaking, as the traffic in slaves in the United States had always been confined to them.[1] And by the other provision the states pledge themselves to each other to maintain the right of property of the master by delivering up to him any slave who may have escaped from his service, and be found within their respective territories. By the first above-mentioned clause, therefore, the right to purchase and hold this property is directly sanctioned and authorized for twenty years by the people who framed the Constitution. And by the second, they pledge themselves to maintain and uphold the right of the master in the manner specified, as long as the government they then formed should endure. And these two provisions show conclusively that neither the description of persons therein referred to nor their descendants were embraced in any of the other provisions of the Constitution, for certainly these two clauses were not intended to confer on them or their posterity the blessings of liberty, or any of the personal rights so carefully provided for the citizen.

No one of that race had ever migrated to the United States voluntarily; all of them had been brought here as articles of merchandise. The number that had been emancipated at that time were but few in comparison with those held in slavery, and they were identified in the public mind with the race to which they belonged, and regarded as a part of the slave population rather than the free. It is obvious that they were not even in the minds of the Framers

---

[1] Taney may have been unaware of the extensive trade in Native American slaves, in which both the settlers and the natives themselves engaged. See, for example, Allan Gallay, *The Indian Slave Trade: The Rise of the English Empire in the American South, 1670–1717* (New Haven: Yale University Press, 2003).

of the Constitution when they were conferring special rights and privileges upon the citizens of a state in every other part of the Union.

Indeed, when we look to the condition of this race in the several states at the time, it is impossible to believe that these rights and privileges were intended to be extended to them....

The only two provisions [in the Constitution] which point to them and include them treat them as property and make it the duty of the government to protect it; no other power, in relation to this race, is to be found in the Constitution; and as it is a government of special, delegated, powers, no authority beyond these two provisions can be constitutionally exercised. The government of the United States had no right to interfere for any other purpose but that of protecting the rights of the owner, leaving it altogether with the several states to deal with this race, whether emancipated or not, as each state may think justice, humanity, and the interests and safety of society, require. The states evidently intended to reserve this power exclusively to themselves.

No one, we presume, supposes that any change in public opinion or feeling, in relation to this unfortunate race, in the civilized nations of Europe or in this country, should induce the court to give to the words of the Constitution a more liberal construction in their favor than they were intended to bear when the instrument was framed and adopted. Such an argument would be altogether inadmissible in any tribunal called on to interpret it. If any of its provisions are deemed unjust, there is a mode prescribed in the instrument itself by which it may be amended; but while it remains unaltered, it must be construed now as it was understood at the time of its adoption. It is not only the same in words, but the same in meaning, and delegates the same powers to the government, and reserves and secures the same rights and privileges to the citizen; and as long as it continues to exist in its present form, it speaks not only in the same words, but with the same meaning and intent with which it spoke when it came from the hands of its framers and was voted on and adopted by the people of the United States. Any other rule of construction would abrogate the judicial character of this court, and make it the mere reflex of the popular opinion or passion of the day. This court was not created by the Constitution for such purposes. Higher and graver trusts have been confided to it, and it must not falter in the path of duty....

And, upon a full and careful consideration of the subject, the court is of opinion, that, upon the facts stated in the plea in abatement, Dred Scott was not a citizen of Missouri within the meaning of the Constitution of the United States, and not entitled as such to sue in its courts....

In considering this part of the controversy [Taney turns from the question of whether Dred Scott was a citizen to the question of whether Scott's time in a free state and territory made him a free man], two questions arise: 1. Was he, together with his family, free in Missouri by reason of the stay in the territory of the United States hereinbefore mentioned? And 2. If they were not, is Scott himself free by reason of his removal to Rock Island, in the state of Illinois, as stated in the above admissions?

We proceed to examine the first question.

The act of Congress[2] upon which the plaintiff relies declares that slavery and involuntary servitude, except as a punishment for crime, shall be forever prohibited in all that part of the territory ceded by France, under the name of Louisiana, which lies north of thirty-six degrees thirty minutes north latitude, and not included within the limits of Missouri. And the difficulty which meets us at the threshold of this part of the inquiry is whether Congress was authorized to pass this law under any of the powers granted to it by the Constitution; for if the authority is not given by that instrument, it is the duty of this court to declare it void and inoperative, and incapable of conferring freedom upon anyone who is held as a slave under the laws of any one of the states.

The counsel for the plaintiff has laid much stress upon that article in the Constitution which confers on Congress the power "to dispose of and make all needful rules and regulations respecting the territory or other property belonging to the United States,"[3] but, in the judgment of the court, that provision has no bearing on the present controversy, and the power there given, whatever it may be, is confined, and was intended to be confined, to the territory which at that time belonged to, or was claimed by, the United States, and was within their boundaries as settled by the treaty with Great Britain, and can have no influence upon a territory afterwards acquired from a foreign government. It was a special provision for a known and particular territory, and to meet a present emergency, and nothing more....

We do not mean, however, to question the power of Congress in this respect. The power to expand the territory of the United States by the admission of new states is plainly given, and, in the construction of this power by all the departments of the government, it has been held to authorize the acquisition of territory not fit for admission at the time, but to be admitted as soon as its population and situation would entitle it to admission....

---

[2] The Missouri Compromise, Document 2

[3] Article IV, section 3

But, until that time arrives, it is undoubtedly necessary that some government should be established in order to organize society and to protect the inhabitants in their persons and property, and as the people of the United States could act in this matter only through the government which represented them and through which they spoke and acted when the territory was obtained, it was not only within the scope of its powers, but it was its duty, to pass such laws and establish such a government as would enable those by whose authority they acted to reap the advantages anticipated from its acquisition and to gather there a population which would enable it to assume the position to which it was destined among the states of the Union....

But the power of Congress over the person or property of a citizen can never be a mere discretionary power under our Constitution and form of government. The powers of the government and the rights and privileges of the citizen are regulated and plainly defined by the Constitution itself. And when the territory becomes a part of the United States, the federal government enters into possession in the character impressed upon it by those who created it. It enters upon it with its powers over the citizen strictly defined, and limited by the Constitution, from which it derives its own existence and by virtue of which alone it continues to exist and act as a government and sovereignty. It has no power of any kind beyond it, and it cannot, when it enters a territory of the United States, put off its character and assume discretionary or despotic powers which the Constitution has denied to it. It cannot create for itself a new character separated from the citizens of the United States and the duties it owes them under the provisions of the Constitution. The territory being a part of the United States, the government and the citizen both enter it under the authority of the Constitution, with their respective rights defined and marked out, and the federal government can exercise no power over his person or property beyond what that instrument confers, nor lawfully deny any right which it has reserved....

The powers over person and property of which we speak are not only not granted to Congress, but are in express terms denied, and they are forbidden to exercise them. And this prohibition is not confined to the states, but the words are general, and extend to the whole territory over which the Constitution gives it power to legislate, including those portions of it remaining under territorial government, as well as that covered by states. It is a total absence of power everywhere within the dominion of the United States, and places the citizens of a territory, so far as these rights are concerned, on the same footing with citizens of the states, and guards them as firmly and plainly against any inroads which the general government might attempt under the plea of implied or incidental powers. And if Congress itself cannot do this—if it is beyond the powers conferred on the federal government—it will be admitted, we presume, that it could not authorize a territorial government to exercise them. It could confer no power on any local government established by its authority to violate the provisions of the Constitution....

Now, as we have already said in an earlier part of this opinion upon a different point, the right of property in a slave is distinctly and expressly affirmed in the Constitution. The right to traffic in it, like an ordinary article of merchandise and property, was guaranteed to the citizens of the United States in every state that might desire it for twenty years. And the government in express terms is pledged to protect it in all future time if the slave escapes from his owner. This is done in plain words—too plain to be misunderstood. And no word can be found in the Constitution which gives Congress a greater power over slave property or which entitles property of that kind to less protection than property of any other description. The only power conferred is the power coupled with the duty of guarding and protecting the owner in his rights.

Upon these considerations, it is the opinion of the court that the act of Congress which prohibited a citizen from holding and owning property of this kind in the territory of the United States north of the line therein mentioned is not warranted by the Constitution, and is therefore void, and that neither Dred Scott himself nor any of his family were made free by being carried into this territory, even if they had been carried there by the owner with the intention of becoming a permanent resident....

Upon the whole, therefore, it is the judgment of this court that it appears by the record before us that the plaintiff [Dred Scott] is not a citizen of Missouri in the sense in which that word is used in the Constitution, and that the Circuit Court of the United States, for that reason, had no jurisdiction in the case, and could give no judgment in it. Its judgment for the defendant must, consequently, be reversed, and a mandate issued directing the suit to be dismissed for want of jurisdiction.

Mr. Justice McLean, dissenting.

...In the argument, it was said that a colored citizen would not be an agreeable member of society. This is more a matter of taste than of law. Several of the states have admitted persons of color to the right of suffrage, and, in this view, have recognized them as citizens, and this has been done in the slave as well as the free states. On the question of citizenship, it must be admitted

that we have not been very fastidious. Under the late treaty with Mexico, we have made citizens of all grades, combinations, and colors. The same was done in the admission of Louisiana and Florida. No one ever doubted, and no court ever held that the people of these territories did not become citizens under the treaty. They have exercised all the rights of citizens, without being naturalized under the acts of Congress. . . .

In the formation of the federal Constitution, care was taken to confer no power on the federal government to interfere with this institution in the states. In the provision respecting the slave trade, in fixing the ratio of representation, and providing for the reclamation of fugitives from labor, slaves were referred to as persons, and in no other respect are they considered in the Constitution.

We need not refer to the mercenary spirit which introduced the infamous traffic in slaves to show the degradation of Negro slavery in our country. This system was imposed upon our colonial settlements by the mother country, and it is due to truth to say that the commercial colonies and states were chiefly engaged in the traffic. But we know as a historical fact that James Madison, that great and good man, a leading member in the Federal Convention, was solicitous to guard the language of that instrument so as not to convey the idea that there could be property in man.

I prefer the lights of Madison, Hamilton, and Jay[4] as a means of construing the Constitution in all its bearings, rather than to look behind that period into a traffic which is now declared to be piracy, and punished with death by Christian nations. I do not like to draw the sources of our domestic relations from so dark a ground. Our independence was a great epoch in the history of freedom, and while I admit the government was not made especially for the colored race, yet many of them were citizens of the New England states, and exercised, the rights of suffrage when the Constitution was adopted, and it was not doubted by any intelligent person that its tendencies would greatly ameliorate their condition.

Many of the states, on the adoption of the Constitution, or shortly afterward, took measures to abolish slavery within their respective jurisdictions, and it is a well-known fact that a belief was cherished by the leading men, South as well as North, that the institution of slavery would gradually decline

[4] Apparently a reference to the Federalist, a commentary on and argument for the adoption of the Constitution, written by Madison, Alexander Hamilton, and John Jay.

until it would become extinct. The increased value of slave labor, in the culture of cotton and sugar, prevented the realization of this expectation. Like all other communities and states, the South were influenced by what they considered to be their own interests.

But if we are to turn our attention to the dark ages of the world, why confine our view to colored slavery? On the same principles, white men were made slaves. All slavery has its origin in power, and is against right....

Mr. Justice Curtis, dissenting.

...On the 25th of June, 1778, the Articles of Confederation being under consideration by the Congress, the delegates from South Carolina moved to amend this fourth article by inserting after the word "free," and before the word "inhabitants," the word "white," so that the privileges and immunities of general citizenship would be secured only to white persons. Two states voted for the amendment, eight states against it, and the vote of one state was divided. The language of the article stood unchanged, and both by its terms of inclusion, "free inhabitants," and the strong implication from its terms of exclusion, "paupers, vagabonds, and fugitives from justice," who alone were excepted, it is clear that under the Confederation, and at the time of the adoption of the Constitution, free colored persons of African descent might be, and, by reason of their citizenship in certain states, were, entitled to the privileges and immunities of general citizenship of the United States....

I can find nothing in the Constitution which, proprio vigore,[5] deprives of their citizenship any class of persons who were citizens of the United States at the time of its adoption, or who should be native-born citizens of any state after its adoption, nor any power enabling Congress to disfranchise persons born on the soil of any state, and entitled to citizenship of such state by its constitution and laws. And my opinion is that, under the Constitution of the United States, every free person born on the soil of a state, who is a citizen of that state by force of its constitution or laws, is also a citizen of the United States....

It has been often asserted that the Constitution was made exclusively by and for the white race. It has already been shown that, in five of the thirteen original states, colored persons then possessed the elective franchise, and were among those by whom the Constitution was ordained and established.

---

[5] by its own force

If so, it is not true, in point of fact, that the Constitution was made exclusively by the white race. And that it was made exclusively for the white race is, in my opinion, not only an assumption not warranted by anything in the Constitution, but contradicted by its opening declaration that it was ordained and established by the people of the United States, for themselves and their posterity. And as free colored persons were then citizens of at least five states, and so in every sense part of the people of the United States, they were among those for whom and whose posterity the Constitution was ordained and established....

I dissent, therefore, from that part of the opinion of the majority of the court in which it is held that a person of African descent cannot be a citizen of the United States, and I regret I must go further and dissent both from what I deem their assumption of authority to examine the constitutionality of the act of Congress commonly called the Missouri Compromise Act[6] and the grounds and conclusions announced in their opinion....

Slavery, being contrary to natural right, is created only by municipal law. This is not only plain in itself, and agreed by all writers on the subject, but is inferable from the Constitution and has been explicitly declared by this court. The Constitution refers to slaves as "persons held to service in one state, under the laws thereof." Nothing can more clearly describe a status created by municipal law. In Prigg v. Pennsylvania, 10 Pet. 611 [1842], this court said: "The state of slavery is deemed to be a mere municipal regulation, founded on and limited to the range of territorial laws." In Rankin v. Lydia, 2 Marsh. 12, 470 [1820], the Supreme Court of Appeals of Kentucky said:

> Slavery is sanctioned by the laws of this state, and the right to hold them under our municipal regulations is unquestionable. But we view this as a right existing by positive law of a municipal character, without foundation in the law of nature or the unwritten common law.

I am not acquainted with any case or writer questioning the correctness of this doctrine....

Is it conceivable that the Constitution has conferred the right on every citizen to become a resident on the territory of the United States with his slaves, and there to hold them as such, but has neither made nor provided for any municipal regulations which are essential to the existence of slavery?

---

[6] Document 2

Is it not more rational to conclude that they who framed and adopted the Constitution were aware that persons held to service under the laws of a state are property only to the extent and under the conditions fixed by those laws that they must cease to be available as property, when their owners voluntarily place them permanently within another jurisdiction, where no municipal laws on the subject of slavery exist . . . ?

DOCUMENT 15

Reply to the *Dred Scott* Decision

Abraham Lincoln

June 26, 1857

One month after the Supreme Court released its decision in the Dred Scott case (Document 14), Abraham Lincoln delivered a response in Springfield, Illinois. Like many Republicans, Lincoln was disgusted with the court's decision. The future of the Republican Party was now at stake, since Chief Justice Roger Taney had declared that the centerpiece of the Republican platform—the right and duty of Congress to prohibit the extension of slavery into the territories—was unconstitutional. Referring to the historical arguments made by Taney and their criticism in the dissenting opinions (Document 14), Lincoln's response to the Dred Scott decision focused on the Founders' understanding of the principles of a just government, in particular the meaning of the equality principle as stated in the Declaration of Independence and its significance for the future of slavery.

Lincoln's speech is also notable for its discussion of white prejudice against African Americans. Lincoln pointed out how his principal political opponent, Senator Stephen A. Douglas (D-Illinois) and the Democratic party, sought to use this prejudice. Lincoln in turn sought to turn this prejudice to the advantage of Republicans. It is in this context that Lincoln brings up the issue of expatriation—sending freed slaves and all African Americans—to Africa. For Lincoln, such expatriation could only be voluntary, but he left the character of expatriation and even its possibility unclear. Doing so was a way of dealing with the prejudice that Lincoln pointed to. Slavery was the cause of the Civil War, and the prejudice against African Americans, as well as the self-interest of those North and South who profited from slavery, as Lincoln also notes, made slavery an intractable political problem.

SOURCE: Frank Crosby, *LIFE OF ABRAHAM LINCOLN, HIS EARLY HISTORY AND POLITICAL CAREER; TOGETHER WITH THE SPEECHES, MESSAGES, PROCLAMATIONS AND OTHER OFFICIAL DOCUMENTS ILLUSTRATIVE OF HIS EVENTFUL ADMINISTRATION* (Philadelphia: John E. Potter, 1865), 431–441, https://quod.lib.umich.edu/l/lincoln2/ACK7441.0001.001/433?rgn=full+text;view=image.

Fellow citizens: I am here to-night, partly by the invitation of some of you, and partly by my own inclination. Two weeks ago, Judge Douglas spoke here on the several subjects of Kansas, the *Dred Scott* decision, and Utah. I listened to the speech at the time, and have read the report of it since. It was intended to controvert opinions which I think just, and to assail (politically, not personally,) those men who, in common with me, entertain those opinions. For this reason I wished then, and still wish, to make some answer to it, which I now take the opportunity of doing....

...[T]he *Dred Scott* decision... declares two propositions—first, that a Negro cannot sue in the U.S. Courts; and secondly, that Congress cannot prohibit slavery in the Territories. It was made by a divided court—dividing differently on the different points. Judge Douglas does not discuss the merits of the decision; and, in that respect, I shall follow his example, believing I could no more improve on McLean and Curtis, than he could on Taney....

There is a natural disgust in the minds of nearly all white people, to the idea of an indiscriminate amalgamation of the white and black races; and Judge Douglas evidently is basing his chief hope, upon the chances of being able to appropriate the benefit of this disgust to himself. If he can, by much drumming and repeating, fasten the odium of that idea upon his adversaries, he thinks he can struggle through the storm. He therefore clings to this hope, as a drowning man to the last plank. He makes an occasion for lugging it in from the opposition to the *Dred Scott* decision. He finds the Republicans insisting that the Declaration of Independence includes all men, black as well as white; and forth-with he boldly denies that it includes Negroes at all, and proceeds to argue gravely that all who contend it does, do so only because they want to vote, and eat, and sleep, and marry with Negroes! He will have it that they cannot be consistent else. Now I protest against that counterfeit logic which concludes that, because I do not want a black woman for a slave I must necessarily want her for a wife. I need not have her for either, I can just leave her alone. In some respects she certainly is not my equal; but in her natural right to eat the bread she earns with her own hands without asking leave of anyone else, she is my equal, and the equal of all others.

Chief Justice Taney, in his opinion in the *Dred Scott* case, admits that the language of the Declaration is broad enough to include the whole human family, but he and Judge Douglas argue that the authors of that instrument did not intend to include Negroes, by the fact that they did not at once, actually place them on an equality with the whites. Now this grave argument comes to just nothing at all, by the other fact, that they did not at once, or ever afterwards, actually place all white people on an equality with one or another. And this is the staple argument of both the chief justice and the senator, for doing this obvious violence to the plain unmistakable language of the Declaration. I think the authors of that notable instrument intended to include all men, but they did not intend to declare all men equal in all respects. They did not mean to say all were equal in color, size, intellect, moral developments, or social capacity. They defined with tolerable distinctness, in what respects they did consider all men created equal—equal in "certain inalienable rights, among which are life, liberty, and the pursuit of happiness." This they said, and this meant. They did not mean to assert the obvious untruth, that all were then actually enjoying that equality, nor yet, that they were about to confer it immediately upon them. In fact, they had no power to confer such a boon. They meant simply to declare the right, so that the enforcement of it might follow as fast as circumstances should permit. They meant to set up a standard maxim for free society, which should be familiar to all, and revered by all; constantly looked to, constantly labored for, and even though never perfectly attained, constantly approximated, and thereby constantly spreading and deepening its influence, and augmenting the happiness and value of life to all people of all colors everywhere. The assertion that "all men are created equal" was of no practical use in effecting our separation from Great Britain; and it was placed in the Declaration, nor for that, but for future use. Its authors meant it to be, thank God, it is now proving itself, a stumbling block to those who in after times might seek to turn a free people back into the hateful paths of despotism. They knew the proneness of prosperity to breed tyrants, and they meant when such should re-appear in this fair land and commence their vocation they should find left for them at least one hard nut to crack.

I have now briefly expressed my view of the meaning and objects of that part of the Declaration of Independence which declares that "all men are created equal."

Now let us hear Judge Douglas' view of the same subject, as I find it in the printed report of his late speech. Here it is:

> "No man can vindicate the character, motives and conduct of the signers of the Declaration of Independence except upon the hypothesis that they referred to the white race alone, and not to the African, when they declared all men to have been created equal—that they were speaking of British subjects on this continent being equal to British subjects born and residing in Great Britain—that they were entitled

to the same inalienable rights, and among them were enumerated life, liberty and the pursuit of happiness. The Declaration was adopted for the purpose of justifying the colonists in the eyes of the civilized world in withdrawing their allegiance from the British crown, and dissolving their connection with the mother country."

My good friends, read that carefully over some leisure hour, and ponder well upon it—see what a mere wreck—mangled ruin—it makes of our once glorious Declaration.

"They were speaking of British subjects on this continent being equal to British subjects born and residing in Great Britain!" Why, according to this, not only Negroes but white people outside of Great Britain and America are not spoken of in that instrument. The English, Irish and Scotch, along with white Americans, were included to be sure, but the French, Germans and other white people of the world are all gone to pot along with the judge's inferior races. I had thought the Declaration promised something better than the condition of British subjects; but no, it only meant that we should be equal to them in their own oppressed and unequal condition. According to that, it gave no promise that having kicked off the king and lords of Great Britain, we should not at once be saddled with a king and lords of our own.

I had thought the Declaration contemplated the progressive improvement in the condition of all men everywhere; but no, it merely "was adopted for the purpose of justifying the colonists in the eyes of the civilized world in withdrawing their allegiance from the British crown, and dissolving their connection with the mother country." Why, that object having been effected some eighty years ago, the Declaration is of no practical use now-mere rubbish-old wadding left to rot on the battle-field after the victory is won.

I understand you are preparing to celebrate the "Fourth," tomorrow week. What for? The doings of that day had no reference to the present; and quite half of you are not even descendants of those who were referred to at that day. But I suppose you will celebrate; and will even go so far as to read the Declaration. Suppose after you read it once in the old fashioned way, you read it once more with Judge Douglas' version. It will then run thus: "We hold these truths to be self-evident that all British subjects who were on this continent eighty-one years ago, were created equal to all British subjects born and then residing in Great Britain."

And now I appeal to all—to Democrats as well as others—are you really willing that the Declaration shall be thus frittered away?—thus left no more at most, than an interesting memorial of the dead past? thus shorn of its vitality, and practical value; and left without the germ or even the suggestion of the individual rights of man in it?

But Judge Douglas is especially horrified at the thought of the mixing blood by the white and black races: agreed for once—a thousand times agreed. There are white men enough to marry all the white women, and black men enough to marry all the black women; and so let them be married. On this point we fully agree with the judge; and when he shall show that his policy is better adapted to prevent amalgamation than ours we shall drop ours, and adopt his. Let us see. In 1850 there were in the United States, 405,751, mulattoes. Very few of these are the offspring of whites and free blacks; nearly all have sprung from black slaves and white masters. A separation of the races is the only perfect preventive of amalgamation but as an immediate separation is impossible the next best thing is to keep them apart where they are not already together. If white and black people never get together in Kansas, they will never mix blood in Kansas. That is at least one self-evident truth. A few free colored persons may get into the free states, in any event; but their number is too insignificant to amount to much in the way of mixing blood. In 1850 there were in the free states, 56,649 mulattoes; but for the most part they were not born there—they came from the slave states, ready made up. In the same year the slave states had 348,874 mulattoes all of home production. The proportion of free mulattoes to free blacks—the only colored classes in the free states—is much greater in the slave than in the free states. It is worthy of note too, that among the free states those which make the colored man the nearest to equal the white, have, proportionably the fewest mulattoes the least of amalgamation. In New Hampshire, the state which goes farthest towards equality between the races, there are just 184 mullatoes while there are in Virginia—how many do you think? 79,775, being 23,126 more than in all the free states together.

These statistics show that slavery is the greatest source of amalgamation; and next to it, not the elevation, but the degeneration of the free blacks. Yet Judge Douglas dreads the slightest restraints on the spread of slavery, and the slightest human recognition of the Negro, as tending horribly to amalgamation.

This very *Dred Scott* case affords a strong test as to which party most favors amalgamation, the Republicans or the dear Union-saving Democracy. Dred Scott, his wife and two daughters were all involved in the suit. We desired the court to have held that they were citizens so far at least as to entitle them to a hearing as to whether they were free or not; and then, also, that they were in fact and in law really free. Could we have had our way, the chances of these black girls, ever mixing their blood with that of white people, would have been diminished at least to the extent that it could not have been without their consent. But Judge Douglas is delighted to have them decided to be slaves, and not human enough to have a hearing, even if they were free, and thus left subject to the forced concubinage of their masters, and liable to become the mothers of mulattoes in spite of themselves—the very state of case that produces nine tenths of all the mulattoes—all the mixing of blood in the nation....

Such separation [of the races], if ever effected at all, must be effected by colonization; and no political party, as such, is now doing anything directly for colonization. Party operations at present only favor or retard colonization incidentally. The enterprise is a difficult one; but "when there is a will there is a way;" and what colonization needs most is a hearty will. Will springs from the two elements of moral sense and self-interest. Let us be brought to believe it is morally right, and, at the same time, favorable to, or, at least, not against, our interest, to transfer the African to his native clime, and we shall find a way to do it, however great the task may be. The children of Israel, to such numbers as to include four hundred thousand fighting men, went out of Egyptian bondage in a body.

How differently the respective courses of the Democratic and Republican parties incidentally bear on the question of forming a will—a public sentiment—for colonization, is easy to see. The Republicans inculcate, with whatever of ability they can, that the Negro is a man; that his bondage is cruelly wrong, and that the field of his oppression ought not to be enlarged. The Democrats deny his manhood; deny, or dwarf to insignificance, the wrong of his bondage; so far as possible, crush all sympathy for him, and cultivate and excite hatred and disgust against him; compliment themselves as Union-savers for doing so; and call the indefinite outspreading of his bondage "a sacred right of self-government."

The plainest print cannot be read through a gold eagle; and it will be ever hard to find many men who will send a slave to Liberia, and pay his passage while they can send him to a new country, Kansas for instance, and sell him for fifteen hundred dollars, and the rise.

DOCUMENT 16

"Mud Sill" Speech

James Henry Hammond

March 4, 1858

A major slavery apologist of the antebellum period, James Henry Hammond served in the U.S. House of Representatives and as governor of South Carolina before entering the U.S. Senate in 1857. Hammond was well known to the public for his strong and spirited defense of slavery, which continued until his resignation from the Senate in 1860, following the secession of South Carolina. His most famous address from the Senate floor came in early 1858. Its occasion was the debate over the admission of Kansas under what was known as the Lecompton Constitution, a pro-slavery document. Stephen A. Douglas (1813–1861) (D-IL), the architect of the Kansas-Nebraska Act (Documents 10 and 11) and a proponent of the people's right to choose whether a territory would be slave or free, opposed the Lecompton Constitution because of the voting fraud that led to its adoption. Hammond claimed that anti-slavery senators were exploiting the rift between Northern and Southern Democrats to destroy the party and take over the national government. Anticipating the consequences of this (the North and South becoming separate governments), Hammond extolled the power of the South. Expressing the confidence, if not arrogance, of the South as the sectional conflict moved toward war, Hammond portrayed the South as a powerful empire that, through its cotton and geographical position, ruled or could rule the world. "Cotton is King," he declared.

The speech also contains Hammond's "mud sill" theory, which stated that in every society there must of necessity be a lower class to provide for the support and maintenance of the upper class. Continuing the argument of George Fitzhugh (Document 13) that the South's social organization was superior to the North's, Hammond's social theory like Fitzhugh's denied the principle of natural human equality found in the Declaration of Independence. To understand the difference between the North and the South, it is useful to compare the accounts of Fitzhugh and Hammond with those of William H. Seward and Abraham Lincoln (Documents 19 and 20).

It is worth noting that in explaining the antagonism of the North and South, Hammond mentions the great issues of antebellum politics: tariffs, internal improvements, and the national bank. All of these issues revolved around the central question of the power of the national government and behind that question was slavery. The more powerful the national government, the more of a threat it posed to slavery, if the government fell into hands hostile to slavery.

SOURCE: *Speech of the Honorable John H. Hammond, of South Carolina, on the Admission of Kansas under the Lecompton Constitution, Delivered in the Senate of the United States,* March 4, 1858 (Washington: Printed by Lemuel Towers, 1858), https://babel.hathitrust.org/cgi/pt?id=loc.ark:/13960/t7jq19w4m;view=1up;seq=3.

... They [opponents of slavery, beginning to coalesce as the Republican party] intend to make [Kansas] a free state as soon as they have effected their purpose of destroying the Democratic Party at the North, and now their chief object here is to agitate slavery. For one, I am not disposed to discuss that question here in any abstract form. I think the time has gone by for that. Our minds are all made up. I may be willing to discuss it—and that is the way it should be and must be discussed—as a practical thing, as a thing that is, and is to be and to discuss its effect upon our political institutions, and ascertain how long those institutions will hold together with slavery ineradicable.

The senator from New York[1] entered very fairly into this field yesterday. ... He said that it was their intention to take this government from unjust and unfaithful hands, and place it in just and faithful hands; that it was their intention to consecrate all the territories of the Union to free labor; and that, to effect their purposes, they intended to reconstruct the Supreme Court....[2]

... But what guarantee have we, when you have this government in your possession, in all its departments, even if we submit quietly to what the senator exhorts us to submit to—the limitation of slavery to its present territory, and even to the reconstruction of the Supreme Court—that you will not plunder us with tariffs; that you will not bankrupt us with internal improvements and bounties on *your* exports; that you will not cramp us with navigation laws, and other laws impeding the facilities of transportation to southern produce? What guarantee have we that you will not create a new bank, and concentrate all the finances of this country at the North, where already, for

---

[1] William H. Seward (1801–1872), who later became Lincoln's Secretary of State, was a well-known opponent of slavery and its expansion into the territories.

[2] The purpose in reconstructing the Supreme Court was to have a majority of anti-slavery justices who would reverse the *Dred Scott* decision (Document 14).

the want of direct trade[3] and a proper system of banking in the South, they are ruinously concentrated? Nay, what guarantee have we that you will not emancipate our slaves, or, at least, make the attempt? We cannot rely on your faith when you have the power. It has been always broken whenever pledged.

As I am disposed to see this question settled as soon as possible, and am perfectly willing to have a final and conclusive settlement now, after what the senator from New York has said, I think it not improper that I should attempt to bring the North and South face to face, and see what resources each of us might have in the contingency of separate organizations.[4]

If we never acquire another foot of territory for the South, look at her. Eight hundred and fifty thousand square miles. As large as Great Britain, France, Austria, Prussia and Spain. Is not that territory enough to make an empire that shall rule the world? With the finest soil, the most delightful climate, whose staple productions none of those great countries can grow, we have three thousand miles of continental seashore line so indented with bays and crowded with islands, that, when their shore lines are added, we have twelve thousand miles. Through the heart of our country runs the great Mississippi, the father of waters, into whose bosom are poured thirty-six thousand miles of tributary rivers; and beyond we have the desert prairie wastes to protect us in our rear. Can you hem in such a territory as that? You talk of putting up a wall of fire around eight hundred and fifty thousand square miles so situated! How absurd.

But, in this territory lies the great valley of the Mississippi, now the real, and soon to be the acknowledged seat of the empire of the world. The sway of that valley will be as great as ever the Nile knew in the earlier ages of mankind. We own the most of it. The most valuable part of it belongs to us now; and although those who have settled above us are now opposed to us, another generation will tell a different tale. They are ours by all the laws of nature; slave-labor will go over every foot of this great valley where it will be found profitable to use it, and some of those who may not use it are soon to be united with us by such ties as will make us one and inseparable. The iron horse will soon be clattering over the sunny plains of the South to bear the products of its upper tributaries of the valley to our Atlantic ports, as it now does through the ice-bound North. And there is the great Mississippi, a bond of union made by nature herself. She will maintain it forever.

---

[3] Northern vessels carried much of the South's cotton to Great Britain, where it was spun into cloth.

[4] that is, if the North and South were separate countries

On this fine territory we have a population four times as large as that with which these colonies separated from the mother country, and a hundred, I might say a thousand fold stronger. Our population is now sixty per cent greater than that of the whole United States when we entered into the second war of independence.[5] It is as large as the whole population of the United States was ten years after the conclusion of that war, and our own exports are three times as great as those of the whole United States then. Upon our muster-rolls we have a million of men. In a defensive war, upon an emergency, every one of them would be available. At any time, the South can raise, equip, and maintain in the field, a larger army than any Power of the earth can send against her, and an army of soldiers—men brought up on horseback, with guns in their hands.

If we take the North, even when the two large states of Kansas and Minnesota shall be admitted, her territory will be one hundred thousand square miles less than ours. I do not speak of California and Oregon; there is no antagonism between the South and those countries, and never will be. The population of the North is fifty per cent greater than ours. I have nothing to say in disparagement either of the soil of the North, or the people of the North, who are a brave and energetic race, full of intellect. But they produce no great staple that the South does not produce; while we produce two or three, and these are the very greatest, that she can never produce. As to her men, I may be allowed to say, they have never proved themselves to be superior to those of the South, either in the field or in the Senate.

But the strength of a nation depends in a great measure upon its wealth, and the wealth of a nation, like that of a man, is to be estimated by its surplus production. . . .[6]

. . . With one-fourth the present tariff, she would have a revenue with the present tariff adequate to all her wants, for the South would never go to war; she would never need an army or a navy, beyond a few garrisons on the frontiers and a few revenue cutters. It is commerce that breeds war.[7] It is manufactures that require to be hawked about the world, and that give rise to

[5] War of 1812

[6] "Surplus product" or "surplus production" is a term associated with Karl Marx. It means roughly that part of the product of labor not necessary to sustain laborers and their families. According to Marx, the capitalist gathers the surplus product by selling what laborers produce but not paying them more than what they need to subsist.

[7] Thomas Jefferson held this view of commerce and war. Thomas Jefferson, *Notes on the State of Virginia*, ed. William Peden (New York: W. W. Norton & Co., 1954), 174–175.

navies and commerce. But we have nothing to do but to take off restrictions on foreign merchandise and open our ports, and the whole world will come to us to trade. They will be too glad to bring and carry us, and we never shall dream of a war. Why the South has never yet had a just cause of war except with the North. Every time she has drawn her sword it has been on the point of honor, and that point of honor has been mainly loyalty to her sister colonies and sister states, who have ever since plundered and calumniated her.

But if there were no other reason why we should never have war, would any sane nation make war on cotton? Without firing a gun, without drawing a sword, should they make war on us we could bring the whole world to our feet.... What would happen if no cotton was furnished for three years? I will not stop to depict what every one can imagine, but this is certain: England would topple headlong and carry the whole civilized world with her, save the South. No, you dare not make war on cotton. No power on earth dares to make war upon it. Cotton is king. Until lately the Bank of England was king; but she tried to put her screws as usual, the fall before last, upon the cotton crop, and was utterly vanquished. The last power has been conquered. Who can doubt, that has looked at recent events, that cotton is supreme? When the abuse of credit had destroyed credit and annihilated confidence; when thousands of the strongest commercial houses in the world were coming down, and hundreds of millions of dollars of supposed property evaporating in thin air; when you came to a dead lock, and revolutions were threatened, what brought you up?[8] Fortunately for you it was the commencement of the cotton season, and we have poured in upon you one million six hundred thousand bales of cotton just at the crisis to save you from destruction....

But, sir, the greatest strength of the South arises from the harmony of her political and social institutions. This harmony gives her a frame of society, the best in the world, and an extent of political freedom, combined with entire security, such as no other people ever enjoyed upon the face of the earth.

In all social systems there must be a class to do the menial duties, to perform the drudgery of life. That is, a class requiring but a low order of intellect and but little skill. Its requisites are vigor, docility, fidelity. Such a class you must have, or you would not have that other class which leads progress, civilization, and refinement. It constitutes the very mud-sill of society and of political government; and you might as well attempt to build a house in the air, as to build either the one or the other, except on this mud-sill. Fortunately for the South, she found a race adapted to that purpose to her hand. A race

[8] Hammond may be referring to the recession and financial panic of 1856–1857.

inferior to her own, but eminently qualified in temper, in vigor, in docility, in capacity to stand the climate, to answer all her purposes. We use them for our purpose, and call them slaves. We found them slaves by the common "consent of mankind," which, according to Cicero, "lex naturae est."[9] The highest proof of what is nature's law. We are old-fashioned at the South yet; slave is a word discarded now by "ears polite;" I will not characterize that class at the North by that term; but you have it; it is there; it is everywhere; it is eternal.

The senator from New York said yesterday that the whole world had abolished slavery. Aye, the name, but not the thing; all the powers of the earth cannot abolish that. God only can do it when he repeals the fiat, "the poor ye always have with you;"[10] for the man who lives by daily labor, and scarcely lives at that, and who has to put out his labor in the market, and take the best he can get for it; in short, your whole hireling class of manual laborers and "operatives," as you call them, are essentially slaves. The difference between us is, that our slaves are hired for life and well compensated; there is no starvation, no begging, no want of employment among our people, and not too much employment either. Yours are hired by the day, not cared for, and scantily compensated, which may be proved in the most painful manner, at any hour in any street of your large towns. Why, you meet more beggars in one day, in any single street of the city of New York, than you would meet in a lifetime in the whole South. We do not think that whites should be slaves either by law or necessity. Our slaves are black, of another and inferior race. The status in which we have placed them is an elevation. They are elevated from the condition in which God first created them, by being made our slaves. None of that race on the whole face of the globe can be compared with the slaves of the South. They are happy, content, unaspiring, and utterly incapable, from intellectual weakness, ever to give us any trouble by their aspirations. Yours are white, of your own race; you are brothers of one blood. They are your equals in natural endowment of intellect, and they feel galled by their degradation. Our slaves do not vote. We give them no political power. Yours do vote, and, being the majority, they are the depositories of all your political power. If they knew the tremendous secret, that the ballot-box is stronger than "an army with banners,"[11] and could combine, where would you be? Your society would be reconstructed, your government overthrown, your property divided, not as they have mistakenly attempted to initiate

---

[9] the law of nature

[10] Matthew 26:11; Mark 14:7

[11] A reference perhaps to Song of Solomon 6:10

such proceedings by meeting in parks, with arms in their hands, but by the quiet process of the ballot-box. You have been making war upon us to our very hearthstones. How would you like for us to send lecturers and agitators North, to teach these people this, to aid in combining, and to lead them? . . .

Transient and temporary causes have thus far been your preservation. The great West has been open to your surplus population, and your hordes of semi-barbarian immigrants, who are crowding in year by year. They make a great movement, and you call it progress. Whither? It is progress; but it is progress toward vigilance committees. The South have sustained you in great measure. You are our factors. You fetch and carry for us. One hundred and fifty million dollars of our money passes annually through your hands. Much of it sticks; all of it assists to keep your machinery together and in motion. Suppose we were to discharge you; suppose we were to take our business out of your hands;—we should consign you to anarchy and poverty. You complain of the rule of the South; that has been another cause that has preserved you. We have kept the government conservative to the great purposes of the Constitution. We have placed it, and kept it, upon the Constitution; and that has been the cause of your peace and prosperity. The senator from New York says that that is about to be at an end; that you intend to take the government from us; that it will pass from our hands into yours. Perhaps what he says is true; it may be; but do not forget—it can never be forgotten—it is written on the brightest page of human history—that we, the slaveholders of the South, took our country in her infancy, and, after ruling her for sixty out of the seventy years of her existence, we surrendered her to you without a stain upon her honor, boundless in prosperity, incalculable in her strength, the wonder and admiration of the world. Time will show what you will make of her; but no time can diminish our glory or your responsibility.

DOCUMENT 17

"House Divided" Speech

Abraham Lincoln

June 16, 1858

Delivered to the Republican State Convention in Springfield, Illinois, Abraham Lincoln's House Divided Speech was intended by its author to be much more than an official announcement accepting his party's nomination for the U.S. Senate. Lincoln's deep-seated belief that slavery was wrong and incompatible with the principles of the Declaration of Independence led him to reject Stephen Douglas's (1813–1861) morally neutral "don't care" policy of popular sovereignty, which was gaining significant public support by 1858. There was even talk that Douglas, out of step with the hardline pro-slavery Democrats of the South, might soon become a Republican and join their ranks. Arguing that evidence suggested a concerted effort by Chief Justice Roger Taney (Document 14) and the leaders of the Democratic Party, including Douglas, to spread slavery across the United States, Lincoln's House Divided Speech was intended to stop Douglas's political rise, especially his growing appeal among Republicans. More importantly, its purpose was to help return "the public mind" to the Founders' belief that slavery was fundamentally unjust and in the course of "ultimate extinction."

SOURCE: *Life and Works of Abraham Lincoln*, Centenary Edition, Volume III, Marion Mills Miller, ed., (New York: The Current Literature Publishing Company, 1907), 35–46, https://archive.org/details/lifeworks03lincuoft/page/n3.

Mr. President and gentlemen of the convention:

If we could first know where we are, and whither we are tending, we could better judge what to do, and how to do it.

We are now far into the fifth year, since a policy was initiated with the avowed object, and confident promise, of putting an end to slavery agitation.[1]

[1] The Kansas-Nebraska Act and the policy of leaving slavery in the territories up to those who lived there, Stephen A. Douglas's policy of popular sovereignty.

Under the operation of that policy, that agitation has not only not ceased, but has constantly augmented.

In my opinion, it will not cease, until a crisis shall have been reached and passed.

"A house divided against itself cannot stand."[2]

I believe this government cannot endure permanently half slave and half free.

I do not expect the Union to be dissolved—I do not expect the house to fall—but I do expect it will cease to be divided.

It will become all one thing, or all the other.

Either the opponents of slavery will arrest the further spread of it, and place it where the public mind shall rest in the belief that it is in the course of ultimate extinction; or its advocates will push it forward, till it shall become alike lawful in all the states, old as well as new—North as well as South.

Have we no tendency to the latter condition?

Let anyone who doubts, carefully contemplate that now almost complete legal combination—piece of machinery, so to speak—compounded of the Nebraska doctrine, and the *Dred Scott* decision.[3] Let him consider not only what work the machinery is adapted to do, and how well adapted; but also, let him study the history of its construction, and trace, if he can, or rather fail, if he can, to trace the evidences of design, and concert of action, among its chief architects, from the beginning.

But, so far, Congress only had acted; and an indorsement by the people, real or apparent, was indispensable, to save the point already gained, and give chance for more.

The new year of 1854 found slavery excluded from more than half the states by state constitutions, and from most of the national territory by Congressional prohibition.

Four days later, commenced the struggle which ended in repealing that Congressional prohibition.[4]

This opened all the national territory to slavery, and was the first point gained.

This necessity had not been overlooked; but had been provided for, as well as might be, in the notable argument of "squatter sovereignty," otherwise

---

[2] Mark 3:25

[3] Documents 11 and 14, respectively.

[4] The Missouri Compromise line of 36 30 north latitude, north of which slavery was prohibited. See Documents 2, 11, and 12.

called "sacred right of self-government," which latter phrase, though expressive of the only rightful basis of any government, was so perverted in this attempted use of it as to amount to just this: That if any one man choose to enslave another, no third man shall be allowed to object.

That argument was incorporated into the Nebraska bill itself, in the language which follows: "It being the true intent and meaning of this act not to legislate slavery into any territory or state, nor to exclude it therefrom; but to leave the people thereof perfectly free to form and regulate their domestic institutions in their own way, subject only to the Constitution of the United States."

Then opened the roar of loose declamation in favor of "squatter sovereignty," and "sacred right of self-government."

"But," said opposition members, "let us amend the bill so as to expressly declare that the people of the territory may exclude slavery." "Not we," said the friends of the measure; and down they voted the amendment.

While the Nebraska bill was passing through Congress, a law case involving the question of a Negro's freedom, by reason of his owner having voluntarily taken him first into a free state and then into a territory covered by the Congressional prohibition, and held him as a slave for a long time in each, was passing through the U. S. Circuit Court for the District of Missouri;[5] and both Nebraska bill and law suit were brought to a decision in the same month of May, 1854. The Negro's name was "Dred Scott," which name now designates the decision finally made in the case.

Before the then next presidential election, the law case came to, and was argued in, the Supreme Court of the United States; but the decision of it was deferred until after the election. Still, before the election, Senator Trumbull,[6] on the floor of the Senate, requested the leading advocate of the Nebraska bill[7] to state his opinion whether the people of a territory can constitutionally exclude slavery from their limits; and the latter answers: "That is a question for the Supreme Court."

The election came. Mr. Buchanan[8] was elected, and the endorsement, such as it was, secured. That was the second point gained. The endorsement,

---

[5] Document 14

[6] Lyman Trumbull (1813-1896) was a senator from Illinois.

[7] Stephen A. Douglas

[8] James Buchanan (1791–1868) was pro-slavery or at least supported the admission of Kansas as a slave state. Buchanan won the election in 1856 in a three-way race with 45 per cent of the popular vote.

however, fell short of a clear popular majority by nearly four hundred thousand votes, and so, perhaps, was not overwhelmingly reliable and satisfactory.

The outgoing president,[9] in his last annual message, as impressively as possible echoed back upon the people the weight and authority of the endorsement.

The Supreme Court met again; did not announce their decision, but ordered a re-argument.

The presidential inauguration came, and still no decision of the court; but the incoming president in his inaugural address, fervently exhorted the people to abide by the forthcoming decision, whatever it might be.

Then, in a few days, came the decision.

The reputed author of the Nebraska bill finds an early occasion to make a speech at this capital endorsing the *Dred Scott* decision, and vehemently denouncing all opposition to it.

The new president, too, seizes the early occasion of the Silliman letter[10] to endorse and strongly construe that decision, and to express his astonishment that any different view had ever been entertained!

At length a squabble springs up between the president and the author of the Nebraska bill, on the mere question of fact, whether the Lecompton Constitution was or was not, in any just sense, made by the people of Kansas; and in that quarrel the latter declares that all he wants is a fair vote for the people, and that he cares not whether slavery be voted down or voted up. I do not understand his declaration that he cares not whether slavery be voted down or voted up, to be intended by him other than as an apt definition of the policy he would impress upon the public mind—the principle for which he declares he has suffered so much, and is ready to suffer to the end.

And well may he cling to that principle. If he has any parental feeling, well may he cling to it. That principle is the only shred left of his original Nebraska doctrine. Under the *Dred Scott* decision "squatter sovereignty" squatted out of existence,[11] tumbled down like temporary scaffolding—like the mould at the foundry served through one blast and fell back into loose sand—helped to carry an election, and then was kicked to the winds. His late joint struggle with the Republicans, against the Lecompton Constitution, involves nothing

---

[9] Franklin Pierce (1804–1869)

[10] Benjamin Silliman (1779–1864), a Yale science Professor, wrote a letter signed with a number of others to Buchanan criticizing the use of troops against anti-slavery settlers in Kansas.

[11] The Supreme Court held that slavery could not be excluded from the territories.

of the original Nebraska doctrine. That struggle was made on a point—the right of a people to make their own constitution—upon which he and the Republicans have never differed.

The several points of the Dred Scott decision, in connection with Senator Douglas's "care not" policy, constitute the piece of machinery, in its present state of advancement. This was the third point gained.

The working points of that machinery are:

First, that no Negro slave, imported as such from Africa, and no descendant of such slave, can ever be a citizen of any state, in the sense of that term as used in the Constitution of the United States.

This point is made in order to deprive the Negro, in every possible event, of the benefit of that provision of the United States Constitution, which declares that "The citizens of each state shall be entitled to all privileges and immunities of citizens in the several states."

Secondly, that "subject to the Constitution of the United States," neither Congress nor a territorial legislature can exclude slavery from any United States territory.

This point is made in order that individual men may fill up the territories with slaves, without danger of losing them as property, and thus to enhance the chances of permanency to the institution through all the future.

Thirdly, that whether the holding a Negro in actual slavery in a free state, makes him free, as against the holder, the United States courts will not decide, but will leave to be decided by the courts of any slave state the Negro may be forced into by the master.

This point is made, not to be pressed immediately; but, if acquiesced in for a while, and apparently endorsed by the people at an election, then to sustain the logical conclusion that what Dred Scott's master might lawfully do with Dred Scott, in the free state of Illinois, every other master may lawfully do with any other one, or one thousand slaves, in Illinois, or in any other free state.

Auxiliary to all this, and working hand in hand with it, the Nebraska doctrine, or what is left of it, is to educate and mould public opinion, at least Northern public opinion, not to care whether slavery is voted down or voted up.

This shows exactly where we now are; and partially, also, whither we are tending.

It will throw additional light on the latter, to go back, and run the mind over the string of historical facts already stated. Several things will now appear less dark and mysterious than they did when they were transpiring.

The people were to be left "perfectly free," "subject only to the Constitution." What the Constitution had to do with it, outsiders could not then see. Plainly enough now, it was an exactly fitted niche, for the *Dred Scott* decision to afterward come in, and declare the perfect freedom of the people to be just no freedom at all.

Why was the amendment, expressly declaring the right of the people, voted down? Plainly enough now: the adoption of it would have spoiled the niche for the *Dred Scott* decision.

Why was the court decision held up? Why even a senator's individual opinion withheld, till after the presidential election? Plainly enough now: the speaking out then would have damaged the perfectly free argument upon which the election was to be carried.

Why the outgoing president's felicitation on the endorsement? Why the delay of a re-argument? Why the incoming president's advance exhortation in favor of the decision?

These things look like the cautious patting and petting of a spirited horse, preparatory to mounting him, when it is dreaded that he may give the rider a fall.

And why the hasty after endorsement of the decision by the president and others?

We cannot absolutely know that all these exact adaptations are the result of preconcert. But when we see a lot of framed timbers, different portions of which we know have been gotten out at different times and places and by different workmen—Stephen, Franklin, Roger and James, for instance—and when we see these timbers joined together, and see they exactly make the frame of a house or a mill, all the tenons and mortices[12] exactly fitting, and all the lengths and proportions of the different pieces exactly adapted to their respective places, and not a piece too many or too few—not omitting even scaffolding—or, if a single piece be lacking, we see the place in the frame exactly fitted and prepared yet to bring such a piece in—in such a case, we find it impossible not to believe that Stephen and Franklin and Roger and James all understood one another from the beginning, and all worked upon a common plan or draft drawn up before the first blow was struck.

It should not be overlooked that, by the Nebraska bill, the people of a state as well as territory, were to be left "perfectly free," "subject only to the Constitution."

Why mention a state? They were legislating for territories, and not for or

[12] a way of connecting pieces of wood

about states. Certainly the people of a state are and ought to be subject to the Constitution of the United States; but why is mention of this lugged into this merely territorial law? Why are the people of a territory and the people of a state therein lumped together, and their relation to the Constitution therein treated as being precisely the same?

While the opinion of the court, by Chief Justice Taney, in the *Dred Scott* case, and the separate opinions of all the concurring judges, expressly declare that the Constitution of the United States neither permits Congress nor a territorial legislature to exclude slavery from any United States territory, they all omit to declare whether or not the same Constitution permits a state, or the people of a state, to exclude it.

Possibly, this is a mere omission; but who can be quite sure, if McLean or Curtis[13] had sought to get into the opinion a declaration of unlimited power in the people of a state to exclude slavery from their limits, just as Chase and Mace[14] sought to get such declaration, in behalf of the people of a territory, into the Nebraska bill;—I ask, who can be quite sure that it would not have been voted down in the one case as it had been in the other?

The nearest approach to the point of declaring the power of a state over slavery, is made by Judge Nelson.[15] He approaches it more than once, using the precise idea, and almost the language, too, of the Nebraska act. On one occasion, his exact language is, "except in cases where the power is restrained by the Constitution of the United States, the law of the state is supreme over the subject of slavery within its jurisdiction."

In what cases the power of the states is so restrained by the United States Constitution, is left an open question, precisely as the same question, as to the restraint on the power of the territories, was left open in the Nebraska act. Put this and that together, and we have another nice little niche, which we may, ere long, see filled with another Supreme Court decision, declaring that the Constitution of the United States does not permit a state to exclude slavery from its limits.

And this may especially be expected if the doctrine of "care not whether slavery be voted down or voted up," shall gain upon the public mind

---

[13] John McLean and Benjamin R. Curtis, the dissenting justices in the Dred Scott case

[14] Senator Salmon P. Chase (1808–1873) (R-Ohio) and Representative Daniel Mace (1811–1867) (D-Indiana)

[15] Justice Samuel Nelson concurred in the Supreme Court's opinion in the *Dred Scott* case

sufficiently to give promise that such a decision can be maintained when made.

Such a decision is all that slavery now lacks of being alike lawful in all the states.

Welcome, or unwelcome, such decision is probably coming, and will soon be upon us, unless the power of the present political dynasty shall be met and overthrown.

We shall lie down pleasantly dreaming that the people of Missouri are on the verge of making their state free, and we shall awake to the reality instead, that the Supreme Court has made Illinois a slave state.

To meet and overthrow the power of that dynasty, is the work now before all those who would prevent that consummation.

That is what we have to do.

How can we best do it?

There are those who denounce us openly to their own friends, and yet whisper us softly, that Senator Douglas is the aptest instrument there is with which to effect that object. They do not tell us, nor has he told us, that he wishes any such object to be effected. They wish us to infer all, from the fact that he now has a little quarrel with the present head of the dynasty; and that he has regularly voted with us on a single point, upon which he and we have never differed.

They remind us that he is a great man, and that the largest of us are very small ones. Let this be granted. But "a living dog is better than a dead lion."[16] Judge Douglas, if not a dead lion, for this work, is at least a caged and toothless one. How can he oppose the advances of slavery? He don't care anything about it. His avowed mission is impressing the "public heart" to care nothing about it.

A leading Douglas democratic newspaper thinks Douglas's superior talent will be needed to resist the revival of the African slave trade.

Does Douglas believe an effort to revive that trade is approaching? He has not said so. Does he really think so? But if it is, how can he resist it? For years he has labored to prove it a sacred right of white men to take Negro slaves into the new territories. Can he possibly show that it is less a sacred right to buy them where they can be bought cheapest? And unquestionably they can be bought cheaper in Africa than in Virginia.

He has done all in his power to reduce the whole question of slavery to one of a mere right of property; and as such, how can he oppose the foreign

---

[16] Ecclesiastes 9:4

slave trade—how can he refuse that trade in that "property" shall be "perfectly free"—unless he does it as a protection to the home production? And as the home producers will probably not ask the protection, he will be wholly without a ground of opposition.

Senator Douglas holds, we know, that a man may rightfully be wiser to-day than he was yesterday—that he may rightfully change when he finds himself wrong.

But can we, for that reason, run ahead, and infer that he will make any particular change, of which he, himself, has given no intimation? Can we safely base our action upon any such vague inference?

Now, as ever, I wish not to misrepresent Judge Douglas's position, question his motives, or do aught that can be personally offensive to him.

Whenever, if ever, he and we can come together on principle so that our cause may have assistance from his great ability, I hope to have interposed no adventitious obstacle.

But clearly, he is not now with us—he does not pretend to be—he does not promise ever to be.

Our cause, then, must be entrusted to, and conducted by, its own undoubted friends—those whose hands are free, whose hearts are in the work—who do care for the result.

Two years ago the Republicans of the nation mustered over thirteen hundred thousand strong.

We did this under the single impulse of resistance to a common danger, with every external circumstance against us.

Of strange, discordant, and even hostile elements, we gathered from the four winds, and formed and fought the battle through, under the constant hot fire of a disciplined, proud and pampered enemy.

Did we brave all then, to falter now?—now, when that same enemy is wavering, dissevered and belligerent?

The result is not doubtful. We shall not fail—if we stand firm, we shall not fail.

Wise counsels may accelerate, or mistakes delay it, but, sooner or later, the victory is sure to come.

DOCUMENT 18

"Homecoming" Speech at Chicago

Stephen A. Douglas

July 9, 1858

Seeking to defend his Senate seat against Abraham Lincoln and the Republicans (Document 17), Stephen Douglas (1813–1861) left Washington, D.C. for Chicago in July 1858. He opened his re-election campaign at the Tremont Hotel, defending the doctrine of popular sovereignty and the right of the people to choose for themselves whether slavery should be voted up or down. "The great principle," Douglas said, referring to popular sovereignty, "is the right of every community to judge and decide for itself, whether a thing is right or wrong." The principal community he had in mind was the people of each state, since Douglas declared the United States "a confederation of sovereign states." Douglas also stated his view that the government of the United States "was made by the white man, for the benefit of the white man, to be administered by white men, in such manner as they should determine." Douglas also went on the offense, attacking Republicans for trying to instigate civil war between North and South over the slavery issue. Douglas singled out Lincoln and the House Divided Speech (Document 17) in particular for limiting the right of the people to choose what laws they wanted and for advocating "a war of sections, a war of the North against the South, of the free states against the slave states—a war of extermination—to be continued relentlessly until the one or the other shall be subdued, and all the states shall either become free or become slave." By trying to paint Lincoln and the Republicans as extremists, Douglas hoped to come across as the candidate of peace, prosperity, and compromise.

In defending popular sovereignty by claiming that it was necessary to "allow the people to decide for themselves whether [slavery] is a good or an evil," Douglas demonstrated that the Civil War was not most fundamentally a war between sections of the country, but a war between those North as well as South who believed slavery was right or could be made right by the will of the people, and those who believed that it was always wrong.

SOURCE: *Political debates between Abraham Lincoln and Stephen A. Douglas in the celebrated campaign of 1858 in Illinois; including the preceding speeches of each at Chicago, Springfield, etc. Also the two great speeches of Abraham Lincoln in Ohio in 1859, and a complete index to the whole* (Cleveland: O.S. Hubbell & company, 1895), 8–20, https://babel.hathitrust.org/cgi/pt?id=loc.ark:/13960/t86h4pg9f;view=1up;seq=18.

... When I found an effort being made during the recent session of Congress to force a constitution upon the people of Kansas against their will,[1] and to force that state into the Union with a constitution which her people had rejected by more than 10,000, I felt bound as a man of honor and a representative of Illinois, bound by every consideration of duty, of fidelity, and of patriotism, to resist to the utmost of my power the consummation of that fraud. With others I did resist it, and resisted it successfully until the attempt was abandoned. We forced them to refer that Constitution back to the people of Kansas, to be accepted or rejected as they shall decide at an election, which is fixed for the first Monday in August next.

I regard the great principle of popular sovereignty, as having been vindicated and made triumphant in this land, as a permanent rule of public policy in the organization of territories and the admission of new states. Illinois took her position upon this principle many years ago. You all recollect that in 1850, after the passage of the compromise measures of that year,[2] when I returned to my home, there was great dissatisfaction expressed at my course in supporting those measures. I appeared before the people of Chicago at a mass meeting, and vindicated each and every one of those measures; and by reference to my speech on that occasion, which was printed and circulated throughout the state at that time, you will find that I then and there said that those measures were all founded upon the great principle that every people ought to possess the right to form and regulate their own domestic institutions in their own way, and that that right being possessed by the people of the states, I saw no reason why the same principle should not be extended to all of the territories of the United States. A general election was held in this state a few months afterward, for members of the legislature, pending which all these questions were thoroughly canvassed and discussed, and the nominees of the different parties instructed in regard to the wishes of their constituents upon them. When that election was over, and the legislature

---

[1] The Lecompton Constitution. See Document 16

[2] The Compromise of 1850, Document 8

assembled, they proceeded to consider the merits of those compromise measures and the principles upon which they were predicated. And what was the result of their action? They passed resolutions, first repealing the Wilmot proviso instructions,[3] and in lieu thereof adopted another resolution, in which they declared the great principle which asserts the right of the people to make their own form of government and establish their own institutions.

That resolution is as follows:

> Resolved, that our liberty and independence are based upon the right of the people to form for themselves such a government as they may choose; that this great principle, the birthright of freemen, the gift of heaven, secured to us by the blood of our ancestors ought to be secured to future generations, and no limitation ought to be applied to this power in the organization of any territory of the United States, of either territorial government or state constitution, provided the government so established shall be Republican, and in conformity with the Constitution of the United States.

That resolution, declaring the great principle of self-government as applicable to the territories and new states, passed the House of Representatives of this state by a vote of sixty-one in the affirmative, to only four in the negative. Thus you find that an expression of public opinion, enlightened, educated, intelligent public opinion on this question by the representatives of Illinois, in 1851, approaches nearer to unanimity than has ever been obtained on any controverted question.

Hence what was my duty, in 1854, when it became necessary to bring forward a bill for the organization of the territories of Kansas and Nebraska? Was it not my duty, in obedience to the Illinois platform, to your standing instructions to your senators, adopted with almost entire unanimity, to incorporate in that bill the great principle of self-government, declaring that it was "the true intent and meaning of the act not to legislate slavery into any state or territory, or to exclude it therefrom, but to leave the people thereof perfectly free to form and regulate their domestic institutions in their own way, subject only to the Constitution of the United States?" I did incorporate that principle in the Kansas-Nebraska bill, and perhaps I did as much as any

---

[3] Instructions to support the Wilmot Proviso, which if adopted would have banned slavery in any territory gained as a consequence of the war with Mexico (1846–1848).

living man in the enactment of that bill, thus establishing the doctrine in the public policy of the country....

...My object was to secure the right of the people of each state and of each territory, North or South, to decide the question for themselves, to have slavery or not, just as they chose.... It is no answer to this argument to say that slavery is an evil, and hence should not be tolerated. You must allow the people to decide for themselves whether it is a good or an evil. You allow them to decide for themselves whether they desire a Maine liquor law or not; you allow them to decide for themselves what kind of common schools they will have; what system of banking they will adopt, or whether they will adopt any at all; you allow them to decide for themselves the relations between husband and wife, parent and child, guardian and ward; in fact, you allow them to decide for themselves all other questions, and why not upon this question? Whenever you put a limitation upon the right of any people to decide what laws they want, you have destroyed the fundamental principle of self-government.

In connection with this subject, perhaps, it will not be improper for me on this occasion to allude to the position of those who have chosen to arraign my conduct on this same subject. I have observed from the public prints, that but a few days ago the Republican Party of the state of Illinois assembled in convention at Springfield, and not only laid down their platform, but nominated a candidate for the United States Senate, as my successor. I take great pleasure in saying that I have known, personally and intimately, for about a quarter of a century, the worthy gentleman who has been nominated for my place,[4] and I will say that I regard him as a kind, amiable, and intelligent gentleman, a good citizen and an honorable opponent; and whatever issue I may have with him will be of principle, and not involving personalities. Mr. Lincoln made a speech before that Republican Convention which unanimously nominated him for the Senate—a speech evidently well prepared and carefully written—in which he states the basis upon which he proposes to carry on the campaign during this summer. In it he lays down two distinct propositions which I shall notice, and upon which I shall take a direct and bold issue with him.

His first and main proposition I will give in his own language, scripture quotations and all [laughter]; I give his exact language: "'A house divided against itself cannot stand.' I believe this government cannot endure,

[4] Abraham Lincoln (Document 17)

permanently, half slave and half free. I do not expect the Union to be dissolved. I do not expect the house to fall; but I do expect it to cease to be divided. It will become all one thing or all the other."

In other words, Mr. Lincoln asserts, as a fundamental principle of this government, that there must be uniformity in the local laws and domestic institutions of each and all the states of the Union; and he therefore invites all the non-slaveholding states to band together, organize as one body, and make war upon slavery in Kentucky, upon slavery in Virginia, upon the Carolinas, upon slavery in all of the slaveholding states in this Union, and to persevere in that war until it shall be exterminated. He then notifies the slaveholding states to stand together as a unit and make an aggressive war upon the free states of this Union with a view of establishing slavery in them all; of forcing it upon Illinois, of forcing it upon New York, upon New England, and upon every other free state, and that they shall keep up the warfare until it has been formally established in them all. In other words, Mr. Lincoln advocates boldly and clearly a war of sections, a war of the North against the South, of the free states against the slave states—a war of extermination—to be continued relentlessly until the one or the other shall be subdued, and all the states shall either become free or become slave.

Now, my friends, I must say to you frankly, that I take bold, unqualified issue with him upon that principle. I assert that it is neither desirable nor possible that there should be uniformity in the local institutions and domestic regulations of the different states of this Union. The framers of our government never contemplated uniformity in its internal concerns. The fathers of the Revolution, and the sages who made the Constitution, well understood . . . that each locality, having separate and distinct interests, required separate and distinct laws, domestic institutions, and police regulations adapted to its own wants and its own condition; and they acted on the presumption, also, that these laws and institutions would be as diversified and as dissimilar as the states would be numerous, and that no two would be precisely alike, because the interests of no two would be precisely the same. Hence, I assert, that the great fundamental principle which underlies our complex system of state and federal governments, contemplated diversity and dissimilarity in the local institutions and domestic affairs of each and every state then in the Union, or thereafter to be admitted into the Confederacy. I therefore conceive that my friend, Mr. Lincoln, has totally misapprehended the great principles upon which our government rests. Uniformity in local and domestic affairs would be destructive of state rights, of state sovereignty, of personal liberty and personal freedom. Uniformity is the parent of despotism the world over, not only in politics, but in religion....

From this view of the case, my friends, I am driven irresistibly to the conclusion that diversity, dissimilarity, variety in all our local and domestic institutions, is the great safeguard of our liberties; and that the framers of our institutions were wise, sagacious, and patriotic, when they made this government a confederation of sovereign states, with a legislature for each, and conferred upon each legislature the power to make all local and domestic institutions to suit the people it represented, without interference from any other state or from the general Congress of the Union. If we expect to maintain our liberties, we must preserve the rights and sovereignty of the states; we must maintain and carry out that great principle of self-government incorporated in the compromise measures of 1850; indorsed by the Illinois legislature in 1851; emphatically embodied and carried out in the Kansas-Nebraska bill, and vindicated this year by the refusal to bring Kansas into the Union with a Constitution distasteful to her people.

The other proposition discussed by Mr. Lincoln in his speech consists in a crusade against the Supreme Court of the United States on account of the *Dred Scott* decision....

... [T]he reason assigned by Mr. Lincoln for resisting the decision of the Supreme Court in the *Dred Scott* case, does not in itself meet my approbation. He objects to it because that decision declared that a Negro descended from African parents, who were brought here and sold as slaves, is not, and cannot be, a citizen of the United States. He says it is wrong, because it deprives the Negro of the benefits of that clause of the Constitution which says that citizens of one state shall enjoy all the privileges and immunities of citizens of the several states; in other words, he thinks it wrong because it deprives the Negro of the privileges, immunities and rights of citizenship, which pertain, according to that decision, only to the white man. I am free to say to you that in my opinion this government of ours is founded on the white basis. It was made by the white man, for the benefit of the white man, to be administered by white men, in such manner as they should determine. It is also true that a Negro, an Indian, or any other man of inferior race to a white man, should be permitted to enjoy, and humanity requires that he should have all the rights, privileges and immunities which he is capable of exercising consistent with the safety of society.... [W]hat are these rights and these privileges? My answer is, that each state must decide for itself the nature and extent of these rights....

. . . I do not subscribe to the doctrine of my friend, Mr. Lincoln, that uniformity is either desirable or possible. I do not acknowledge that the states must all be free or must all be slave.

I do not acknowledge that the Negro must have civil and political rights everywhere or nowhere. I do not acknowledge that the Chinese must have the same rights in California that we would confer upon him here. I do not acknowledge that the cooley[5] imported into this country must necessarily be put upon an equality with the white race. I do not acknowledge any of these doctrines of uniformity in the local and domestic regulations in the different states.

Thus you see, my fellow-citizens, that the issues between Mr. Lincoln and myself, as respective candidates for the U.S. Senate, as made up, are direct, unequivocal, and irreconcilable. He goes for uniformity in our domestic institutions, for a war of sections, until one or the other shall be subdued. I go for the great principle of the Kansas-Nebraska bill, the right of the people to decide for themselves.

[5] Cooly or Coolie is a term used to refer to a day laborer. In the United States, it was used to describe Chinese immigrants and is considered derogatory.

DOCUMENT 19

"An Irrepressible Conflict"

William Henry Seward

October 25, 1858

Before becoming Abraham Lincoln's Secretary of State, and one of his most trusted advisors, William Henry Seward (1801–1872) served as governor of New York, U.S. senator, and was the favorite to win the Republican nomination for president in 1860. During the 1858 midterm elections, Seward spoke to a crowd in Rochester, New York, delivering what was arguably the most impressive, yet politically disastrous, speech of his career. Seward claimed that an "irrepressible conflict" was brewing over slavery and that the United States, as a result, must sooner or later become all slave or all free. The Democratic Party was the party of the slave power, Seward argued, its survival dependent on the support of the slave interest. The Republican Party had to replace it. But Seward's fiery rhetoric and uncompromising attitude earned him the reputation throughout the South, and even in parts of the North, as a war-monger. The speech weakened his appeal among Republicans and severely damaged his chances of securing the 1860 nomination.

Seward's speech is also notable for its description and defense of the system of free labor, which he contrasts to the system of slavery. Seward's account of free labor should be compared with Senator James Henry Hammond's defense of the slave system (Document 16) and Abraham Lincoln's defense of free labor (Document 20). It was the far-reaching political, moral, and economic effects of the two different labor systems that made the Civil War an "irrepressible conflict."

SOURCE: *The Irrepressible Conflict: A Speech Delivered at Rochester, Monday, Oct. 25, 1858* (New York: New York Tribune, 1858), https://babel.hathitrust.org/cgi/pt?id=coo.31924032259578;view=1up;seq=1.

The unmistakable outbreaks of zeal which occur all around me show that you are earnest men—and such a man am I. Let us, therefore, at least for a time, pass all secondary and collateral questions, whether of a personal or of a general nature, and consider the main subject of the present canvass. The

Democratic Party, or, to speak more accurately, the party which wears that attractive name—is in possession of the federal government. The Republicans propose to dislodge that party, and dismiss it from its high trust.

The main subject, then, is whether the Democratic Party deserves to retain the confidence of the American people. In attempting to prove it unworthy, I think that I am not actuated by prejudices against that party, or by prepossessions in favor of its adversary; for I have learned, by some experience, that virtue and patriotism, vice and selfishness, are found in all parties, and that they differ less in their motives than in the policies they pursue.

Our country is a theatre, which exhibits, in full operation, two radically different political systems; the one resting on the basis of servile or slave labor, the other on voluntary labor of freemen.

The laborers who are enslaved are all Negroes, or persons more or less purely of African derivation. But this is only accidental. The principle of the system is, that labor in every society, by whomsoever performed, is necessarily unintellectual, groveling and base; and that the laborer, equally for his own good and for the welfare of the state, ought to be enslaved. The white laboring man, whether native or foreigner, is not enslaved, only because he cannot, as yet, be reduced to bondage.

You need not be told now that the slave system is the older of the two, and that once it was universal.

The emancipation of our own ancestors, Caucasians and Europeans as they were, hardly dates beyond a period of five hundred years. The great melioration of human society which modern times exhibits is mainly due to the incomplete substitution of the system of voluntary labor for the one of servile labor, which has already taken place. This African slave system is one which, in its origin and in its growth, has been altogether foreign from the habits of the races which colonized these states, and established civilization here. It was introduced on this continent as an engine of conquest, and for the establishment of monarchical power, by the Portuguese and the Spaniards, and was rapidly extended by them all over South America, Central America, Louisiana, and Mexico. Its legitimate fruits are seen in the poverty, imbecility, and anarchy which now pervade all Portuguese and Spanish America. The free-labor system is of German extraction, and it was established in our country by emigrants from Sweden, Holland, Germany, Great Britain, and Ireland.

We justly ascribe to its influences the strength, wealth, greatness, intelligence, and freedom, which the whole American people now enjoy. One of the chief elements of the value of human life is freedom in the pursuit of happiness. The slave system is not only intolerable, unjust, and inhuman, toward the laborer, whom, only because he is a laborer, it loads down with chains and converts into merchandise, but is scarcely less severe upon the freeman, to whom, only because he is a laborer from necessity, it denies facilities for employment, and whom it expels from the community because it cannot enslave and convert into merchandise also. It is necessarily improvident and ruinous, because, as a general truth, communities prosper and flourish, or droop and decline, in just the degree that they practice or neglect to practice the primary duties of justice and humanity. The free-labor system conforms to the divine law of equality, which is written in the hearts and consciences of man, and therefore is always and everywhere beneficent.

The slave system is one of constant danger, distrust, suspicion, and watchfulness. It debases those whose toil alone can produce wealth and resources for defense, to the lowest degree of which human nature is capable, to guard against mutiny and insurrection, and thus wastes energies which otherwise might be employed in national development and aggrandizement.

The free-labor system educates all alike, and by opening all the fields of industrial employment and all the departments of authority, to the unchecked and equal rivalry of all classes of men, at once secures universal contentment, and brings into the highest possible activity all the physical, moral, and social energies of the whole state. In states where the slave system prevails, the masters, directly or indirectly, secure all political power, and constitute a ruling aristocracy. In states where the free-labor system prevails, universal suffrage necessarily obtains, and the state inevitably becomes, sooner or later, a republic or democracy....

...The two systems are at once perceived to be incongruous. But they are more than incongruous—they are incompatible. They never have permanently existed together in one country, and they never can. It would be easy to demonstrate this impossibility, from the irreconcilable contrast between their great principles and characteristics. But the experience of mankind has conclusively established it. Slavery, as I have intimated, existed in every state in Europe. Free labor has supplanted it everywhere except in Russia and Turkey. State necessities developed in modern times are now obliging even those two nations to encourage and employ free labor; and already, despotic as they are, we find them engaged in abolishing slavery. In the United States, slavery came into collision with free labor at the close of the last century, and fell before it in New England, New York, New Jersey, and Pennsylvania, but triumphed over it effectually, and excluded it for a period yet undetermined, from Virginia, the Carolinas, and Georgia. Indeed, so incompatible are the two systems, that every new state which is organized within our ever-extending domain makes its first political act a choice of the one and the exclusion of the other, even at the cost of civil war, if necessary. The slave states, without law, at the last national election, successfully forbade, within their own limits, even the casting of votes for a candidate for president of the United States supposed to be favorable to the establishment of the free-labor system in new states.

Hitherto, the two systems have existed in different states, but side by side within the American Union. This has happened because the Union is a confederation of states. But in another aspect the United States constitute only one nation. Increase of population, which is filling the states out to their very borders, together with a new and extended network of railroads and other avenues, and an internal commerce which daily becomes more intimate, is rapidly bringing the states into a higher and more perfect social unity or consolidation. Thus, these antagonistic systems are continually coming into closer contact, and collision results.

Shall I tell you what this collision means? They who think that it is accidental, unnecessary, the work of interested or fanatical agitators, and therefor ephemeral, mistake the case altogether. It is an irrepressible conflict between opposing and enduring forces, and it means that the United States must and will, sooner or later, become either entirely a slaveholding nation, or entirely a free-labor nation. Either the cotton and rice fields of South Carolina and the sugar plantations of Louisiana will ultimately be tilled by free labor, and Charleston and New Orleans become markets of legitimate merchandise alone, or else the rye fields and wheat fields of Massachusetts and New York must again be surrendered by their farmers to slave culture and to the production of slaves, and Boston and New York become once more markets for trade in the bodies and souls of men. It is the failure to apprehend this great truth that induces so many unsuccessful attempts at final compromises between the slave and free states, and it is the existence of this great fact that renders all such pretended compromises, when made, vain and ephemeral. Startling as this saying may appear to you, fellow-citizens, it is by no means an original or even a modern one. Our forefathers knew it to be true, and unanimously acted upon it when they framed the Constitution of the United States. They regarded the existence of the servile system in so many of the states with sorrow and shame, which they openly confessed, and they looked upon the collision between them, which was then just revealing itself, and which we are now accustomed to deplore, with favor and hope. They knew that one or the other system must exclusively prevail.

Unlike too many of those who in modem time invoke their authority, they had a choice between the two. They preferred the system of free labor, and they determined to organize the government, and so direct its activity, that that system should surely and certainly prevail. For this purpose, and no other, they based the whole structure of the government broadly on the principle that all men are created equal, and therefore free—little dreaming that, within the short period of one hundred years, their descendants would bear to be told by any orator, however popular, that the utterance of that principle was merely a rhetorical rhapsody; or by any judge, however venerated, that it was attended by mental reservation, which rendered it hypocritical and false. By the ordinance of 1787[1] they dedicated all of the national domain not yet polluted by slavery to free labor immediately, thenceforth and forever; while by the new Constitution and laws they invited foreign free labor from all lands under the sun, and interdicted the importation of African slave labor, at all times, in all places, and under all circumstances whatsoever. It is true that they necessarily and wisely modified this policy of freedom by leaving it to the several states, affected as they were by different circumstances, to abolish slavery in their own way and at their own pleasure, instead of confiding that duty to Congress; and that they secured to the slave states, while yet retaining the system of slavery, a three-fifths representation of slaves in the federal government, until they should find themselves able to relinquish it with safety. But the very nature of these modifications fortifies my position, that the fathers knew that the two systems could not endure within the Union, and expected within a short period slavery would disappear forever. Moreover, in order that these modifications might not altogether defeat their grand design of a republic maintaining universal equality, they provided that two thirds of the states might amend the Constitution....

... How, then, and in what way, shall the necessary resistance [to slavery] be made? There is only one way. The Democratic Party must be permanently dislodged from the government. The reason is, that the Democratic Party is inextricably committed to the designs of the slaveholders, which I have described.

Such is the Democratic Party. It has no policy, state or federal, for finance, or trade, or manufacture, or commerce, or education, or internal improvements, or for the protection or even the security of civil or religious liberty. It is positive and uncompromising in the interest of slavery—negative, compromising, and vacillating, in regard to everything else. It boasts its love

[1] The Northwest Ordinance

of equality, and wastes its strength, and even its life, in fortifying the only aristocracy known in the land. It professes fraternity, and, so often as slavery requires, allies itself with proscription. It magnifies itself for conquests in foreign lands, but it sends the national eagle forth always with chains, and not the olive branch, in his fangs.

This dark record shows you, fellow-citizens, what I was unwilling to announce at an earlier stage of this argument, that of the whole nefarious schedule of slaveholding designs which I have submitted to you, the Democratic Party has left only one yet to be consummated-the abrogation of the law which forbids the African slave trade.

I know—few, I think, know better than I—the resources and energies of the Democratic Party, which is identical with the slave power. I do ample justice to its traditional popularity. I know further—few, I think, know better than I—the difficulties and disadvantages of organizing a new political force, like the Republican Party, and the obstacles it must encounter in laboring without prestige and without patronage. But, understanding all this, I know that the Democratic Party must go down, and that the Republican Party must rise into its place. The Democratic Party derived its strength, originally, from its adoption of the principles of equal and exact justice to all men. So long as it practiced this principle faithfully it was invulnerable. It became vulnerable when it renounced the principle, and since that time it has maintained itself, not by virtue of its own strength, or even of its traditional merits, but because there as yet had appeared in the political field no other party that had the conscience and the courage to take up, and avow, and practice the life-inspiring principle which the Democratic Party had surrendered. At last, the Republican Party has appeared. It avows, now, as the Republican Party of 1800 did, in one word, its faith and its works, "Equal and exact justice to all men." Even when it first entered the field, only half organized, it struck a blow which only just failed to secure complete and triumphant victory. In this, its second campaign, it has already won advantages which render that triumph now both easy and certain.

The secret of its assured success lies in that very characteristic which, in the mouth of scoffers, constitutes its great and lasting imbecility and reproach. It lies in the fact that it is a party of one idea; but that is a noble one—an idea that fills and expands all generous souls; the idea of equality—the equality of all men before human tribunals and human laws, as they all are equal before the divine tribunal and divine laws.

I know, and you know, that a revolution has begun. I know, and all the world knows, that revolutions never go backward. Twenty senators and a hundred representatives proclaim boldly in Congress today sentiments and opinions and principles of freedom which hardly so many men, even in this free state, dared to utter in their own homes twenty years ago. While the government of the United States, under the conduct of the Democratic Party, has been all that time surrendering one plain and castle after another to slavery, the people of the United States have been no less steadily and perseveringly gathering together the forces with which to recover back again all the fields and all the castles which have been lost, and to confound and overthrow, by one decisive blow, the betrayers of the Constitution and freedom forever.

DOCUMENT 20

Address before the Wisconsin State Agricultural Society

Abraham Lincoln

September 30, 1859

Abraham Lincoln won the popular vote against Stephen A. Douglas (1813–1861) in the 1858 Illinois senatorial race (Documents 17 and 18), but Douglas was chosen senator because the Democrats maintained their majority in the Illinois Senate, where senators were chosen at the time. (This changed with the ratification of the 17th Amendment, April 8, 1913.) In 1859, Lincoln continued to work as a lawyer, but his campaign against Douglas raised his national profile and made him a possible presidential candidate. Lincoln continued to build his following outside of Illinois with speaking tours in Ohio, Indiana, Wisconsin, and Kansas. In this speech given on the tour, Lincoln defended free labor from attacks made by those in favor of slavery (Documents 7, 13, and 16; for a view similar to Lincoln's, see Document 19). In doing so, Lincoln showed not only how different were the views of those who favored and opposed slavery, he also addressed a question fundamental to the possibility and the goodness of a way of life based on human equality: was it possible to satisfy the requirements of both the body and mind through human labor? His answer depends on bringing technology, and therefore education, to the service of man's needs. In human history, during which slavery had been a universal practice, this was a revolutionary change in point of view.

SOURCE: *Life and Works of Abraham Lincoln*, Centenary Edition, Volume II, Marion Mills Miller, ed., (New York: The Current Literature Publishing Company, 1907), 277–293, https://archive.org/details/lifeworksofabraho4linc/page/n9.

... The world is agreed that labor is the source from which human wants are mainly supplied. There is no dispute upon this point. From this point, however, men immediately diverge. Much disputation is maintained as to the best way of applying and controlling the labor element. By some it is assumed that labor is available only in connection with capital—that nobody labors, unless somebody else, owning capital, somehow, by the use of that capital, induces him to do it. Having assumed this, they proceed to consider whether it is best that capital shall hire laborers, and thus induce them to work by their own consent; or buy them, and drive them to it without their consent. Having proceeded so far they naturally conclude that all laborers are necessarily either hired laborers, or slaves. They further assume that whoever is once a hired laborer, is fatally fixed in that condition for life; and thence again that his condition is as bad as, or worse than that of a slave. This is the "mud sill" theory.[1]

But another class of reasoners hold the opinion that there is no such relation between capital and labor, as assumed; and that there is no such thing as a freeman being fatally fixed for life, in the condition of a hired laborer, that both these assumptions are false, and all inferences from them groundless. They hold that labor is prior to, and independent of, capital; that, in fact, capital is the fruit of labor, and could never have existed if labor had not first existed—that labor can exist without capital, but that capital could never have existed without labor. Hence they hold that labor is the superior—greatly the superior—of capital.

They do not deny that there is, and probably always will be, a relation between labor and capital. The error, as they hold, is in assuming that the whole labor of the world exists within that relation. A few men own capital; and that few avoid labor themselves, and with their capital, hire, or buy, another few to labor for them. A large majority belong to neither class—neither work for others, nor have others working for them. Even in all our slave states, except South Carolina, a majority of the whole people of all colors, are neither slaves nor masters. In these free states, a large majority are neither hirers or hired. Men, with their families—wives, sons and daughters—work for themselves, on their farms, in their houses and in their shops, taking the whole product to themselves, and asking no favors of capital on the one hand, nor of hirelings or slaves on the other. It is not forgotten that a considerable number of persons mingle their own labor with capital; that is, labor with their own hands, and also buy slaves or hire freemen to labor for them; but this is only a mixed, and not a distinct class. No principle stated is disturbed by the existence of this mixed class. Again, as has already been said, the opponents of the "mud sill" theory insist that there is not, of necessity, any such thing as the free hired laborer being fixed to that condition for

[1] See Document 16.

life. There is demonstration for saying this. Many independent men, in this assembly, doubtless a few years ago were hired laborers. And their case is almost if not quite the general rule.

The prudent, penniless beginner in the world, labors for wages awhile, saves a surplus with which to buy tools or land, for himself; then labors on his own account another while, and at length hires another new beginner to help him. This, say its advocates, is free labor—the just and generous, and prosperous system, which opens the way for all—gives hope to all, and energy, and progress, and improvement of condition to all. If any continue through life in the condition of the hired laborer, it is not the fault of the system, but because of either a dependent nature which prefers it, or improvidence, folly, or singular misfortune. I have said this much about the elements of labor generally, as introductory to the consideration of a new phase which that element is in process of assuming. The old general rule was that educated people did not perform manual labor. They managed to eat their bread, leaving the toil of producing it to the uneducated. This was not an insupportable evil to the working bees, so long as the class of drones remained very small. But now, especially in these free states, nearly all are educated—quite too nearly all, to leave the labor of the uneducated, in any wise adequate to the support of the whole. It follows from this that henceforth educated people must labor. Otherwise, education itself would become a positive and intolerable evil. No country can sustain, in idleness, more than a small percentage of its numbers. The great majority must labor at something productive. From these premises the problem springs, "How can labor and education be the most satisfactory combined?"

By the "mud sill" theory it is assumed that labor and education are incompatible; and any practical combination of them impossible. According to that theory, a blind horse upon a tread-mill, is a perfect illustration of what a laborer should be—all the better for being blind, that he could not tread out of place, or kick understandingly. According to that theory, the education of laborers is not only useless, but pernicious, and dangerous. In fact, it is, in some sort, deemed a misfortune that laborers should have heads at all. Those same heads are regarded as explosive materials, only to be safely kept in damp places, as far as possible from that peculiar sort of fire which ignites them. A Yankee who could invent a strong-handed man without a head would receive the everlasting gratitude of the "mud sill" advocates.

But free labor says "no!" Free labor argues that, as the Author of man makes every individual with one head and one pair of hands, it was probably intended that heads and hands should cooperate as friends; and that that particular head, should direct and control that particular pair of hands. As each man has one mouth to be fed, and one pair of hands to furnish food, it was probably intended that that particular pair of hands should feed that particular mouth—that each head is the natural guardian, director, and protector of the hands and mouth inseparably connected with it; and that being so, every head should be cultivated, and improved, by whatever will add to its capacity for performing its charge. In one word free labor insists on universal education....

This leads to the further reflection, that no other human occupation opens so wide a field for the profitable and agreeable combination of labor with cultivated thought, as agriculture. I know of nothing so pleasant to the mind, as the discovery of anything which is at once new and valuable—nothing which so lightens and sweetens toil, as the hopeful pursuit of such discovery. And how vast, and how varied a field is agriculture, for such discovery. The mind, already trained to thought, in the country school, or higher school, cannot fail to find there an exhaustless source of profitable enjoyment. Every blade of grass is a study; and to produce two, where there was but one, is both a profit and a pleasure. And not grass alone; but soils, seeds, and seasons—hedges, ditches, and fences, draining, droughts, and irrigation—plowing, hoeing, and harrowing—reaping, mowing, and threshing—saving crops, pests of crops, diseases of crops, and what will prevent or cure them—implements, utensils, and machines, their relative merits, and [how] to improve them—hogs, horses, and cattle—sheep, goats, and poultry—trees, shrubs, fruits, plants, and flowers—the thousand things of which these are specimens—each a world of study within itself.

In all this, book-learning is available. A capacity, and taste, for reading, gives access to whatever has already been discovered by others. It is the key, or one of the keys, to the already solved problems. And not only so. It gives a relish, and facility, for successfully pursuing the [yet] unsolved ones. The rudiments of science, are available, and highly valuable. Some knowledge of botany assists in dealing with the vegetable world—with all growing crops. Chemistry assists in the analysis of soils, selection, and application of manures, and in numerous other ways. The mechanical branches of natural philosophy, are ready help in almost everything; but especially in reference to implements and machinery.

The thought recurs that education—cultivated thought—can best be combined with agricultural labor, or any labor, on the principle of thorough work—that careless, half performed, slovenly work, makes no place for such combination. And thorough work, again, renders sufficient, the smallest quantity of ground to each man. And this again, conforms to what must occur in a world less inclined to wars, and more devoted to the arts of peace, than heretofore. Population must increase rapidly—more rapidly than in former times—and ere long the most valuable of all arts, will be the art of deriving a comfortable subsistence from the smallest area of soil. No community whose every member possesses this art, can ever be the victim of oppression of any of its forms. Such community will be alike independent of crowned kings, money kings, and land kings.

DOCUMENT 21

Republican Party Platform

May 17, 1860

The Republican Party was formed in 1854, the same year the Missouri Compromise was repealed under the Kansas-Nebraska Act. Two years later, during the election of 1856, the Republicans drafted their first presidential party platform, declaring the right and the duty of Congress "to prohibit in the territories those twin relics of barbarism—polygamy and slavery." (Polygamy was a reference to the Mormons in the Utah territory, created in 1850 as part of the laws that made up the Compromise of 1850 [Document 8].) The Republican candidate for president that year, John C. Fremont (1813–1890), narrowly lost to James Buchanan (1791–1868), the Democratic candidate. In 1860, the Republicans drafted a party platform dominated by the slavery issue and, after several ballots, nominated Abraham Lincoln for president and Hannibal Hamlin of Maine for vice president.

SOURCE: Republican Party Platform of 1860, online by Gerhard Peters and John T. Woolley, The American Presidency Project, https://www.presidency.ucsb.edu/node/273296.

Resolved that we, the delegated representatives of the Republican electors of the United States, in convention assembled, in discharge of the duty we owe to our constituents and our country, unite in the following declarations:

First. That the history of the nation during the last four years has fully established the propriety and necessity of the organization and perpetuation of the Republican party, and that the causes which called it into existence are permanent in their nature, and now more than ever before demand its peaceful and constitutional triumph.

Second. That the maintenance of the principles promulgated in the Declaration of Independence and embodied in the federal Constitution, "That all men are created equal; that they are endowed by their Creator with certain inalienable rights; that among these are life, liberty, and the pursuit of happiness; that to secure these rights, governments are instituted among men, deriving their just powers from the consent of the governed," is essential to the preservation of our Republican institutions; and that the federal Constitution, the rights of the states, and the Union of the states, must and shall be preserved.

Third. That to the Union of the states this nation owes its unprecedented increase in population; its surprising development of material resources; its rapid augmentation of wealth; its happiness at home and its honor abroad; and we hold in abhorrence all schemes for disunion, come from whatever source they may; and we congratulate the country that no Republican member of Congress has uttered or countenanced the threats of disunion so often made by Democratic members, without rebuke and with applause from their political associates; and we denounce those threats of disunion, in case of a popular overthrow of their ascendency, as denying the vital principles of a free government, and as an avowal of contemplated treason, which it is the imperative duty of an indignant people sternly to rebuke and forever silence.

Fourth. That the maintenance inviolate of the rights of the states, and especially the right of each state, to order and control its own domestic institutions according to its own judgment exclusively, is essential to that balance of power on which the perfection and endurance of our political fabric depends, and we denounce the lawless invasion by armed force of the soil of any state or territory, no matter under what pretext, as among the gravest of crimes.

Fifth. That the present Democratic Administration has far exceeded our worst apprehension in its measureless subserviency to the exactions of a sectional interest, as is especially evident in its desperate exertions to force the infamous Lecompton Constitution[1] upon the protesting people of Kansas; in construing the personal relation between master and servant to involve an unqualified property in persons; in its attempted enforcement everywhere, on land and sea, through the intervention of Congress and of the federal courts, of the extreme pretensions of a purely local interest, and in its general and unvarying abuse of the power entrusted to it by a confiding people.

Sixth. That the people justly view with alarm the reckless extravagance which pervades every department of the federal government; that a return to rigid economy and accountability is indispensable to arrest the systematic plunder of the public treasury by favored partisans; while the recent startling developments of frauds and corruptions at the federal metropolis, show that an entire change of administration is imperatively demanded.

---

[1] See the introduction to Document 16.

Seventh. That the new dogma that the Constitution of its own force carries slavery into any or all of the territories of the United States, is a dangerous political heresy, at variance with the explicit provisions of that instrument itself, with cotemporaneous exposition, and with legislative and judicial precedent, is revolutionary in its tendency and subversive of the peace and harmony of the country.

Eighth. That the normal condition of all the territory of the United States is that of freedom; that as our Republican fathers, when they had abolished slavery in all our national territory, ordained that no "person should be deprived of life, liberty or property, without due process of law,"[2] it becomes our duty, by legislation, whenever such legislation is necessary, to maintain this provision of the Constitution against all attempts to violate it; and we deny the authority of Congress, of a territorial legislature, or of any individuals, to give legal existence to slavery in any territory of the United States.

Ninth. That we brand the recent reopening of the African slave trade, under the cover of our national flag, aided by perversions of judicial power, as a crime against humanity, and a burning shame to our country and age, and we call upon Congress to take prompt and efficient measures for the total and final suppression of that execrable traffic.

Tenth. That in the recent vetoes by the federal governors of the acts of the legislatures of Kansas and Nebraska, prohibiting slavery in those territories, we find a practical illustration of the boasted Democratic principle of non-intervention and popular sovereignty, embodied in the Kansas-Nebraska bill, and a demonstration of the deception and fraud involved therein.

Eleventh. That Kansas should of right be immediately admitted as a state, under the Constitution recently formed and adopted by her people, and accepted by the House of Representatives.

Twelfth. That while providing revenue for the support of the general government by duties upon imports, sound policy requires such an adjustment of these imposts as to encourage the development of the industrial interests of the whole country, and we commend that policy of national exchanges which  secures to the workingmen liberal wages, to agriculture remunerating prices, to mechanics and manufacturers an adequate reward for their skill, labor and enterprise, and to the nation commercial prosperity and independence.

Thirteenth. That we protest against any sale or alienation to others of the public lands held by actual settlers, and against any view of the free homestead

[2] a paraphrase of a portion of the Fifth Amendment to the Constitution

policy which regards the settlers as paupers or suppliants for public bounty, and we demand the passage by Congress of the complete and satisfactory homestead measure which has already passed the House.

Fourteenth. That the Republican party is opposed to any change in our naturalization laws, or any state legislation by which the rights of citizenship hitherto accorded by emigrants from foreign lands shall be abridged or impaired; and in favor of giving a full and efficient protection to the rights of all classes of citizens, whether native or naturalized, both at home and abroad.

Fifteenth. That appropriation by Congress for river and harbor improvements of a national character, required for the accommodation and security of an existing commerce, are authorized by the Constitution and justified by the obligation of government to protect the lives and property of its citizens.

Sixteenth. That a railroad to the Pacific Ocean is imperatively demanded by the interests of the whole country; that the federal government ought to render immediate and efficient aid in its construction; and that, as preliminary thereto, a daily overland mail should be promptly established.

Seventeenth. Finally, having thus set forth our distinctive principles and views, we invite the cooperation of all citizens, however differing on other questions who substantially agree with us in their affirmance and support.

DOCUMENT 22

Democratic Party Platforms

June 2, 1856 and June 18, 1860

The Democratic Party first met in Charleston, South Carolina and, failing to come to a consensus, later in Baltimore, Maryland, where it eventually nominated for president Stephen A. Douglas, Abraham Lincoln's former rival in the 1858 Illinois Senatorial election and the author of the Kansas-Nebraska Act (Documents 17 and 18). But the delegates from the Lower South, bolstered by the recent Supreme Court ruling in the Dred Scott case (Document 14), refused to accept Douglas's popular sovereignty compromise on the principle that slavery was right and rejected his selection. They immediately withdrew and nominated a hardline pro-slavery advocate, John C. Breckinridge of Kentucky. To complicate matters further, a fourth candidate entered the race: Senator John Bell from Tennessee was nominated by the Constitutional Union Party, composed of ex-Whigs and former members of the American or "Know-Nothing" Party. With the Democratic Party split over the issue of slavery, the rejuvenated Republicans sensed that victory was near. The stage was now set for the most important election in American history.

We reproduce here the 1860 platform in its entirety and the portion of the 1856 platform that deals with slavery, because the 1860 nominating convention unanimously adopted the 1856 platform.

SOURCE: 1860 Democratic Party Platform, online by Gerhard Peters and John T. Woolley, The American Presidency Project, https://www.presidency.ucsb.edu/node/273172 and 1856 Democratic Party Platform, online by Gerhard Peters and John T. Woolley, The American Presidency Project, https://www.presidency.ucsb.edu/node/273169. The American Presidency Project used the first day of the national nominating conventions as the "date" of the platforms since the original documents are undated.

The 1860 Platform

1. Resolved, that we, the Democracy of the Union in Convention assembled, hereby declare our affirmance of the resolutions unanimously adopted and

declared as a platform of principles by the Democratic Convention at Cincinnati, in the year 1856, believing that Democratic principles are unchangeable in their nature, when applied to the same subject matters; and we recommend, as the only further resolutions, the following:

2. Inasmuch as difference of opinion exists in the Democratic Party as to the nature and extent of the powers of a territorial legislature, and as to the powers and duties of Congress, under the Constitution of the United States, over the institution of slavery within the territories,

Resolved, that the Democratic Party will abide by the decision of the Supreme Court of the United States upon these questions of Constitutional law.[1]

3. Resolved, that it is the duty of the United States to afford ample and complete protection to all its citizens, whether at home or abroad, and whether native or foreign born.

4. Resolved, that one of the necessities of the age, in a military, commercial, and postal point of view, is speedy communication between the Atlantic and Pacific states; and the Democratic Party pledge such constitutional government aid as will insure the construction of a railroad to the Pacific coast, at the earliest practicable period.

5. Resolved, that the Democratic Party is in favor of the acquisition of the Island of Cuba on such terms as shall be honorable to ourselves and just to Spain.

6. Resolved, that the enactments of the state legislatures to defeat the faithful execution of the Fugitive Slave Law, are hostile in character, subversive of the Constitution, and revolutionary in their effect.

7. Resolved, that it is in accordance with the interpretation of the Cincinnati platform,[2] that during the existence of the territorial governments the measure of restriction, whatever it may be, imposed by the federal Constitution on the power of the territorial legislature over the subject of the domestic relations, as the same has been, or shall hereafter be finally determined by the Supreme Court of the United States, should be respected by all good citizens, and enforced with promptness and fidelity by every branch of the general government.

---

[1] an implicit endorsement of the *Dred Scott* decision (Document 14)

[2] the 1856 convention

The 1856 Platform

Resolved, that we reiterate with renewed energy of purpose the well-considered declarations of former conventions upon the sectional issue of domestic slavery, and concerning the reserved rights of the states.

1. that Congress has no power under the Constitution, to interfere with or control the domestic institutions of the several states, and that such states are the sole and proper judges of everything appertaining to their own affairs, not prohibited by the Constitution; that all efforts of the abolitionists, or others, made to induce Congress to interfere with questions of slavery, or to take incipient steps in relation thereto, are calculated to lead to the most alarming and dangerous consequences; and that all such efforts have an inevitable tendency to diminish the happiness of the people and endanger the stability and permanency of the Union, and ought not to be countenanced by any friend of our political institutions.

2. that the foregoing proposition covers, and was intended to embrace the whole subject of slavery agitation in Congress; and therefore, the Democratic Party of the Union, standing on this national platform, will abide by and adhere to a faithful execution of the acts known as the compromise measures,[3] settled by the Congress of 1850; "the act for reclaiming fugitives from service or labor," included; which act being designed to carry out an express provision of the Constitution, cannot, with fidelity thereto, be repealed, or so changed as to destroy or impair its efficiency.

3. that the Democratic Party will resist all attempts at renewing, in Congress or out of it, the agitation of the slavery question under whatever shape or color the attempt may be made.

4. that the Democratic Party will faithfully abide by and uphold, the principles laid down in the Kentucky and Virginia resolutions of 1798, and in the report of Mr. Madison to the Virginia Legislature in 1799;[4] that it adopts those principles as constituting one of the main foundations of its political creed, and is resolved to carry them out in their obvious meaning and import.

And that we may more distinctly meet the issue on which a sectional party, subsisting exclusively on slavery agitation, now relies to test the fidelity of the people, North and South, to the Constitution and the Union—

[3] The Compromise of 1850 (Document 8)

[4] The Kentucky and Virginia resolutions and James Madison's report asserted the right of a state to decide if the actions of the federal government were constitutional.

1. Resolved, that claiming fellowship with, and desiring the co-operation of all who regard the preservation of the Union under the Constitution as the paramount issue—and repudiating all sectional parties and platforms concerning domestic slavery, which seek to embroil the states and incite to treason and armed resistance to law in the territories; and whose avowed purposes, if consummated, must end in civil war and disunion, the American Democracy recognize and adopt the principles contained in the organic laws establishing the territories of Kansas and Nebraska as embodying the only sound and safe solution of the "slavery question" upon which the great national idea of the people of this whole country can repose in its determined conservatism of the Union—non-interference by Congress with slavery in state and territory, or in the District of Columbia.

2. that this was the basis of the compromises of 1850 confirmed by both the Democratic and Whig parties in national conventions—ratified by the people in the election of 1852, and rightly applied to the organization of territories in 1854.

3. that by the uniform application of this Democratic principle to the organization of territories, and to the admission of new states, with or without domestic slavery, as they may elect—the equal rights, of all the states will be preserved intact; the original compacts of the Constitution maintained inviolate; and the perpetuity and expansion of this Union insured to its utmost capacity of embracing, in peace and harmony, every future American state that may be constituted or annexed, with a republican form of government.

Resolved, that we recognize the right of the people of all the territories, including Kansas and Nebraska, acting through the legally and fairly expressed will of a majority of actual residents, and whenever the number of their inhabitants justifies it, to form a Constitution, with or without domestic slavery, and be admitted into the Union upon terms of perfect equality with the other states.

Resolved, finally, that in view of the condition of popular institutions in the Old World (and the dangerous tendencies of sectional agitation, combined with the attempt to enforce civil and religious disabilities against the rights of acquiring and enjoying citizenship, in our own land) a high and sacred duty is devolved with increased responsibility upon the Democratic Party of this country, as the party of the Union, to uphold and maintain the rights of every state, and thereby the Union of the states; and to sustain and advance among us constitutional liberty, by continuing to resist all monopolies and exclusive legislation for the benefit of the few, at the expense of the many, and by a vigilant and constant adherence to those principles and compromises of the Constitution, which are broad enough and strong enough to embrace and uphold the Union as it was, the Union as it is, and the Union as it shall be, in the full expansion of the energies and capacity of this great and progressive people.

DOCUMENT 23

Declaration of the Immediate Causes Which Induce and Justify the Secession of South Carolina from the Federal Union

December 24, 1860

Abraham Lincoln won the presidential election of 1860 with about 40 per cent of the popular vote, the rest divided among three other candidates (Document 22). Lincoln would have won the electoral college vote and become president even if all the votes for the other candidates had gone to just one of them, since the free states Lincoln won had sufficient electoral votes to elect a president. As a consequence of Lincoln's election, South Carolina was the first state to secede from the Union, after decades threatening nullification and secession under the banner of states' rights. On November 10, 1860, only days after Lincoln's election to the presidency, the South Carolina General Assembly called for a convention of the people of the state to consider secession, members of which were elected early the next month. The convention, composed of 169 delegates, voted unanimously in favor of secession and quickly drew up the declaration of secession to explain its reasons for dissolving the Union.

President James Buchanan (1791–1868), who had not run for re-election, in his last State of the Union Address (December 3, 1860) denied the right of states to secede, disappointing the South, and blamed anti-slavery sentiment for creating discord and disunion, aggravating the North. He then denied that the president or the federal government had any authority to prevent secession. He remained in office until March 4, 1861. During that time, six states—Mississippi, Florida, Alabama, Georgia, Louisiana, and Texas—joined South Carolina in declaring their secession from the Union.

As others had since the time of the Missouri Compromise (Document 2), the authors of the South Carolina Declaration addressed the character of the Union and defended the justice of their decision by offering a history of the founding of the United States. (Compare the account here with Abraham Lincoln's, Appendix E.) The South Carolina Declaration also echoes the argument and even some of the phrases of the Declaration of Independence, without, of course, mentioning its key premise, human equality.

SOURCE: *Declaration of the Immediate Causes Which Induce and Justify the Secession of South Carolina from the Federal Union and the Ordinance of Secession* (Charleston: Printed by Evans and Cogswell, 1860, https://digital.scetv.org/teachingAmerhistory/pdfs/DeclImm Causes.pdf

---

The people of the state of South Carolina, in Convention assembled, on the 26th day of April, A.D., 1852, declared that the frequent violations of the Constitution of the United States, by the federal government, and its encroachments upon the reserved rights of the states, fully justified this state in then withdrawing from the federal Union; but in deference to the opinions and wishes of the other slaveholding states, she forbore at that time to exercise this right. Since that time, these encroachments have continued to increase, and further forbearance ceases to be a virtue.

And now the state of South Carolina having resumed her separate and equal place among nations, deems it due to herself, to the remaining United States of America, and to the nations of the world, that she should declare the immediate causes which have led to this act.

In the year 1765, that portion of the British Empire embracing Great Britain, undertook to make laws for the government of that portion composed of the thirteen American Colonies. A struggle for the right of self-government ensued, which resulted, on the 4th of July, 1776, in a Declaration, by the Colonies, "that they are, and of right ought to be, free and independent states; and that, as free and independent states, they have full power to levy war, conclude peace, contract alliances, establish commerce, and to do all other acts and things which independent states may of right do."

They further solemnly declared that whenever any "form of government becomes destructive of the ends for which it was established, it is the right of the people to alter or abolish it, and to institute a new government." Deeming the government of Great Britain to have become destructive of these ends, they declared that the colonies "are absolved from all allegiance to the British Crown, and that all political connection between them and the State of Great Britain is, and ought to be, totally dissolved."

In pursuance of this Declaration of Independence, each of the thirteen states proceeded to exercise its separate sovereignty; adopted for itself a Constitution, and appointed officers for the administration of government in all its departments—Legislative, Executive and Judicial. For purposes of defense, they united their arms and their counsels; and, in 1778, they entered into a league known as the Articles of Confederation, whereby they agreed to entrust the administration of their external relations to a common agent, known as the Congress of the United States, expressly declaring, in the first article "that each state retains its sovereignty, freedom and independence, and every power, jurisdiction and right which is not, by this Confederation, expressly delegated to the United States in Congress assembled."

Under this Confederation the war of the Revolution was carried on, and on the 3rd of September, 1783, the contest ended, and a definite treaty was signed by Great Britain, in which she acknowledged the independence of the colonies in the following terms:

"ARTICLE 1—His Britannic Majesty acknowledges the said United States, viz: New Hampshire, Massachusetts Bay, Rhode Island and Providence Plantations, Connecticut, New York, New Jersey, Pennsylvania, Delaware, Maryland, Virginia, North Carolina, South Carolina and Georgia, to be free, sovereign and independent states; that he treats with them as such; and for himself, his heirs and successors, relinquishes all claims to the government, propriety and territorial rights of the same and every part thereof."

Thus were established the two great principles asserted by the colonies, namely: the right of a state to govern itself; and the right of a people to abolish a government when it becomes destructive of the ends for which it was instituted. And concurrent with the establishment of these principles, was the fact, that each colony became and was recognized by the mother country a free, sovereign and independent state.

In 1787, deputies were appointed by the states to revise the Articles of Confederation, and on 17th September, 1787, these deputies recommended for the adoption of the states, the Articles of Union, known as the Constitution of the United States.

The parties to whom this Constitution was submitted, were the several sovereign states; they were to agree or disagree, and when nine of them agreed the compact was to take effect among those concurring; and the general government, as the common agent, was then invested with their authority.

If only nine of the thirteen states had concurred, the other four would have remained as they then were—separate, sovereign states, independent of any of the provisions of the Constitution. In fact, two of the states did not accede to the Constitution until long after it had gone into operation among the other eleven;[1] and during that interval, they each exercised the functions of an independent nation.

By this Constitution, certain duties were imposed upon the several states, and the exercise of certain of their powers was restrained, which necessarily implied their continued existence as sovereign states. But to remove all doubt, an amendment was added, which declared that the powers not delegated to the United States by the Constitution, nor prohibited by it to the states, are reserved to the states, respectively, or to the people.[2] On the 23d May, 1788, South Carolina, by a convention of her people, passed an ordinance assenting to this Constitution, and afterwards altered her own Constitution, to conform herself to the obligations she had undertaken.

Thus was established, by compact between the states, a government with definite objects and powers, limited to the express words of the grant. This limitation left the whole remaining mass of power subject to the clause reserving it to the states or to the people, and rendered unnecessary any specification of reserved rights.

We hold that the government thus established is subject to the two great principles asserted in the Declaration of Independence; and we hold further, that the mode of its formation subjects it to a third fundamental principle, namely: the law of compact. We maintain that in every compact between two or more parties, the obligation is mutual; that the failure of one of the contracting parties to perform a material part of the agreement, entirely releases the obligation of the other; and that where no arbiter is provided, each party is remitted to his own judgment to determine the fact of failure, with all its consequences.

In the present case, that fact is established with certainty. We assert that fourteen of the states have deliberately refused, for years past, to fulfill their constitutional obligations, and we refer to their own statutes for the proof.

The Constitution of the United States, in its fourth article, provides as follows: "No person held to service or labor in one state, under the laws thereof, escaping into another, shall, in consequence of any law or regulation therein, be discharged from such service or labor, but shall be delivered up, on claim of the party to whom such service or labor may be due."

---

[1] Nine states ratified the Constitution and the new government began March 4, 1789. North Carolina did not ratify until November 1789, followed by Rhode Island in May 1790.

[2] The 10th Amendment

This stipulation was so material to the compact, that without it that compact would not have been made. The greater number of the contracting parties held slaves, and they had previously evinced their estimate of the value of such a stipulation by making it a condition in the Ordinance[3] for the government of the territory ceded by Virginia, which now composes the states north of the Ohio River.

The same article of the Constitution stipulates also for rendition by the several states of fugitives from justice from the other states.

The general government, as the common agent, passed laws to carry into effect these stipulations of the states. For many years these laws were executed. But an increasing hostility on the part of the non-slaveholding states to the institution of slavery, has led to a disregard of their obligations, and the laws of the general government have ceased to effect the objects of the Constitution. The states of Maine, New Hampshire, Vermont, Massachusetts, Connecticut, Rhode Island, New York, Pennsylvania, Illinois, Indiana, Michigan, Wisconsin and Iowa, have enacted laws which either nullify the acts of Congress or render useless any attempt to execute them. In many of these states the fugitive is discharged from service or labor claimed, and in none of them has the state government complied with the stipulation made in the Constitution. The state of New Jersey, at an early day, passed a law in conformity with her constitutional obligation; but the current of anti-slavery feeling has led her more recently to enact laws which render inoperative the remedies provided by her own law and by the laws of Congress. In the state of New York even the right of transit for a slave has been denied by her tribunals; and the states of Ohio and Iowa have refused to surrender to justice fugitives charged with murder, and with inciting servile insurrection in the state of Virginia. Thus the constituted compact has been deliberately broken and disregarded by the non-slaveholding states, and the consequence follows that South Carolina is released from her obligation.

The ends for which the Constitution was framed are declared by itself to be "to form a more perfect union, establish justice, insure domestic

---

[3] The Northwest Ordinance. Its sixth article states that "There shall be neither slavery nor involuntary servitude in the said territory, otherwise than in the punishment of crimes whereof the party shall have been duly convicted: Provided, always, that any person escaping into the same, from whom labor or service is lawfully claimed in any one of the original states, such fugitive may be lawfully reclaimed and conveyed to the person claiming his or her labor or service as aforesaid."

tranquility, provide for the common defence, promote the general welfare, and secure the blessings of liberty to ourselves and our posterity."[4]

These ends it endeavored to accomplish by a federal government, in which each state was recognized as an equal, and had separate control over its own institutions. The right of property in slaves was recognized by giving to free persons distinct political rights, by giving them the right to represent, and burthening them with direct taxes for three-fifths of their slaves; by authorizing the importation of slaves for twenty years; and by stipulating for the rendition of fugitives from labor.

We affirm that these ends for which this government was instituted have been defeated, and the government itself has been made destructive of them by the action of the non-slaveholding states. Those states have assumed the right of deciding upon the propriety of our domestic institutions; and have denied the rights of property established in fifteen of the states and recognized by the Constitution; they have denounced as sinful the institution of slavery; they have permitted open establishment among them of societies, whose avowed object is to disturb the peace and to eloign[5] the property of the citizens of other states. They have encouraged and assisted thousands of our slaves to leave their homes; and those who remain, have been incited by emissaries, books and pictures to servile insurrection.

For twenty-five years this agitation has been steadily increasing, until it has now secured to its aid the power of the common government. Observing the forms of the Constitution, a sectional party has found within that article establishing the Executive Department, the means of subverting the Constitution itself. A geographical line has been drawn across the Union, and all the states north of that line have united in the election of a man to the high office of president of the United States, whose opinions and purposes are hostile to slavery.[6] He is to be entrusted with the administration of the common government, because he has declared that that "Government cannot endure permanently half slave, half free,"[7] and that the public mind must rest in the belief that slavery is in the course of ultimate extinction.

This sectional combination for the submersion of the Constitution, has been aided in some of the states by elevating to citizenship, persons who, by

---

[4] the preamble

[5] to remove or carry away

[6] Abraham Lincoln

[7] Document 17

the supreme law of the land, are incapable of becoming citizens;[8] and their votes have been used to inaugurate a new policy, hostile to the South, and destructive of its beliefs and safety.

On the 4th day of March next, this party will take possession of the government. It has announced that the South shall be excluded from the common territory, that the judicial tribunals shall be made sectional, and that a war must be waged against slavery until it shall cease throughout the United States.

The guarantees of the Constitution will then no longer exist; the equal rights of the states will be lost. The slaveholding states will no longer have the power of self-government, or self-protection, and the federal government will have become their enemy.

Sectional interest and animosity will deepen the irritation, and all hope of remedy is rendered vain, by the fact that public opinion at the North has invested a great political error with the sanction of more erroneous religious belief.

We, therefore, the people of South Carolina, by our delegates in Convention assembled, appealing to the Supreme Judge of the world for the rectitude of our intentions, have solemnly declared that the Union heretofore existing between this state and the other states of North America, is dissolved, and that the state of South Carolina has resumed her position among the nations of the world, as a separate and independent state; with full power to levy war, conclude peace, contract alliances, establish commerce, and to do all other acts and things which independent states may of right.

---

[8] African-Americans. This may be a reference to the ruling in the *Dred Scott* case (Document 14) that African-Americans or descendants of slaves were not American citizens.

DOCUMENT 24

Fragment on the Constitution and Union

Abraham Lincoln

January 1861

Nestled among the complete speeches and writings of Abraham Lincoln are several fragments, or brief notes, that represent Lincoln's thoughts on a variety of issues. Some of these carefully prepared fragments eventually found their way into major speeches, while others did not. Likely written sometime during the four months between his election on November 6, 1860 and his inauguration on March 4, 1861, this particular fragment expresses what must have been on Lincoln's mind as the nation stood on the precipice of Civil War. Drawing inspiration from the Bible, specifically Proverbs 25:11, Lincoln reflects that the Union and the Constitution are a "picture of silver" framed around the principle of liberty to all, or an "apple of gold," from the Declaration of Independence. From this, Lincoln seems to have chartered his course for the coming struggle. In focusing on the connection between the Declaration and Constitution, Lincoln was focusing on what was in the deepest sense the cause of the Civil War. The nation was divided over how to understand the connection between its two founding documents, the Declaration and Constitution. Was the latter and popular sovereignty or the will of the people an authority in its own right? Or did its authority derive from the Declaration's assertion of human equality and thus liberty for all?

SOURCE: *New Letters and Papers of Lincoln, compiled by Paul M. Angle* (Boston: Houghton Mifflin Company, 1930), 240–241, https://catalog.hathitrust.org/Record/000318262.

All this is not the result of accident. It has a philosophical cause. Without the Constitution and the Union, we could not have attained the result; but even these are not the primary cause of our great prosperity. There is something back of these, entwining itself more closely about the human heart. That something is the principle of "liberty to all"—the principle that clears the path for all—gives hope to all—and by consequence, enterprise, and industry to all.

The expression of that principle, in our Declaration of Independence, was most happy and fortunate. Without this, as well as with it, we could have declared our independence of Great Britain; but without it, we could not, I think, have secured our free government and consequent prosperity. No oppressed people will fight and endure, as our fathers did, without the promise of something better than a mere change of masters.

The assertion of that principle, at that time, was the word "fitly spoken" which has proved an "apple of gold" to us. The Union and the Constitution are the picture of silver, subsequently framed around it. The picture was made not to conceal or destroy the apple but to adorn, and preserve it. The picture was made for the apple—not the apple for the picture.

So let us act, that neither picture or apple shall ever be blurred or bruised or broken.

That we may so act, we must study, and understand the points of danger.

DOCUMENT 25

Inaugural Address

Jefferson Davis

February 18, 1861

Jefferson Davis, Senator from Mississippi and former Secretary of War, publicly resigned his Senate seat during an emotional farewell address to Congress on January 21, 1861, only days after his home state had seceded from the Union. Less than a month later, Davis was sworn in as the first and—as it turned out—only President of the Confederate States of America at the first Confederate capital in Montgomery, Alabama. (Richmond, Virginia became the capital a few months after Davis gave his speech.) In his inaugural address, Davis explained secession by referring to the argument of the Declaration of Independence that government must be by the consent of the governed, but he ignored the Declaration's statement about the equality of men, the truth that makes consent necessary. (The South Carolina secession declaration also echoed the Declaration but ignored equality [Document 23]). Davis explained what he believed to be the principal reasons justifying secession. In plotting a course for the new country's future, Davis expressed the hope that the seceded states would be permitted to leave the Union in peace.

SOURCE: *A Compilation of the Messages and Papers of the Confederacy: Including the Diplomatic Correspondence, 1861-1865* (Nashville: United States Publishing Company, 1906), 32–36, https://babel.hathitrust.org/cgi/pt?id=mdp.35112102583558;view=1up;seq=62.

Gentlemen of the Congress of the Confederate States of America, Friends, and Fellow Citizens:

Called to the difficult and responsible station of Chief Magistrate of the Provisional Government which you have instituted, I approach the discharge of the duties assigned to me with humble distrust of my abilities, but with a sustaining confidence in the wisdom of those who are to guide and aid me in the administration of public affairs, and an abiding faith in the virtue and patriotism of the people. Looking forward to the speedy establishment of a permanent government to take the place of this, which by its greater moral and physical power will be better able to combat with many difficulties that arise from the conflicting interests of separate nations, I enter upon the duties of the office to which I have been chosen with the hope that the beginning of our career, as a Confederacy, may not be obstructed by hostile opposition to our enjoyment of the separate existence and independence we have asserted, and which, with the blessing of Providence, we intend to maintain.

Our present political position has been achieved in a manner unprecedented in the history of nations. It illustrates the American idea that governments rest on the consent of the governed, and that it is the right of the people to alter or abolish them at will whenever they become destructive of the ends for which they were established. The declared purpose of the compact of the Union from which we have withdrawn was to "establish justice, insure domestic tranquility, provide for the common defense, promote the general welfare, and secure the blessings of liberty to ourselves and our posterity;"[1] and when, in the judgment of the sovereign states composing this Confederacy, it has been perverted from the purposes for which it was ordained, and ceased to answer the ends for which it was established, a peaceful appeal to the ballot box declared that, so far as they are concerned, the government created by that compact should cease to exist. In this they merely asserted the right which the Declaration of Independence of July 4, 1776, defined to be "inalienable." Of the time and occasion of its exercise they as sovereigns were the final judges, each for itself. The impartial and enlightened verdict of mankind will vindicate the rectitude of our conduct; and He who knows the hearts of men will judge of the sincerity with which we have labored to preserve the government of our fathers in its spirit.

The right solemnly proclaimed at the birth of the United States, and which has been solemnly affirmed and reaffirmed in the Bills of Rights of the states subsequently admitted into the Union of 1789, undeniably recognizes in the people the power to resume the authority delegated for the purposes of government. Thus the sovereign states here represented have proceeded to form this Confederacy; and it is by abuse of language that their act has been denominated a revolution. They formed a new alliance, but within each state its government has remained; so that the rights of person and property have not been disturbed. The agent through which they communicated with foreign nations is changed, but this does not necessarily interrupt their international relations. Sustained by the consciousness that the transition from the former Union to the present Confederacy has not proceeded from a disregard on our part of just obligations, or any failure to perform every

---

[1] preamble of the Constitution

constitutional duty, moved by no interest or passion to invade the rights of others, anxious to cultivate peace and commerce with all nations, if we may not hope to avoid war, we may at least expect that posterity will acquit us of having needlessly engaged in it. Doubly justified by the absence of wrong on our part, and by wanton aggression on the part of others, there can be no cause to doubt that the courage and patriotism of the people of the Confederate States will be found equal to any measure of defense which their honor and security may require.

An agricultural people, whose chief interest is the export of commodities required in every manufacturing country, our true policy is peace, and the freest trade which our necessities will permit. It is alike our interest and that of all those to whom we would sell, and from whom we would buy, that there should be the fewest practicable restrictions upon the interchange of these commodities. There can, however, be but little rivalry between ours and any manufacturing or navigating community, such as the northeastern states of the American Union. It must follow, therefore, that mutual interest will invite to good will and kind offices on both parts. If, however, passion or lust of dominion should cloud the judgment or inflame the ambition of those states, we must prepare to meet the emergency and maintain, by the final arbitrament of the sword, the position which we have assumed among the nations of the earth.

We have entered upon the career of independence, and it must be inflexibly pursued. Through many years of controversy with our late associates of the Northern states, we have vainly endeavored to secure tranquility and obtain respect for the rights to which we were entitled. As a necessity, not a choice, we have resorted to the remedy of separation, and henceforth our energies must be directed to the conduct of our own affairs, and the perpetuity of the Confederacy which we have formed. If a just perception of mutual interest shall permit us peaceably to pursue our separate political career, my most earnest desire will have been fulfilled. But if this be denied to us, and the integrity of our territory and jurisdiction be assailed, it will but remain for us with firm resolve to appeal to arms and invoke the blessing of Providence on a just cause.

As a consequence of our new condition and relations, and with a view to meet anticipated wants, it will be necessary to provide for the speedy and efficient organization of branches of the Executive department having special charge of foreign intercourse, finance, military affairs, and the postal service. For purposes of defense, the Confederate States may, under ordinary circumstances, rely mainly upon the militia; but it is deemed advisable, in the present condition of affairs, that there should be a well-instructed and disciplined army, more numerous than would usually be required on a peace establishment. I also suggest that, for the protection of our harbors and commerce on the high seas, a navy adapted to those objects will be required. But this, as well as other subjects appropriate to our necessities, have doubtless engaged the attention of Congress.

With a Constitution differing only from that of our fathers in so far as it is explanatory of their well-known intent, freed from sectional conflicts, which have interfered with the pursuit of the general welfare, it is not unreasonable to expect that states from which we have recently parted may seek to unite their fortunes to ours under the Government which we have instituted. For this your Constitution makes adequate provision; but beyond this, if I mistake not the judgment and will of the people, a reunion with the states from which we have separated is neither practicable nor desirable. To increase the power, develop the resources, and promote the happiness of the Confederacy, it is requisite that there should be so much of homogeneity that the welfare of every portion shall be the aim of the whole. When this does not exist, antagonisms are engendered which must and should result in separation.

Actuated solely by the desire to preserve our own rights, and promote our own welfare, the separation by the Confederate States has been marked by no aggression upon others, and followed by no domestic convulsion. Our industrial pursuits have received no check, the cultivation of our fields has progressed as heretofore, and, even should we be involved in war, there would be no considerable diminution in the production of the staples which have constituted our exports, and in which the commercial world has an interest scarcely less than our own. This common interest of the producer and consumer can only be interrupted by exterior force which would obstruct the transmission of our staples to foreign markets—a course of conduct which would be as unjust, as it would be detrimental, to manufacturing and commercial interests abroad.

Should reason guide the action of the government from which we have separated, a policy so detrimental to the civilized world, the Northern states included, could not be dictated by even the strongest desire to inflict injury upon us; but, if the contrary should prove true, a terrible responsibility will rest upon it, and the suffering of millions will bear testimony to the folly and wickedness of our aggressors. In the meantime there will remain to us, besides the ordinary means before suggested, the well-known resources for retaliation upon the commerce of an enemy.

Experience in public stations, of subordinate grade to this which your kindness has conferred, has taught me that care and toil and disappointment are the price of official elevation. You will see many errors to forgive, many deficiencies to tolerate; but you shall not find in me either want of zeal or fidelity to the cause that is to me the highest in hope, and of most enduring affection. Your generosity has bestowed upon me an undeserved distinction, one which I neither sought nor desired. Upon the continuance of that sentiment, and upon your wisdom and patriotism, I rely to direct and support me in the performance of the duties required at my hands.

We have changed the constituent parts, but not the system of government. The Constitution framed by our fathers is that of these Confederate States. In their exposition of it, and in the judicial construction it has received, we have a light which reveals its true meaning.

Thus instructed as to the true meaning and just interpretation of that instrument, and ever remembering that all offices are but trusts held for the people, and that powers delegated are to be strictly construed, I will hope by due diligence in the performance of my duties, though I may disappoint your expectations, yet to retain, when retiring, something of the good will and confidence which welcome my entrance into office.

It is joyous in the midst of perilous times to look around upon a people united in heart, where one purpose of high resolve animates and actuates the whole; where the sacrifices to be made are not weighed in the balance against honor and right and liberty and equality. Obstacles may retard, but they cannot long prevent, the progress of a movement sanctified by its justice and sustained by a virtuous people. Reverently let us invoke the God of our fathers to guide and protect us in our efforts to perpetuate the principles which by his blessing they were able to vindicate, establish, and transmit to their posterity. With the continuance of his favor ever gratefully acknowledged, we may hopefully look forward to success, to peace, and to prosperity.

DOCUMENT 26

First Inaugural Address

Abraham Lincoln

March 4, 1861

By the time Abraham Lincoln delivered his First Inaugural Address, seven states claimed to have seceded from the Union. These states were South Carolina, Mississippi, Florida, Alabama, Georgia, Louisiana, and Texas. Delivered from the East Portico of the federal Capitol, Lincoln's First Inaugural Address sought to calm and pacify southerners by convincing them that they had nothing to fear from a Republican administration. Part philosophical treatise on the nature of the Union, the address also reminded Americans of the practical problems with separating North and South. Appealing to "the better angels of our nature," the speech concluded with an urgent plea for peace, yet one that would ultimately fall on deaf ears. Four more states—Virginia, Arkansas, North Carolina, and Tennessee—seceded after President Lincoln called into federal service 75,000 men of the militias from several states on April 15, less than twenty-four hours after the garrison at Fort Sumter surrendered. The Civil War had begun.

SOURCE: Abraham Lincoln, Inaugural Address Online by Gerhard Peters and John T. Woolley, The American Presidency Project https://www.presidency.ucsb.edu/node/202167.

Fellow citizens of the United States:

In compliance with a custom as old as the government itself, I appear before you to address you briefly, and to take, in your presence, the oath prescribed by the Constitution of the United States, to be taken by the president "before he enters on the execution of his office."[1]

I do not consider it necessary, at present, for me to discuss those matters of administration about which there is no special anxiety, or excitement.

Apprehension seems to exist among the people of the Southern states, that by the accession of a Republican administration, their property, and their peace, and personal security, are to be endangered. There has never

[1] Constitution Article II, section 1

been any reasonable cause for such apprehension. Indeed, the most ample evidence to the contrary has all the while existed. And been open to their inspection. It is found in nearly all the published speeches of him who now addresses you. I do but quote from one of those speeches when I declare that "I have no purpose, directly or indirectly, to interfere with the institution of slavery in the states where it exists. I believe I have no lawful right to do so, and I have no inclination to do so."[2] Those who nominated and elected me did so with full knowledge that I had made this, and many similar declarations, and had never recanted them. And more than this, they placed in the platform, for my acceptance, and as a law to themselves, and to me, the clear and emphatic resolution which I now read:

> Resolved, That the maintenance inviolate of the rights of the states, and especially the right of each state to order and control its own domestic institutions according to its own judgment exclusively, is essential to that balance of power on which the perfection and endurance of our political fabric depend; and we denounce the lawless invasion by armed force of the soil of any state or territory, no matter under what pretext, as among the gravest of crimes.[3]

I now reiterate these sentiments: and in doing so, I only press upon the public attention the most conclusive evidence of which the case is susceptible, that the property, peace and security of no section are to be in anywise endangered by the now incoming administration. I add, too, that all the protection which, consistently with the Constitution and the laws, can be given, will be cheerfully given to all the states when lawfully demanded, for whatever cause—as cheerfully to one section, as to another.

There is much controversy about the delivering up of fugitives from service or labor. The clause I now read is as plainly written in the Constitution as any other of its provisions:

"No person held to service or labor in one state, under the laws thereof, escaping into another, shall, in consequence of any law or regulation therein, be discharged from such service or labor, but shall be delivered up on claim of the party to whom such service or labor may be due."[4]

It is scarcely questioned that this provision was intended by those who

---

[2] First debate with Stephen A. Douglas, Ottawa, Illinois, August 21, 1858.

[3] 1860 Republican Party Platform, Document 21

[4] Article IV, section 2

made it, for the reclaiming of what we call fugitive slaves; and the intention of the lawgiver is the law. All members of Congress swear their support to the whole Constitution—to this provision as much as to any other. To the proposition, then, that slaves whose cases come within the terms of this clause, "shall be delivered up," their oaths are unanimous. Now, if they would make the effort in good temper, could they not, with nearly equal unanimity, frame and pass a law, by means of which to keep good that unanimous oath?

There is some difference of opinion whether this clause should be enforced by national or by state authority; but surely that difference is not a very material one. If the slave is to be surrendered, it can be of but little consequence to him, or to others, by which authority it is done. And should any one, in any case, be content that his oath shall go unkept, on a merely unsubstantial controversy as to how it shall be kept?

Again, in any law upon this subject, ought not all the safeguards of liberty known in civilized and humane jurisprudence to be introduced, so that a free man be not, in any case surrendered as a slave? And might it not be well, at the same time, to provide by law for the enforcement of that clause in the Constitution which guarantees that "The citizens of each state shall be entitled to all privileges and immunities of citizens in the several states?"[5]

I take the official oath today, with no mental reservations, and with no purpose to construe the Constitution or laws, by any hypercritical rules. And while I do not choose now to specify particular acts of Congress as proper to be enforced, I do suggest, that it will be much safer for all, both in official and private stations, to conform to and abide by, all those acts which stand unrepealed, than to violate any of them, trusting to find impunity in having them held to be unconstitutional.

It is seventy-two years since the first inauguration of a president under our national Constitution. During that period fifteen different and greatly distinguished citizens, have, in succession, administered the executive branch of the government. They have conducted it through many perils; and, generally, with great success. Yet, with all this scope for precedent, I now enter upon the same task for the brief constitutional term of four years, under great and peculiar difficulty. A disruption of the federal Union heretofore only menaced, is now formidably attempted.

I hold, that in contemplation of universal law, and of the Constitution, the Union of these states is perpetual. Perpetuity is implied, if not expressed, in the fundamental law of all national governments. It is safe to assert that no

[5] Article IV, section 2

government proper, ever had a provision in its organic law for its own termination. Continue to execute all the express provisions of our national Constitution, and the Union will endure forever—it being impossible to destroy it, except by some action not provided for in the instrument itself.

Again, if the United States be not a government proper, but an association of states in the nature of contract merely, can it, as a contract, be peaceably unmade, by less than all the parties who made it? One party to a contract may violate it—break it, so to speak; but does it not require all to lawfully rescind it?

Descending from these general principles, we find the proposition that, in legal contemplation, the Union is perpetual, confirmed by the history of the Union itself. The Union is much older than the Constitution. It was formed in fact, by the Articles of Association in 1774. It was matured and continued by the Declaration of Independence in 1776. It was further matured and the faith of all the then thirteen states expressly plighted and engaged that it should be perpetual, by the Articles of Confederation in 1778. And finally, in 1787, one of the declared objects for ordaining and establishing the Constitution, was "to form a more perfect union."

But if destruction of the Union, by one, or by a part only, of the states, be lawfully possible, the Union is less perfect than before the Constitution, having lost the vital element of perpetuity.

It follows from these views that no state, upon its own mere motion, can lawfully get out of the Union; that resolves and ordinances to that effect are legally void; and that acts of violence, within any state or states, against the authority of the United States, are insurrectionary or revolutionary, according to circumstances.

I therefore consider that, in view of the Constitution and the laws, the Union is unbroken; and, to the extent of my ability, I shall take care, as the Constitution itself expressly enjoins upon me, that the laws of the Union be faithfully executed in all the states. Doing this I deem to be only a simple duty on my part; and I shall perform it, so far as practicable, unless my rightful masters, the American people, shall withhold the requisite means, or, in some authoritative manner, direct the contrary. I trust this will not be regarded as a menace, but only as the declared purpose of the Union that it will constitutionally defend, and maintain itself.

In doing this there needs to be no bloodshed or violence; and there shall be none, unless it be forced upon the national authority. The power confided to me, will be used to hold, occupy, and possess the property, and places belonging to the government, and to collect the duties and imposts; but beyond what may be necessary for these objects, there will be no invasion—no using of force against, or among the people anywhere. Where hostility to the United States, in any interior locality, shall be so great and so universal, as to prevent competent resident citizens from holding the federal offices, there will be no attempt to force obnoxious strangers among the people for that object. While the strict legal right may exist in the government to enforce the exercise of these offices, the attempt to do so would be so irritating, and so nearly impracticable with all, that I deem it better to forego, for the time, the uses of such offices.

The mails, unless repelled, will continue to be furnished in all parts of the Union. So far as possible, the people everywhere shall have that sense of perfect security which is most favorable to calm thought and reflection. The course here indicated will be followed, unless current events, and experience, shall show a modification, or change, to be proper; and in every case and exigency, my best discretion will be exercised, according to circumstances actually existing, and with a view and a hope of a peaceful solution of the national troubles, and the restoration of fraternal sympathies and affections.

That there are persons in one section, or another who seek to destroy the Union at all events, and are glad of any pretext to do it, I will neither affirm nor deny; but if there be such, I need address no word to them. To those, however, who really love the Union, may I not speak?

Before entering upon so grave a matter as the destruction of our national fabric, with all its benefits, its memories, and its hopes, would it not be wise to ascertain precisely why we do it? Will you hazard so desperate a step, while there is any possibility that any portion of the ills you fly from, have no real existence? Will you, while the certain ills you fly to, are greater than all the real ones you fly from? Will you risk the commission of so fearful a mistake?

All profess to be content in the Union, if all constitutional rights can be maintained. Is it true, then, that any right, plainly written in the Constitution, has been denied? I think not. Happily the human mind is so constituted, that no party can reach to the audacity of doing this. Think, if you can, of a single instance in which a plainly written provision of the Constitution has ever been denied. If, by the mere force of numbers, a majority should deprive a minority of any clearly written constitutional right, it might, in a moral point of view, justify revolution—certainly would, if such right were a vital one. But such is not our case. All the vital rights of minorities, and of individuals, are so plainly assured to them, by affirmations and negations, guaranties and prohibitions, in the Constitution, that controversies never arise concerning them. But no organic law can ever be framed with a provision specifically applicable to every question which may occur in practical administration. No foresight can anticipate, nor any document of reasonable length contain express provisions for all possible questions. Shall fugitives from labor be surrendered by national or by state authority? The Constitution does not expressly say. May Congress prohibit slavery in the territories? The Constitution does not expressly say. Must Congress protect slavery in the territories? The Constitution does not expressly say.

From questions of this class spring all our constitutional controversies, and we divide upon them into majorities and minorities. If the minority will not acquiesce, the majority must, or the government must cease. There is no other alternative; for continuing the government, is acquiescence on one side or the other. If a minority, in such case, will secede rather than acquiesce, they make a precedent which, in turn, will divide and ruin them; for a minority of their own will secede from them, whenever a majority refuses to be controlled by such minority. For instance, why may not any portion of a new confederacy, a year or two hence, arbitrarily secede again, precisely as portions of the present Union now claim to secede from it. All who cherish disunion sentiments, are now being educated to the exact temper of doing this. Is there such perfect identity of interests among the states to compose a new Union, as to produce harmony only, and prevent renewed secession?

Plainly, the central idea of secession, is the essence of anarchy. A majority, held in restraint by constitutional checks, and limitations, and always changing easily, with deliberate changes of popular opinions and sentiments, is the only true sovereign of a free people. Whoever rejects it, does, of necessity, fly to anarchy or to despotism. Unanimity is impossible; the rule of a minority, as a permanent arrangement, is wholly inadmissible; so that, rejecting the majority principle, anarchy, or despotism in some form, is all that is left.

I do not forget the position assumed by some, that constitutional questions are to be decided by the Supreme Court; nor do I deny that such decisions must be binding in any case, upon the parties to a suit, as to the object of that suit, while they are also entitled to very high respect and consideration, in all parallel cases, by all other departments of the government. And while it is obviously possible that such decision may be erroneous in any given case, still the evil effect following it, being limited to that particular case, with the chance that it may be over-ruled, and never become a precedent for other cases, can better be borne than could the evils of a different practice. At the same time the candid citizen must confess that if the policy of the government, upon vital questions, affecting the whole people, is to be irrevocably fixed by decisions of the Supreme Court, the instant they are made, in ordinary litigation between parties, in personal actions, the people will have ceased, to be their own rulers, having, to that extent, practically resigned their government, into the hands of that eminent tribunal. Nor is there, in this view, any assault upon the court, or the judges. It is a duty, from which they may not shrink, to decide cases properly brought before them; and it is no fault of theirs, if others seek to turn their decisions to political purposes.

One section of our country believes slavery is right, and ought to be extended, while the other believes it is wrong, and ought not to be extended. This is the only substantial dispute. The fugitive slave clause of the Constitution, and the law for the suppression of the foreign slave trade, are each as well enforced, perhaps, as any law can ever be in a community where the moral sense of the people imperfectly supports the law itself. The great body of the people abide by the dry legal obligation in both cases, and a few break over in each. This, I think, cannot be perfectly cured; and it would be worse in both cases after the separation of the sections, than before. The foreign slave trade, now imperfectly suppressed, would be ultimately revived without restriction, in one section; while fugitive slaves, now only partially surrendered, would not be surrendered at all, by the other.

Physically speaking, we cannot separate. We cannot remove our respective sections from each other, nor build an impassable wall between them. A husband and wife may be divorced, and go out of the presence, and beyond the reach of each other; but the different parts of our country cannot do this. They cannot but remain face to face; and intercourse, either amicable or hostile, must continue between them. Is it possible then to make that intercourse more advantageous, or more satisfactory, after separation than before? Can aliens make treaties easier than friends can make laws? Can treaties be more faithfully enforced between aliens, than laws can among friends? Suppose you go to war, you cannot fight always; and when, after much loss on both sides, and no gain on either, you cease fighting, the identical old questions, as to terms of intercourse, are again upon you.

This country, with its institutions, belongs to the people who inhabit it. Whenever they shall grow weary of the existing government, they can exercise their constitutional right of amending it, or their revolutionary right to dismember, or overthrow it. I cannot be ignorant of the fact that many worthy, and patriotic citizens are desirous of having the national Constitution amended. While I make no recommendation of amendments, I fully recognize the rightful authority of the people over the whole subject, to be exercised in either of the modes prescribed in the instrument itself; and I should, under existing circumstances, favor, rather than oppose, a fair opportunity being afforded the people to act upon it.

I will venture to add that, to me, the convention mode seems preferable, in that it allows amendments to originate with the people themselves, instead of only permitting them to take, or reject, propositions, originated by others, not especially chosen for the purpose, and which might not be precisely such, as they would wish to either accept or refuse. I understand a proposed amendment to the Constitution—which amendment, however, I have not seen, has passed Congress, to the effect that the federal government, shall never interfere with the domestic institutions of the states, including that of persons held to service. To avoid misconstruction of what I have said, I depart from my purpose not to speak of particular amendments, so far as to say that, holding such a provision to now be implied constitutional law, I have no objection to its being made express, and irrevocable.

The chief magistrate derives all his authority from the people, and they have conferred none upon him to fix terms for the separation of the states. The people themselves can do this also if they choose; but the executive, as such, has nothing to do with it. His duty is to administer the present government, as it came to his hands, and to transmit it, unimpaired by him, to his successor.

Why should there not be a patient confidence in the ultimate justice of the people? Is there any better, or equal hope, in the world? In our present differences, is either party without faith of being in the right? If the Almighty Ruler of nations, with his eternal truth and justice, be on your side of the North, or on yours of the South, that truth, and that justice, will surely prevail, by the judgment of this great tribunal, the American people.

By the frame of the government under which we live, this same people have wisely given their public servants but little power for mischief; and have, with equal wisdom, provided for the return of that little to their own hands at very short intervals.

While the people retain their virtue, and vigilance, no administration, by any extreme of wickedness or folly, can very seriously injure the government, in the short space of four years.

My countrymen, one and all, think calmly and well, upon this whole subject. Nothing valuable can be lost by taking time. If there be an object to hurry any of you, in hot haste, to a step which you would never take deliberately, that object will be frustrated by taking time; but no good object can be frustrated by it. Such of you as are now dissatisfied, still have the old Constitution unimpaired, and, on the sensitive point, the laws of your own framing under it; while the new administration will have no immediate power, if it would, to change either. If it were admitted that you who are dissatisfied, hold the right side in the dispute, there still is no single good reason for precipitate action. Intelligence, patriotism, Christianity, and a firm reliance on Him, who has never yet forsaken this favored land, are still competent to adjust, in the best way, all our present difficulty.

In your hands, my dissatisfied fellow countrymen, and not in mine, is the momentous issue of civil war. The government will not assail you. You can have no conflict, without being yourselves the aggressors. You have no oath registered in Heaven to destroy the government, while I shall have the most solemn one to "preserve, protect and defend" it.

I am loth to close. We are not enemies, but friends. We must not be enemies. Though passion may have strained, it must not break our bonds of affection. The mystic chords of memory, stretching from every battle-field, and patriot grave, to every living heart and hearthstone, all over this broad land, will yet swell the chorus of the Union, when again touched, as surely they will be, by the better angels of our nature.

APPENDIX A

Declaration of Independence

In CONGRESS, July 4, 1776

The unanimous Declaration of the thirteen united States of America, When in the Course of human events, it becomes necessary for one people to dissolve the political bands which have connected them with another, and to assume among the powers of the earth, the separate and equal station to which the Laws of Nature and of Nature's God entitle them, a decent respect to the opinions of mankind requires that they should declare the causes which impel them to the separation.

We hold these truths to be self-evident, that all men are created equal, that they are endowed by their Creator with certain unalienable Rights, that among these are Life, Liberty and the pursuit of Happiness.—That to secure these rights, Governments are instituted among Men, deriving their just powers from the consent of the governed,—that whenever any Form of Government becomes destructive of these ends, it is the Right of the People to alter or to abolish it, and to institute new Government, laying its foundation on such principles and organizing its powers in such form, as to them shall seem most likely to effect their Safety and Happiness. Prudence, indeed, will dictate that Governments long established should not be changed for light and transient causes; and accordingly all experience hath shewn, that mankind are more disposed to suffer, while evils are sufferable, than to right themselves by abolishing the forms to which they are accustomed. But when a long train of abuses and usurpations, pursuing invariably the same Object evinces a design to reduce them under absolute Despotism, it is their right, it is their duty, to throw off such Government, and to provide new Guards for their future security.—Such has been the patient sufferance of these Colonies; and such is now the necessity which constrains them to alter their former Systems of Government. The history of the present King of Great Britain is a history of repeated injuries and usurpations, all having in direct object the establishment of an absolute Tyranny over these States. To prove this, let Facts be submitted to a candid world.

He has refused his Assent to Laws, the most wholesome and necessary for the public good.

He has forbidden his Governors to pass Laws of immediate and pressing importance, unless suspended in their operation till his Assent should be obtained; and when so suspended, he has utterly neglected to attend to them.

He has refused to pass other Laws for the accommodation of large districts of people, unless those people would relinquish the right of Representation in the Legislature, a right inestimable to them and formidable to tyrants only.

He has called together legislative bodies at places unusual, uncomfortable, and distant from the depository of their public Records, for the sole purpose of fatiguing them into compliance with his measures.

He has dissolved Representative Houses repeatedly, for opposing with manly firmness his invasions on the rights of the people.

He has refused for a long time, after such dissolutions, to cause others to be elected; whereby the Legislative powers, incapable of Annihilation, have returned to the People at large for their exercise; the State remaining in the mean time exposed to all the dangers of invasion from without, and convulsions within.

He has endeavoured to prevent the population of these States; for that purpose obstructing the Laws for Naturalization of Foreigners; refusing to pass others to encourage their migrations hither, and raising the conditions of new Appropriations of Lands.

He has obstructed the Administration of Justice, by refusing his Assent to Laws for establishing Judiciary powers.

He has made Judges dependent on his Will alone, for the tenure of their offices, and the amount and payment of their salaries.

He has erected a multitude of New Offices, and sent hither swarms of Officers to harrass our people, and eat out their substance.

He has kept among us, in times of peace, Standing Armies without the Consent of our legislatures.

He has affected to render the Military independent of and superior to the Civil power.

He has combined with others to subject us to a jurisdiction foreign to our constitution, and unacknowledged by our laws; giving his Assent to their Acts of pretended Legislation:

For Quartering large bodies of armed troops among us:

For protecting them, by a mock Trial, from punishment for any Murders which they should commit on the Inhabitants of these States:

For cutting off our Trade with all parts of the world:

For imposing Taxes on us without our Consent:

For depriving us in many cases, of the benefits of Trial by Jury:

For transporting us beyond Seas to be tried for pretended offences:

For abolishing the free System of English Laws in a neighbouring Province, establishing therein an Arbitrary government, and enlarging its Boundaries so as to render it at once an example and fit instrument for introducing the same absolute rule into these Colonies:

For taking away our Charters, abolishing our most valuable Laws, and altering fundamentally the Forms of our Governments:

For suspending our own Legislatures, and declaring themselves invested with power to legislate for us in all cases whatsoever.

He has abdicated Government here, by declaring us out of his Protection and waging War against us.

He has plundered our seas, ravaged our Coasts, burnt our towns, and destroyed the lives of our people.

He is at this time transporting large Armies of foreign Mercenaries to compleat the works of death, desolation and tyranny, already begun with circumstances of Cruelty & perfidy scarcely paralleled in the most barbarous ages, and totally unworthy the Head of a civilized nation.

He has constrained our fellow Citizens taken Captive on the high Seas to bear Arms against their Country, to become the executioners of their friends and Brethren, or to fall themselves by their Hands.

He has excited domestic insurrections amongst us, and has endeavoured to bring on the inhabitants of our frontiers, the merciless Indian Savages, whose known rule of warfare, is an undistinguished destruction of all ages, sexes and conditions.

In every stage of these Oppressions We have Petitioned for Redress in the most humble terms: Our repeated Petitions have been answered only by repeated injury. A Prince whose character is thus marked by every act which may define a Tyrant, is unfit to be the ruler of a free people.

Nor have We been wanting in attentions to our British brethren. We have warned them from time to time of attempts by their legislature to extend an unwarrantable jurisdiction over us. We have reminded them of the circumstances of our emigration and settlement here. We have appealed to their native justice and magnanimity, and we have conjured them by the ties of our common kindred to disavow these usurpations, which, would inevitably interrupt our connections and correspondence. They too have been deaf to the voice of justice and of consanguinity. We must, therefore, acquiesce in the necessity, which denounces our Separation, and hold them, as we hold the rest of mankind, Enemies in War, in Peace Friends.

We, THEREFORE, the Representatives of the UNITED STATES OF AMERICA, in General Congress, Assembled, appealing to the Supreme Judge of the world for the rectitude of our intentions, do, in the Name, and by Authority of the good People of these Colonies, solemnly publish and declare, That these United Colonies are, and of Right ought to be FREE AND INDEPENDENT STATES; that they are Absolved from all Allegiance to the British Crown, and that all political connection between them and the State of Great Britain, is and ought to be totally dissolved; and that as Free and Independent States, they have full Power to levy War, conclude Peace, contract Alliances, establish Commerce, and to do all other Acts and Things which Independent States may of right do. And for the support of this Declaration, with a firm reliance on the protection of divine Providence, we mutually pledge to each other our Lives, our Fortunes and our sacred Honor.

[Georgia:]
Button Gwinnett
Lyman Hall
George Walton

[North Carolina:]
William Hooper
Joseph Hewes
John Penn

[South Carolina:]
Edward Rutledge
Thomas Heyward, Jr.
Thomas Lynch, Jr.
Arthur Middleton

[Maryland:]
Samuel Chase
William Paca
Thomas Stone
Charles Carroll of Carrollton

[Virginia:]
George Wythe
Richard Henry Lee
Thomas Jefferson
Benjamin Harrison
Thomas Nelson, Jr.
Francis Lightfoot Lee
Carter Braxton

[Pennsylvania:]
Robert Morris
Benjamin Rush
Benjamin Franklin
John Morton
George Clymer
James Smith
George Taylor
James Wilson
George Ross

[Delaware:]
Caesar Rodney
George Read
Thomas McKean

[New York:]
William Floyd
Philip Livingston
Francis Lewis
Lewis Morris

[New Jersey:]
Richard Stockton
John Witherspoon
Francis Hopkinson
John Hart
Abraham Clark

[New Hampshire:]
Josiah Bartlett
William Whipple
Matthew Thornton

[Massachusetts:]
John Hancock
Samuel Adams
John Adams
Robert Treat Paine
Elbridge Gerry

[Rhode Island:]
Stephen Hopkins
William Ellery

[Connecticut:]
Roger Sherman
Samuel Huntington
William Williams
Oliver Wolcott

APPENDIX B

Constitution of the United States of America

September 17, 1787

[Editors' note: Bracketed sections in the text of the Constitution have been superceded or modified by Constitutional amendments.]

We **the People** of the United States, in Order to form a more perfect Union, establish Justice, insure domestic Tranquility, provide for the common defence, promote the general Welfare, and secure the Blessings of Liberty to ourselves and our Posterity, do ordain and establish this Constitution for the United States of America.

Article I

Section 1. All legislative Powers herein granted shall be vested in a Congress of the United States, which shall consist of a Senate and House of Representatives.

Section 2. The House of Representatives shall be composed of Members chosen every second Year by the People of the several States, and the Electors in each State shall have the Qualifications requisite for Electors of the most numerous Branch of the State Legislature.

No Person shall be a Representative who shall not have attained to the Age of twenty five Years, and been seven Years a Citizen of the United States, and who shall not, when elected, be an Inhabitant of that State in which he shall be chosen.

[Representatives and direct Taxes shall be apportioned among the several States which may be included within this Union, according to their respective Numbers, which shall be determined by adding to the whole Number of free Persons, including those bound to Service for a Term of Years, and excluding Indians not taxed, three fifths of all other Persons.][1] The actual Enumeration shall be made within three Years after the first

[1] modified by Section 2 of the Fourteenth Amendment

Meeting of the Congress of the United States, and within every subsequent Term of ten Years, in such Manner as they shall by Law direct. The Number of Representatives shall not exceed one for every thirty Thousand, but each State shall have at Least one Representative; and until such enumeration shall be made, the State of New Hampshire shall be entitled to chuse three, Massachusetts eight, Rhode-Island and Providence Plantations one, Connecticut five, New-York six, New Jersey four, Pennsylvania eight, Delaware one, Maryland six, Virginia ten, North Carolina five, South Carolina five, and Georgia three.

When vacancies happen in the Representation from any State, the Executive Authority thereof shall issue Writs of Election to fill such Vacancies.

The House of Representatives shall chuse their Speaker and other Officers; and shall have the sole Power of Impeachment.

Section 3. The Senate of the United States shall be composed of two Senators from each State, [*chosen by the Legislature thereof,*][2] for six Years; and each Senator shall have one Vote.

Immediately after they shall be assembled in Consequence of the first Election, they shall be divided as equally as may be into three Classes. The Seats of the Senators of the first Class shall be vacated at the Expiration of the second Year, of the second Class at the Expiration of the fourth Year, and of the third Class at the Expiration of the sixth Year, so that one third may be chosen every second Year; [*and if Vacancies happen by Resignation, or otherwise, during the Recess of the Legislature of any State, the Executive thereof may make temporary Appointments until the next Meeting of the Legislature, which shall then fill such Vacancies.*][3]

No Person shall be a Senator who shall not have attained to the Age of thirty Years, and been nine Years a Citizen of the United States, and who shall not, when elected, be an Inhabitant of that State for which he shall be chosen.

The Vice President of the United States shall be President of the Senate, but shall have no Vote, unless they be equally divided.

The Senate shall chuse their other Officers, and also a President pro tempore, in the Absence of the Vice President, or when he shall exercise the Office of President of the United States.

The Senate shall have the sole Power to try all Impeachments. When sitting for that Purpose, they shall be on Oath or Affirmation. When the

[2] superseded by the Seventeenth Amendment

[3] modified by the Seventeenth Amendment

President of the United States is tried, the Chief Justice shall preside: And no Person shall be convicted without the Concurrence of two thirds of the Members present.

Judgment in Cases of Impeachment shall not extend further than to removal from Office, and disqualification to hold and enjoy any Office of honor, Trust or Profit under the United States: but the Party convicted shall nevertheless be liable and subject to Indictment, Trial, Judgment and Punishment, according to Law.

Section 4. The Times, Places and Manner of holding Elections for Senators and Representatives, shall be prescribed in each State by the Legislature thereof; but the Congress may at any time by Law make or alter such Regulations, except as to the Places of chusing Senators.

The Congress shall assemble at least once in every Year, and such Meeting shall be [on the first Monday in December,][4] unless they shall by Law appoint a different Day.

Section 5. Each House shall be the Judge of the Elections, Returns and Qualifications of its own Members, and a Majority of each shall constitute a Quorum to do Business; but a smaller Number may adjourn from day to day, and may be authorized to compel the Attendance of absent Members, in such Manner, and under such Penalties as each House may provide.

Each House may determine the Rules of its Proceedings, punish its Members for disorderly Behaviour, and, with the Concurrence of two thirds, expel a Member.

Each House shall keep a Journal of its Proceedings, and from time to time publish the same, excepting such Parts as may in their Judgment require Secrecy; and the Yeas and Nays of the Members of either House on any question shall, at the Desire of one fifth of those Present, be entered on the Journal.

Neither House, during the Session of Congress, shall, without the Consent of the other, adjourn for more than three days, nor to any other Place than that in which the two Houses shall be sitting.

Section 6. The Senators and Representatives shall receive a Compensation for their Services, to be ascertained by Law, and paid out of the Treasury of the United States. They shall in all Cases, except Treason, Felony and

[4] modified by Section 2 of the Twentieth Amendment

Breach of the Peace, be privileged from Arrest during their Attendance at the Session of their respective Houses, and in going to and returning from the same; and for any Speech or Debate in either House, they shall not be questioned in any other Place.

No Senator or Representative shall, during the Time for which he was elected, be appointed to any civil Office under the Authority of the United States, which shall have been created, or the Emoluments whereof shall have been encreased during such time; and no Person holding any Office under the United States, shall be a Member of either House during his Continuance in Office.

Section 7. All Bills for raising Revenue shall originate in the House of Representatives; but the Senate may propose or concur with Amendments as on other Bills.

Every Bill which shall have passed the House of Representatives and the Senate, shall, before it become a Law, be presented to the President of the United States; If he approve he shall sign it, but if not he shall return it, with his Objections to that House in which it shall have originated, who shall enter the Objections at large on their Journal, and proceed to reconsider it. If after such Reconsideration two thirds of that House shall agree to pass the Bill, it shall be sent, together with the Objections, to the other House, by which it shall likewise be reconsidered, and if approved by two thirds of that House, it shall become a Law. But in all such Cases the Votes of both Houses shall be determined by yeas and Nays, and the Names of the Persons voting for and against the Bill shall be entered on the Journal of each House respectively. If any Bill shall not be returned by the President within ten Days (Sundays excepted) after it shall have been presented to him, the Same shall be a Law, in like Manner as if he had signed it, unless the Congress by their Adjournment prevent its Return, in which Case it shall not be a Law.

Every Order, Resolution, or Vote to which the Concurrence of the Senate and House of Representatives may be necessary (except on a question of Adjournment) shall be presented to the President of the United States; and before the Same shall take Effect, shall be approved by him, or being disapproved by him, shall be repassed by two thirds of the Senate and House of Representatives, according to the Rules and Limitations prescribed in the Case of a Bill.

Section 8. The Congress shall have Power To lay and collect Taxes, Duties, Imposts and Excises, to pay the Debts and provide for the common Defence and general Welfare of the United States; but all Duties, Imposts and Excises shall be uniform throughout the United States;

To borrow Money on the credit of the United States;

To regulate Commerce with foreign Nations, and among the several States, and with the Indian Tribes;

To establish an uniform Rule of Naturalization, and uniform Laws on the subject of Bankruptcies throughout the United States;

To coin Money, regulate the Value thereof, and of foreign Coin, and fix the Standard of Weights and Measures;

To provide for the Punishment of counterfeiting the Securities and current Coin of the United States;

To establish Post Offices and post Roads;

To promote the Progress of Science and useful Arts, by securing for limited Times to Authors and Inventors the exclusive Right to their respective Writings and Discoveries;

To constitute Tribunals inferior to the supreme Court;

To define and punish Piracies and Felonies committed on the high Seas, and Offenses against the Law of Nations;

To declare War, grant Letters of Marque and Reprisal, and make Rules concerning Captures on Land and Water;

To raise and support Armies, but no Appropriation of Money to that Use shall be for a longer Term than two Years;

To provide and maintain a Navy;

To make Rules for the Government and Regulation of the land and naval Forces;

To provide for calling forth the Militia to execute the Laws of the Union, suppress Insurrections and repel Invasions;

To provide for organizing, arming, and disciplining, the Militia, and for governing such Part of them as may be employed in the Service of the United States, reserving to the States respectively, the Appointment of the Officers, and the Authority of training the Militia according to the discipline prescribed by Congress;

To exercise exclusive Legislation in all Cases whatsoever, over such District (not exceeding ten Miles square) as may, by Cession of particular States, and the Acceptance of Congress, become the Seat of the Government of the United States, and to exercise like Authority over all Places purchased by the Consent of the Legislature of the State in which the Same shall be, for the Erection of Forts, Magazines, Arsenals, dock-Yards, and other needful Buildings;—And

To make all Laws which shall be necessary and proper for carrying into Execution the foregoing Powers, and all other Powers vested by this Constitution in the Government of the United States, or in any Department or Officer thereof.

Section 9. The Migration or Importation of such Persons as any of the States now existing shall think proper to admit, shall not be prohibited by the Congress prior to the Year one thousand eight hundred and eight, but a Tax or duty may be imposed on such Importation, not exceeding ten dollars for each Person.

The Privilege of the Writ of Habeas Corpus shall not be suspended, unless when in Cases of Rebellion or Invasion the public Safety may require it.

No Bill of Attainder or ex post facto Law shall be passed.

No Capitation, or other direct, Tax shall be laid, unless in Proportion to the Census or Enumeration herein before directed to be taken.[5]

No Tax or Duty shall be laid on Articles exported from any State.

No Preference shall be given by any Regulation of Commerce or Revenue to the Ports of one State over those of another: nor shall Vessels bound to, or from, one State, be obliged to enter, clear, or pay Duties in another.

No Money shall be drawn from the Treasury, but in Consequence of Appropriations made by Law; and a regular Statement and Account of the Receipts and Expenditures of all public Money shall be published from time to time.

No Title of Nobility shall be granted by the United States: And no Person holding any Office of Profit or Trust under them, shall, without the Consent of the Congress, accept of any present, Emolument, Office, or Title, of any kind whatever, from any King, Prince, or foreign State.

Section 10. No State shall enter into any Treaty, Alliance, or Confederation; grant Letters of Marque and Reprisal; coin Money; emit Bills of Credit; make any Thing but gold and silver Coin a Tender in Payment of Debts; pass any Bill of Attainder, ex post facto Law, or Law impairing the Obligation of Contracts, or grant any Title of Nobility.

No State shall, without the Consent of the Congress, lay any Imposts or Duties on Imports or Exports, except what may be absolutely necessary for executing it's inspection Laws: and the net Produce of all Duties and Imposts, laid by any State on Imports or Exports, shall be for the Use of the Treasury

---

[5] modified by the Sixteenth Amendment

of the United States; and all such Laws shall be subject to the Revision and Controul of the Congress.

No State shall, without the Consent of Congress, lay any Duty of Tonnage, keep Troops, or Ships of War in time of Peace, enter into any Agreement or Compact with another State, or with a foreign Power, or engage in War, unless actually invaded, or in such imminent Danger as will not admit of delay.

Article II

Section 1. The executive Power shall be vested in a President of the United States of America. He shall hold his Office during the Term of four Years, and, together with the Vice President, chosen for the same Term, be elected, as follows:

Each State shall appoint, in such Manner as the Legislature thereof may direct, a Number of Electors, equal to the whole Number of Senators and Representatives to which the State may be entitled in the Congress: but no Senator or Representative, or Person holding an Office of Trust or Profit under the United States, shall be appointed an Elector.

[The Electors shall meet in their respective States, and vote by Ballot for two Persons, of whom one at least shall not be an Inhabitant of the same State with themselves. And they shall make a List of all the Persons voted for, and of the Number of Votes for each; which List they shall sign and certify, and transmit sealed to the Seat of the Government of the United States, directed to the President of the Senate. The President of the Senate shall, in the Presence of the Senate and House of Representatives, open all the Certificates, and the Votes shall then be counted. The Person having the greatest Number of Votes shall be the President, if such Number be a Majority of the whole Number of Electors appointed; and if there be more than one who have such Majority, and have an equal Number of Votes, then the House of Representatives shall immediately chuse by Ballot one of them for President; and if no Person have a Majority, then from the five highest on the List the said House shall in like Manner chuse the President. But in chusing the President, the Votes shall be taken by States, the Representation from each State having one Vote; A quorum for this purpose shall consist of a Member or Members from two thirds of the States, and a Majority of all the States shall be necessary to a Choice. In every Case, after the Choice of the President, the Person having the greatest Number of Votes of the Electors shall be the Vice President. But if there should remain two or more who have equal Votes, the Senate shall chuse from them by Ballot the Vice President.][6]

The Congress may determine the Time of chusing the Electors, and the Day on which they shall give their Votes; which Day shall be the same throughout the United States.

No Persons except a natural born Citizen, or a Citizen of the United States, at the time of the Adoption of this Constitution, shall be eligible to the Office of President; neither shall any Person be eligible to that Office who shall not have attained to the Age of thirty five Years, and been fourteen Years a Resident within the United States.

[In Case of the Removal of the President from Office, or of his Death, Resignation, or Inability to discharge the Powers and Duties of the said Office, the Same shall devolve on the Vice President, and the Congress may by Law provide for the Case of Removal, Death, Resignation or Inability, both of the President and Vice President, declaring what Officer shall then act as President, and such Officer shall act accordingly, until the Disability be removed, or a President shall be elected.][7]

The President shall, at stated Times, receive for his Services, a Compensation, which shall neither be increased nor diminished during the Period for which he shall have been elected, and he shall not receive within that Period any other Emolument from the United States, or any of them.

Before he enter on the Execution of his Office, he shall take the following Oath or Affirmation:—"I do solemnly swear (or affirm) that I will faithfully execute the Office of President of the United States, and will to the best of my Ability, preserve, protect and defend the Constitution of the United States."

Section 2. The President shall be Commander in Chief of the Army and Navy of the United States, and of the Militia of the several States, when called into the actual Service of the United States; he may require the Opinion, in writing, of the principal Officer in each of the executive Departments, upon any Subject relating to the Duties of their respective Offices, and he shall have Power to grant Reprieves and Pardons for Offences against the United States, except in Cases of Impeachment.

He shall have Power, by and with the Advice and Consent of the Senate, to make Treaties, provided two thirds of the Senators present concur; and he

---

[6] modifed by the Twelfth Amendment
[7] modified by the Twenty-Fifth Amendment

shall nominate, and by and with the Advice and Consent of the Senate, shall appoint Ambassadors, other public Ministers and Consuls, Judges of the supreme Court, and all other Officers of the United States, whose Appointments are not herein otherwise provided for, and which shall be established by Law: but the Congress may by Law vest the Appointment of such inferior Officers, as they think proper, in the President alone, in the Courts of Law, or in the Heads of Departments.

The President shall have Power to fill up all Vacancies that may happen during the Recess of the Senate, by granting Commissions which shall expire at the End of their next Session.

Section 3. He shall from time to time give to the Congress Information of the State of the Union, and recommend to their Consideration such Measures as he shall judge necessary and expedient; he may, on extraordinary Occasions, convene both Houses, or either of them, and in Case of Disagreement between them, with Respect to the Time of Adjournment, he may adjourn them to such Time as he shall think proper; he shall receive Ambassadors and other public Ministers; he shall take Care that the Laws be faithfully executed, and shall Commission all the Officers of the United States.

Section 4. The President, Vice President and all civil Officers of the United States, shall be removed from Office on Impeachment for, and Conviction of, Treason, Bribery, or other high Crimes and Misdemeanors.

Article III

Section 1. The judicial Power of the United States, shall be vested in one supreme Court, and in such inferior Courts as the Congress may from time to time ordain and establish. The Judges, both of the supreme and inferior Courts, shall hold their Offices during good Behaviour, and shall, at stated Times, receive for their Services, a Compensation, which shall not be diminished during their Continuance in Office.

Section 2. The judicial Power shall extend to all Cases, in Law and Equity, arising under this Constitution, the Laws of the United States, and Treaties made, or which shall be made, under their Authority;—to all Cases affecting Ambassadors, other public Ministers and Consuls;—to all Cases of admiralty and maritime Jurisdiction;—to Controversies to which the United States shall be a Party;—to Controversies between two or more States;—[*between a State and Citizens of another State;—*][8] between Citizens of different States;—between Citizens of the same State claiming Lands under Grants of different States, [*and between a State, or the Citizens thereof, and foreign States, Citizens or Subjects.*][9]

In all Cases affecting Ambassadors, other public Ministers and Consuls, and those in which a State shall be Party, the supreme Court shall have original Jurisdiction. In all the other Cases before mentioned, the supreme Court shall have appellate Jurisdiction, both as to Law and Fact, with such Exceptions, and under such Regulations as the Congress shall make.

The Trial of all Crimes, except in Cases of Impeachment, shall be by Jury; and such Trial shall be held in the State where the said Crimes shall have been committed; but when not committed within any State, the Trial shall be at such Place or Places as the Congress may by Law have directed.

Section 3. Treason against the United States, shall consist only in levying War against them, or in adhering to their Enemies, giving them Aid and Comfort. No Person shall be convicted of Treason unless on the Testimony of two Witnesses to the same overt Act, or on Confession in open Court.

The Congress shall have Power to declare the Punishment of Treason, but no Attainder of Treason shall work Corruption of Blood, or Forfeiture except during the Life of the Person attained.

Article IV

Section 1. Full Faith and Credit shall be given in each State to the public Acts, Records, and judicial Proceedings of every other State. And the Congress may by general Laws prescribe the Manner in which such Acts, Records and Proceedings shall be proved, and the Effect thereof.

Section 2. The Citizens of each State shall be entitled to all Privileges and Immunities of Citizens in the several States.

A Person charged in any State with Treason, Felony, or other Crime, who shall flee from Justice, and be found in another State, shall on Demand of

---

[8] superseded by the Eleventh Amendment

[9] superseded by the Eleventh Amendment

the executive Authority of the State from which he fled, be delivered up, to be removed to the State having Jurisdiction of the Crime.

[No Person held to Service or Labour in one State, under the Laws thereof, escaping into another, shall, in Consequence of any Law or Regulation therein, be discharged from such Service or Labour, but shall be delivered up on Claim of the Party to whom such Service or Labour may be due.][10]

Section 3. New States may be admitted by the Congress into this Union; but no new State shall be formed or erected within the Jurisdiction of any other State; nor any State be formed by the Junction of two or more States, or Parts of States, without the Consent of the Legislatures of the States concerned as well as of the Congress.

The Congress shall have Power to dispose of and make all needful Rules and Regulations respecting the Territory or other Property belonging to the United States; and nothing in this Constitution shall be so construed as to Prejudice any Claims of the United States, or of any particular State.

Section 4. The United States shall guarantee to every State in this Union a Republican Form of Government, and shall protect each of them against Invasion; and on Application of the Legislature, or of the Executive (when the Legislature cannot be convened) against domestic Violence.

Article V

The Congress, whenever two thirds of both Houses shall deem it necessary, shall propose Amendments to this Constitution, or, on the Application of the Legislatures of two thirds of the several States, shall call a Convention for proposing Amendments, which, in either Case, shall be valid to all Intents and Purposes, as Part of this Constitution, when ratified by the Legislatures of three fourths of the several States, or by Conventions in three fourths thereof, as the one or the other Mode of Ratification may be proposed by the Congress; Provided that no Amendment which may be made prior to the Year One thousand eight hundred and eight shall in any Manner affect the first and fourth Clauses in the Ninth Section of the first Article; and that no State, without its Consent, shall be deprived of its equal Suffrage in the Senate.

---

[10] superseded by the Thirteenth Amendment

Article VI

All Debts contracted and Engagements entered into, before the Adoption of this Constitution, shall be as valid against the United States under this Constitution, as under the Confederation.

This Constitution, and the Laws of the United States which shall be made in Pursuance thereof; and all Treaties made, or which shall be made, under the Authority of the United States, shall be the supreme Law of the Land; and the Judges in every State shall be bound thereby, any Thing in the Constitution or Laws of any State to the Contrary notwithstanding.

The Senators and Representatives before mentioned, and the Members of the several State Legislatures, and all executive and judicial Officers, both of the United States and of the several States, shall be bound by Oath or Affirmation, to support this Constitution; but no religious Test shall ever be required as a Qualification to any Office or public Trust under the United States.

Article VII

The Ratification of the Conventions of nine States, shall be sufficient for the Establishment of this Constitution between the States so ratifying the Same.

Done in Convention by the Unanimous Consent of the States present the Seventeenth Day of September in the Year of our Lord one thousand seven hundred and Eighty seven and of the Independence of the United States of America the Twelfth In Witness whereof We have hereunto subscribed our Names,

Go. Washington—
Presidt. and deputy from Virginia

New Hampshire
John Langdon
Nicholas Gilman

Massachusetts
Nathaniel Gorham
Rufus King

Connecticut
Wm. Saml. Johnson
Roger Sherman

New York
Alexander Hamilton

New Jersey
Wil: Livingston
David Brearley
Wm. Paterson
Jona: Dayton

Pennsylvania
B Franklin
Thomas Mifflin
Robt. Morris
Geo. Clymer
Thos. FitzSimons
Jared Ingersoll
James Wilson
Gouv Morris

Delaware
Geo: Read
Gunning Bedford jun
John Dickinson
Richard Bassett
Jaco: Broom

Maryland
James McHenry
Dan of St Thos. Jenifer
Danl. Carroll

Virginia
John Blair—
James Madison Jr.

North Carolina
Wm. Blount
Richd. Dobbs Spaight
Hu Williamson

South Carolina
J. Rutledge
Charles Cotesworth Pinckney
Charles Pinckney
Pierce Butler

Georgia
William Few
Abr Baldwin

Attest William Jackson Secretary

AMENDMENTS TO THE CONSTITUTION OF THE UNITED STATES OF AMERICA

Amendment I

Ratified December 15, 1791

Congress shall make no law respecting an establishment of religion, or prohibiting the free exercise thereof; or abridging the freedom of speech, or of the press; or the right of the people peaceably to assemble, and to petition the Government for a redress of grievances.

Amendment II

Ratified December 15, 1791

A well regulated Militia, being necessary to the security of a free State, the right of the people to keep and bear Arms, shall not be infringed.

Amendment III

Ratified December 15, 1791

No Soldier shall, in time of peace be quartered in any house, without the consent of the Owner, nor in time of war, but in a manner to be prescribed by law.

Amendment IV

Ratified December 15, 1791

The right of the people to be secure in their persons, houses, papers, and effects, against unreasonable searches and seizures, shall not be violated, and no Warrants shall issue, but upon probable cause, supported by Oath or affirmation, and particularly describing the place to be searched, and the persons or things to be seized.

Amendment V

Ratified December 15, 1791

No person shall be held to answer for a capital, or otherwise infamous crime, unless on a presentment or indictment of a Grand Jury, except in cases arising in the land or naval forces, or in the Militia, when in actual service in time of War or public danger; nor shall any person be subject for the same offence to be twice put in jeopardy of life or limb, nor shall be compelled in any criminal case to be a witness against himself, nor be deprived of life, liberty, or property, without due process of law; nor shall private property be taken for public use, without just compensation.

Amendment VI

Ratified December 15, 1791

In all criminal prosecutions, the accused shall enjoy the right to a speedy and public trial, by an impartial jury of the State and district wherein the crime shall have been committed, which district shall have been previously ascertained by law, and to be informed of the nature and cause of the accusation; to be confronted with the witnesses against him; to have compulsory process for obtaining witnesses in his favor, and to have the assistance of counsel for his defence.

Amendment VII

Ratified December 15, 1791

In Suits at common law, where the value in controversy shall exceed twenty dollars, the right of trial by jury shall be preserved, and no fact tried by a jury, shall be otherwise reexamined in any Court of the United States, than according to the rules of the common law.

Amendment VIII

Ratified December 15, 1791

Excessive bail shall not be required, nor excessive fines imposed, nor cruel and unusual punishments inflicted.

Amendment IX

Ratified December 15, 1791

The enumeration in the Constitution, of certain rights, shall not be construed to deny or disparage others retained by the people.

Amendment X

Ratified December 15, 1791

The powers not delegated to the United States by the Constitution, nor prohibited by it to the States, are reserved to the States respectively, or to the people.

APPENDIX C

Thematic Table of Contents

Anti-slavery Arguments

Pro-slavery Arguments

Popular Sovereignty

Political Compromises over Slavery

Constitutional Arguments over Slavery

The Constitution and the Union

Party Platforms

APPENDIX D

Study Questions

For each of the documents in this collection, we suggest below in section A questions relevant for that document alone and in section B questions that require comparison between documents.

1. James Tallmadge Jr., Speech to Congress, 1819

A. How does Tallmadge understand slavery and what are his views on the possibility of a sectional crisis, or even a civil war, regarding the status of slavery in the territories? What legal and constitutional arguments does Tallmadge make in defense of prohibiting slavery in the territories, and how might the Southern opposition at this time respond?

B. How does Tallmadge's approach to the legal status of slavery in the territories compare to the Missouri Compromise (Document 2)?

2. Henry Clay, Missouri Compromise Act, 1820

A. Why does Section 4 of the law require Missouri to have a "republican" constitution and form of government, and what does that mean exactly? What does the Missouri Compromise say about the status of slavery, both in regards to Missouri and the rest of the Louisiana Territory, and what is the significance of the 36°30′ line? How, and in what ways, does the law represent a compromise between North and South on the question of slavery?

B. How would William Lloyd Garrison (Document 5) and Abraham Lincoln (Document 12) think differently about the Missouri Compromise? What explains the difference in their respective approaches?

3. Thomas Jefferson, Letter to John Holmes, 1820

A. What was Jefferson's reaction to the Missouri question, and why does he characterize it as "a fire bell in the night"? What does Jefferson mean when he says that, in regard to slavery, "we have the wolf by the ears," with justice on one side, and self-preservation on the other? What does this tell us about his views on slavery? How does Jefferson compare the generation of 1776 to the younger generation of Americans?

B. How do Jefferson's views on slavery compare to others in this collection?

4. Daniel Webster and Robert Y. Hayne, Webster-Hayne Debates, 1830

A. What are the main points of difference between Webster and Hayne, especially on the question of the nature of the Union and the Constitution? How do Webster and Hayne differ in regard to their understandings of the proper relationship among the several states and between the states and the national government? Where in these debates do we see a possible argument in defense of Constitutional secession by the states, later claimed by the Southern Confederacy before, during, and after the Civil War?

B. In what way(s) does South Carolina's Declaration of the Causes of Secession (Document 23) and Jefferson Davis's Inaugural Address (Document 25) represent a fulfillment of the arguments put forth by Hayne in the debates? In what way(s) does Lincoln's First Inaugural (Document 26) represent a fulfillment of the arguments put forth by Webster in the debates?

5. William Lloyd Garrison, "On the Constitution and the Union," 1832

A. Why does Garrison characterize the Constitution as an "infamous bargain" and an "unholy alliance"? What is the relationship between the Constitution of the United States and the Declaration of Independence, according to Garrison? How does Garrison view the potential splitting up of the Union between North and South over the slavery question?

B. How does Garrison's understanding of the Constitution and Union compare to Daniel Webster's (Document 4) and Abraham Lincoln's (Documents 24 and 26)? Does Frederick Douglass agree or disagree with Garrison's understanding of the Constitution as a pro-slavery document, based on Document 9?

6. John C. Calhoun, Speech on Abolition Petitions, 1837

A. What does Calhoun mean when he refers to slavery as "a positive good"? Why is it better to be a slave than a poor man, according to Calhoun?

B. Does Calhoun have the same understanding of slavery as Thomas Jefferson (Document 3)? Which authors in this collection would Calhoun classify as "fanatics"?

7. John C. Calhoun, Speech on the Oregon Bill, 1848

A. According to Calhoun, what will a future historian of the decline and fall of the American Union think was the cause of its failure? Why does Calhoun reject the principles of natural liberty and natural equality? What does Calhoun mean, exactly, when he says that liberty is a "reward" or a "prize to be won"? How does Calhoun's understanding of liberty depart from that of the American Founders?

B. Does Calhoun's understanding of the Declaration of Independence come closer to the ideas expressed by Chief Justice Roger Taney (Document 14) or George Fitzhugh (Document 13)?

8. Henry Clay, Compromise of 1850, 1850

A. What reasons are given for the enactment of the law in the preamble? What does the law say about the future status of slavery in California, the Mexican Territory, and the District of Columbia? What reasons are given in each case? How, and in what ways, does the law represent a compromise between North and South on the question of slavery?

B. How would Frederick Douglass (Document 9) and John C. Calhoun (Document 7) think differently about the Compromise of 1850? What explains the difference in their respective approaches?

9. Frederick Douglass, "What to the Slave is the Fourth of July?," 1852

A. Why would Douglass want to deliver this speech on July fifth instead of the fourth? What is the meaning and significance of the Fourth of July, from the slave's point of view? Why is slavery a violation of the Founders' principles from the Declaration of Independence, according to Douglass, and why does he call the Founders "statesmen, patriots and heroes"? Does Douglass believe that the United States Constitution is a pro-slavery or an anti-slavery document?

B. In his views on slavery and the Constitution, how does Douglass differ from his fellow abolitionist William Lloyd Garrison (Document 5) and from Abraham Lincoln (Documents 12 and 26)?

10. Appeal of the Independent Democrats to the People of America, 1854

A. Why do the Independent Democrats say slavery and the Union are incompatible?

B. In what ways do the Independent Democrats differ from their fellow Democrat, Stephen A. Douglas (Document 11), on the Kansas-Nebraska Act? What explains these differences?

11. Stephen A. Douglas, Nebraska Territory, 1854

A. How does Douglas defend the principle of popular sovereignty? On what ideas or principles does it rely?

B. In Documents 12 and 15, what is Lincoln's criticism of popular sovereignty? Is he right to say that the people can't vote to make slavery morally right?

12. Abraham Lincoln, Speech on the Repeal of the Missouri Compromise, 1854

A. Why does Lincoln believe that Stephen Douglas's policy of being indifferent to whether people of a territory permitted slavery or not is equivalent to "covert real zeal for the spread of slavery"? What is "the sheet anchor" of American republicanism, according to Lincoln, and how does the Kansas-Nebraska Act of 1854 violate it? What does Lincoln mean when he says that the Union must be made "worthy of the saving"?

B. How does the Kansas-Nebraska Act of 1854 compare to earlier compromises on slavery, such as the Missouri Compromise of 1820 (Document 2) and the Compromise of 1850 (Document 8)? Based on Document 3, how would Thomas Jefferson view the repeal of the Missouri Compromise?

13. George Fitzhugh, *Sociology for the South, or The Failure of Free Society,* 1854

A. How does Fitzhugh attempt to defend the institution of Southern slavery? How does Fitzhugh compare the way of life in the South versus the way of life in the North? Which does he prefer and why?

B. How might Frederick Douglass (Document 9), a former slave, respond to Fitzhugh's claims about slavery?

14. Roger Taney, *Dred Scott v. Sandford,* 1857

A. What were the main issues in the case of Dred Scott, and what were Chief Justice Taney's main arguments for deciding them in the way that he did?

B. Does Taney's understanding of the Declaration of Independence have more in common with John C. Calhoun's (Document 7) or Stephen Douglas's (Document 11)? Would Taney agree or disagree with George Fitzhugh's reading of the Declaration (Document 13)? How would Taney reply to Abraham Lincoln's objections in Document 15?

15. Abraham Lincoln, Reply to the *Dred Scott* Decision, 1857

A. How does Lincoln respond to Chief Justice Roger Taney's interpretations of the Declaration of Independence and the Constitution of the United States? How does Lincoln understand the equality principle of the Declaration?

B. Based on Document 14, how would Taney reply to Lincoln's objections to the Dred Scott case?

16. James Henry Hammond, "Mud Sill Speech," 1858

A. Upon what grounds does Hammond justify slavery? What exactly is the "mud sill" theory, and how has it manifested differently in the North compared to the South? Which approach does Hammond prefer, and why?

B. How might Frederick Douglass (Document 9), a former slave, respond to Hammond's claims about slavery? Would John C. Calhoun (Document 7) and George Fitzhugh (Document 13) accept or reject Hammond's "mud sill" theory?

17. Abraham Lincoln, "House Divided" Speech, 1858

A. What does Lincoln mean when he says, "A house divided against itself cannot stand"? It is sometimes argued that the House Divided Speech helped to bring on the Civil War; what justification could be given for Lincoln's making such an inflammatory speech?

B. How does Stephen Douglas (Document 18) interpret Lincoln's House Divided Speech? Is that interpretation accurate? Does William H. Seward's Irrepressible Conflict speech (Document 19) differ from the House Divided Speech?

18. Stephen A. Douglas, "Homecoming" Speech at Chicago, 1858

A. What is the basis of Douglas's opposition to the Lecompton Constitution? What is the fundamental principle of self-government, according to Douglas, and how does the Kansas-Nebraska Act of 1854 fulfill that principle?

B. Does Abraham Lincoln agree or disagree with Douglas's opposition to the Lecompton Constitution (Document 17)? How does Douglas interpret Lincoln's House Divided Speech (Document 17)? Is that interpretation accurate? What reason(s) does Douglas give for supporting Chief Justice Taney's ruling in the Dred Scott case (Document 14)?

19. William H. Seward, "The Irrepressible Conflict," 1858

A. How does the slave system differ from the free labor system, and why are the two systems incongruous and incompatible? What does this mean for the future of the United States? What is the "irrepressible conflict," according to Seward, and why is it unavoidable?

B. How does Seward's address compare to the arguments of Abraham Lincoln's House Divided Speech (Document 17)? How would John C. Calhoun (Document 6) or George Fitzhugh (Document 13) or James Henry

Hammond (Document 16) reply to Seward's statements about the differences between the slave and free labor systems?

20. Abraham Lincoln, Address before the Wisconsin State Agricultural Society, 1859

A. How does Lincoln explain the free labor system? Why does it need technology and education?

B. Do Lincoln and William H. Seward (Document 19) differ in their understanding of the free labor system? How would John C. Calhoun (Document 6) or George Fitzhugh (Document 13) or James Henry Hammond (Document 16) reply to Lincoln's statements about the difference between the slave and free labor systems?

21. Republican Party Platform, 1860

A. What position does the Republican Party take in regard to secession and the possible breakup of the Union? How does the Republican Party view the extension of slavery into the territories?

B. How does the Republican platform differ from the Democratic platform (Document 22)? In what way(s) does Abraham Lincoln's First Inaugural Address (Document 26) represent a culmination of Republican principles, as expressed in their 1860 platform?

22. Democratic Party Platform, 1856 and 1860

A. What position does the Democratic Party take in regard to secession and the possible breakup of the Union? How does the Democratic Party view the extension of slavery into the territories?

B. How does the Democratic platform differ from the Republican platform (Document 21)? In what way(s) does Stephen Douglas's speeches (Documents 11 and 18) foreshadow the Democratic platform?

23. Declaration of the Immediate Causes Which Induce and Justify the Secession of South Carolina from the Federal Union, 1860

A. What reasons are given for South Carolina's decision to secede from the Union? What role has slavery played in the determination of that decision, and what does the election of Abraham Lincoln mean to the South?

B. Is Lincoln guilty of the charges held against him by the state of South Carolina, based on his House Divided Speech (Document 17), his First Inaugural Address (Document 26), or any of his other speeches and writings in this collection?

24. Abraham Lincoln, Fragment on the Constitution and Union, 1861

A. What does it mean that the Union has a "philosophical cause"? What is the relationship between the Declaration of Independence and the Constitution, according to Lincoln? How is that relationship demonstrated by Lincoln's analogy of the "apple of gold" and the "picture of silver"? What are "the points of danger" that Lincoln might have in mind?

B. How does Lincoln's understanding of the Constitution and Union compare to John C. Calhoun's (Documents 6 and 7) and, especially, William Lloyd Garrison's (Document 5)? Does this fragment inform, in any significant way, the argument of Lincoln's First Inaugural Address (Document 26)?

25. Jefferson Davis, Inaugural Address, 1861

A. Upon what grounds does Davis justify separation from the American Union? Why does Davis reject the notion that the Southern Confederacy represents a revolution, and what is the difference between revolution and secession?

B. How would Davis respond to Abraham Lincoln's arguments against secession in Documents 26?

26. Abraham Lincoln, First Inaugural Address, 1861

A. What is Lincoln willing to do in order to pacify the South? What is he not willing to do? What arguments does Lincoln give in defense of the perpetuity of the Union? What is the difference between "secession" and "revolution," according to Lincoln? Why is that significant, given the circumstances? What does Lincoln think constitutes "the only substantial dispute" between the North and the South? Why does responsibility for initiating Civil War rest squarely on the shoulders of the South, according to Lincoln's argument at the end of the speech?

B. What are the main similarities and differences between Lincoln's First Inaugural and Jefferson Davis's (Document 25)?

APPENDIX E

Lincoln's History of the Slavery Issue

October 16, 1854

The following history of slavery in the American republic is taken from Abraham Lincoln's speech on the Kansas-Nebraska Act's repeal of the Missouri Compromise (Document 12). The long debate over slavery leading up to the Civil War turned on numerous historical incidents and their interpretation. Lincoln's account thus provides useful background for all the documents in this collection.

SOURCE: *Life and Works of Abraham Lincoln, Centenary Edition, Volume II* (New York: The Current Literature Publishing Company, 1907), 219–275, https://archive.org/details/lifeworks02lincuoft/page/n7.

In order to get a clear understanding of what the Missouri Compromise is, a short history... will perhaps be proper. When we established our independence, we did not own, or claim, the country to which this compromise applies. Indeed, strictly speaking, the confederacy then owned no country at all; the states respectively owned the country within their limits; and some of them owned territory beyond their strict state limits. Virginia thus owned the northwestern territory the country out of which the principal part of Ohio, all Indiana, all Illinois, all Michigan and all Wisconsin, have since been formed. She also owned (perhaps within her then limits) what has since been formed into the state of Kentucky. North Carolina thus owned what is now the state of Tennessee; and South Carolina and Georgia, in separate parts, owned what are now Mississippi and Alabama. Connecticut, I think, owned the little remaining part of Ohio—being the same where they now send Giddings[1] to Congress, and beat all creation at making cheese. These territories, together with the states themselves, constituted all the country over which the confederacy then claimed any sort of jurisdiction. We were then living under the Articles of Confederation, which were superseded by the Constitution several years afterwards. The question of ceding

[1] Joshua R. Giddings (1795-1864) was a representative from Ohio

these territories to the general government was set on foot. Mr. Jefferson, the author of the Declaration of Independence, and otherwise a chief actor in the Revolution; then a delegate in Congress; afterwards twice president; who was, is, and perhaps will continue to be, the most distinguished politician of our history; a Virginian by birth and continued residence, and withal, a slaveholder; conceived the idea of taking that occasion, to prevent slavery ever going into the northwestern territory. He prevailed on the Virginia legislature to adopt his views, and to cede the territory, making the prohibition of slavery therein, a condition of the deed. Congress accepted the cession, with the condition; and in the first ordinance (which the acts of Congress were then called) for the government of the territory, provided that slavery should never be permitted therein. This is the famed ordinance of '87 so often spoken of.[2] Thenceforward, for sixty-one years, and until in 1848, the last scrap of this territory came into the Union as the State of Wisconsin, all parties acted in quiet obedience to this ordinance. It is now what Jefferson foresaw and intended—the happy home of teeming millions of free, white, prosperous people, and no slave amongst them.

Thus, with the author of the Declaration of Independence, the policy of prohibiting slavery in new territory originated. Thus, away back of the Constitution, in the pure fresh, free breath of the revolution, the state of Virginia, and the national Congress put that policy in practice. Thus, through sixty odd of the best years of the republic did that policy steadily work to its great and beneficent end. And thus, in those five states, and five millions of free, enterprising people, we have before us the rich fruits of this policy. But now new light breaks upon us. Now Congress declares this ought never to have been; and the like of it, must never be again. The sacred right of self-government is grossly violated by it![3] We even find some men, who drew their first breath, and every other breath of their lives, under this very restriction, now live in dread of absolute suffocation, if they should be restricted in the "sacred right" of taking slaves to Nebraska. That perfect liberty they sigh for—the liberty of making slaves of other people—Jefferson never thought of; their own father never thought of; they never thought of themselves, a year ago.

[2] The Northwest Ordinance

[3] Stephen A. Douglas justified the repeal of the Missouri Compromise in the Kansas-Nebraska Act (signed into law May 30, 1854) by arguing that giving the residents of a territory the right to decide whether it would be slave or free was an exercise of self-government, and thus in accord with the fundamental principle of American government. See Document 11.

How fortunate for them, they did not sooner become sensible of their great misery! Oh, how difficult it is to treat with respect, such assaults upon all we have ever really held sacred!

But to return to history. In 1803 we purchased what was then called Louisiana, of France. It included the now states of Louisiana, Arkansas, Missouri, and Iowa; also the territory of Minnesota, and the present bone of contention, Kansas and Nebraska. Slavery already existed among the French at New Orleans; and to some extent at St. Louis. In 1812 Louisiana came into the Union as a slave state, without controversy. In 1818 or '19, Missouri showed signs of a wish to come in with slavery. This was resisted by northern members of Congress; and thus began the first great slavery agitation in the nation. This controversy lasted several months, and became very angry and exciting; the House of Representatives voting steadily for the prohibition of slavery in Missouri, and the Senate voting as steadily against it. Threats of breaking up the Union were freely made; and the ablest public men of the day became seriously alarmed. At length a compromise was made, in which, like all compromises, both sides yielded something. It was a law passed on the 6th day of March, 1820, providing that Missouri might come into the Union with slavery, but that in all the remaining part of the territory purchased of France, which lies north of 36 degrees and 30 minutes north latitude, slavery should never be permitted. This provision of law is the Missouri Compromise.[4] In excluding slavery north of the line, the same language is employed as in the Ordinance of '87. It directly applied to Iowa, Minnesota, and to the present bone of contention, Kansas and Nebraska. Whether there should or should not, be slavery south of that line, nothing was said in the law; but Arkansas constituted the principal remaining part, south of the line; and it has since been admitted as a slave state without serious controversy. More recently, Iowa, north of the line, came in as a free state without controversy. Still later, Minnesota, north of the line, had a territorial organization without controversy. Texas principally south of the line, and west of Arkansas; though originally within the purchase from France, had, in 1819, been traded off to Spain, in our treaty for the acquisition of Florida. It had thus become a part of Mexico. Mexico revolutionized and became independent of Spain. American citizens began settling rapidly, with their slaves in the southern part of Texas. Soon they revolutionized against Mexico, and established an independent government of their own, adopting a constitution, with slavery,

[4] Document 2

strongly resembling the constitutions of our slave states. By still another rapid move, Texas, claiming a boundary much further West, than when we parted with her in 1819, was brought back to the United States, and admitted into the Union as a slave state. There then was little or no settlement in the northern part of Texas, a considerable portion of which lay north of the Missouri line; and in the resolutions admitting her into the Union, the Missouri restriction was expressly extended westward across her territory. This was in 1845, only nine years ago.

Thus originated the Missouri Compromise; and thus has it been respected down to 1845. And even four years later, in 1849, our distinguished senator,[5] in a public address, held the following language in relation to it:

The Missouri Compromise had been in practical operation for about a quarter of a century, and had received the sanction and approbation of men of all parties in every section of the Union. It had allayed all sectional jealousies and irritations growing out of this vexed question, and harmonized and tranquilized the whole country. It had given to Henry Clay, as its prominent champion, the proud sobriquet of the "Great Pacificator," and by that title and for that service, his political friends had repeatedly appealed to the people to rally under his standard, as a presidential candidate, as the man who had exhibited the patriotism and the power to suppress, an unholy and treasonable agitation, and preserve the Union. He was not aware that any man or any party from any section of the Union, had ever urged as an objection to Mr. Clay, that he was the great champion of the Missouri Compromise. On the contrary, the effort was made by the opponents of Mr. Clay, to prove that he was not entitled to the exclusive merit of that great patriotic measure, and that the honor was equally due to others as well as to him, for securing its adoption—that it had its origin in the hearts of all patriotic men, who desired to preserve and perpetuate the blessings of our glorious Union—an origin akin that of the Constitution of the United States, conceived in the same spirit of fraternal affection, and calculated to remove forever, the only danger, which seemed to threaten, at some distant day, to sever the social bond of union. All the evidences of public opinion at that day, seemed to indicate that this Compromise had been canonized in the hearts of the American people, as a sacred thing which no ruthless hand would ever be reckless enough to disturb.

I do not read this extract to involve Judge Douglas in an inconsistency. If

---

[5] Stephen A. Douglas

he afterwards thought he had been wrong, it was right for him to change. I bring this forward merely to show the high estimate placed on the Missouri Compromise by all parties up to so late as the year 1849.

But, going back a little, in point of time, our war with Mexico broke out in 1846. When Congress was about adjourning that session, President Polk asked them to place two millions of dollars under his control, to be used by him in the recess, if found practicable and expedient, in negotiating a treaty of peace with Mexico, and acquiring some part of her territory. A bill was duly got up, for the purpose, and was progressing swimmingly, in the House of Representatives, when a member by the name of David Wilmot, a Democrat from Pennsylvania, moved as an amendment "Provided that in any territory thus acquired, there shall never be slavery."

This is the origin of the far-famed "Wilmot Proviso." It created a great flutter; but it stuck like wax, was voted into the bill, and the bill passed with it through the House. The Senate, however, adjourned without final action on it and so both appropriation and proviso were lost, for the time. The war continued, and at the next session, the president renewed his request for the appropriation, enlarging the amount, I think, to three million. Again came the proviso; and defeated the measure. Congress adjourned again, and the war went on. In Dec. 1847, the new congress assembled. I was in the lower House that term. The "Wilmot Proviso" or the principle of it, was constantly coming up in some shape or other, and I think I may venture to say I voted for it at least forty times; during the short term I was there. The Senate, however, held it in check, and it never became law. In the spring of 1848 a treaty of peace was made with Mexico; by which we obtained that portion of her country which now constitutes the territories of New Mexico and Utah, and the now state of California. By this treaty the Wilmot Proviso was defeated, as so far as it was intended to be a condition of the acquisition of territory. Its friends, however, were still determined to find some way to restrain slavery from getting into the new country. This new acquisition lay directly west of our old purchase from France, and extended west to the Pacific Ocean—and was so situated that if the Missouri line should be extended straight west, the new country would be divided by such extended line, leaving some north and some south of it. On Judge Douglas' motion a bill, or provision of a bill, passed the Senate to so extend the Missouri line. The Proviso men in the House, including myself, voted it down, because by implication, it gave up the Southern part to slavery, while we were bent on having it all free.

In the fall of 1848 the gold mines were discovered in California. This attracted people to it with unprecedented rapidity, so that on, or soon after, the meeting of the new congress in December 1849, she already had a population of nearly a hundred thousand, had called a convention, formed a state constitution, excluding slavery, and was knocking for admission into the Union. The Proviso men, of course were for letting her in, but the Senate, always true to the other side would not consent to her admission. And there California stood, kept out of the Union, because she would not let slavery into her borders. Under all the circumstances perhaps this was not wrong. There were other points of dispute, connected with the general question of slavery, which equally needed adjustment. The South clamored for a more efficient fugitive slave law. The North clamored for the abolition of a peculiar species of slave trade in the District of Columbia, in connection with which, in view from the windows of the capitol, a sort of Negro-livery stable, where droves of Negroes were collected, temporarily kept, and finally taken to Southern markets, precisely like droves of horses, had been openly maintained for fifty years. Utah and New Mexico needed territorial governments; and whether slavery should or should not be prohibited within them, was another question. The indefinite western boundary of Texas was to be settled. She was received a slave state; and consequently the farther west the slavery men could push her boundary, the more slave country they secured. And the farther east the slavery opponents could thrust the boundary back, the less slave ground was secured. Thus this was just as clearly a slavery question as any of the others.

These points all needed adjustment; and they were all held up, perhaps wisely, to make them help to adjust one another. The Union, now, as in 1820, was thought to be in danger; and devotion to the Union rightfully inclined men to yield somewhat, in points where nothing else could have so inclined them. A compromise was finally effected. The South got their new fugitive-slave law; and the North got California, (the far best part of our acquisition from Mexico,) as a free state. The South got a provision that New Mexico and Utah, when admitted as states, may come in with or without slavery as they may then choose; and the North got the slave trade abolished in the District of Columbia. The North got the western boundary of Texas, thence further back eastward than the south desired; but, in turn, they gave Texas ten millions of dollars, with which to pay her old debts. This is the compromise of 1850.

Preceding the presidential election of 1852, each of the great political parties, Democrats and Whigs, met in convention, and adopted resolutions endorsing the compromise of '50; as a "finality," a final settlement, so far as these parties could make it so, of all slavery agitation. Previous to this, in 1851, the Illinois legislature had endorsed it.

During this long period of time Nebraska had remained, substantially an uninhabited country, but now emigration to, and settlement within it began to take place. It is about one third as large as the present United States, and its importance so long overlooked, begins to come into view. The restriction of slavery by the Missouri Compromise directly applies to it; in fact, was first made, and has since been maintained, expressly for it. In 1853, a bill to give it a territorial government passed the House of Representatives, and, in the hands of Judge Douglas, failed of passing the Senate only for want of time. This bill contained no repeal of the Missouri Compromise. Indeed, when it was assailed because it did not contain such repeal, Judge Douglas defended it in its existing form. On January 4th, 1854, Judge Douglas introduces a new bill to give Nebraska territorial government. He accompanies this bill with a report, in which last, he expressly recommends that the Missouri Compromise shall neither be affirmed nor repealed.

Before long the bill is so modified as to make two territories instead of one; calling the southern one Kansas.

Also, about a month after the introduction of the bill, on the judge's own motion, it is so amended as to declare the Missouri Compromise inoperative and void; and, substantially, that the people who go and settle there may establish slavery, or exclude it, as they may see fit. In this shape the bill passed both branches of Congress, and became a law.

This is the repeal of the Missouri Compromise...

It is not contended, I believe, that any such command [by the people] has ever been given in express terms [to repeal the Missouri Compromise]. It is only said that it was done in principle. The support of the Wilmot Proviso, is the first fact mentioned, to prove that the Missouri restriction was repudiated in principle, and the second is, the refusal to extend the Missouri line over the country acquired from Mexico. These are near enough alike to be treated together. The one was to exclude the chances of slavery from the whole new acquisition by the lump; and the other was to reject a division of it, by which one half was to be given up to those chances. Now whether this was a repudiation of the Missouri line, in principle, depends upon whether the Missouri law contained any principle requiring the line to be extended over the country acquired from Mexico. I contend it did not. I insist that it contained no general principle, but that it was, in every sense, specific. That its terms limit it to the country purchased from France, is undenied and undeniable.

It could have no principle beyond the intention of those who made it. They did not intend to extend the line to country which they did not own. If they intended to extend it, in the event of acquiring additional territory, why did they not say so? It was just as easy to say, that "in all the country west of the Mississippi, which we now own, or may hereafter acquire there shall never be slavery," as to say, what they did say; and they would have said it if they had meant it. An intention to extend the law is not only not mentioned in the law, but is not mentioned in any contemporaneous history. Both the law itself, and the history of the times are a blank as to any principle of extension; and by neither the known rules for construing statutes and contracts, nor by common sense, can any such principle be inferred.

Another fact showing the specific character of the Missouri law—showing that it intended no more than it expressed—showing that the line was not intended as a universal dividing line between free and slave territory, present and prospective—north of which slavery could never go—is the fact that by that very law, Missouri came in as a slave state, north of the line. If that law contained any prospective principle, the whole law must be looked to in order to ascertain what the principle was. And by this rule, the South could fairly contend that inasmuch as they got one slave state north of the line at the inception of the law, they have the right to have another given them north of it occasionally—now and then in the indefinite westward extension of the line. This demonstrates the absurdity of attempting to deduce a prospective principle from the Missouri Compromise line.

When we voted for the Wilmot Proviso, we were voting to keep slavery out of the whole Mexican acquisition; and little did we think we were thereby voting, to let it into Nebraska, laying several hundred miles distant. When we voted against extending the Missouri line, little did we think we were voting to destroy the old line, then of near thirty years standing. To argue that we thus repudiated the Missouri Compromise is no less absurd than it would be to argue that because we have, so far, forborne to acquire Cuba, we have thereby, in principle, repudiated our former acquisitions, and determined to throw them out of the Union! No less absurd than it would be to say that because I may have refused to build an addition to my house, I thereby have decided to destroy the existing house! And if I catch you setting fire to my house, you will turn upon me and say I instructed you to do it! The most conclusive argument, however, that, while voting for the Wilmot Proviso, and while voting against the extension of the Missouri line, we never thought of disturbing the original Missouri Compromise, is found in the facts that there was then, and still is, an unorganized tract of fine country, nearly as large as the state of Missouri, lying immediately west of Arkansas, and south of the Missouri Compromise line;[6] and that we never attempted to prohibit slavery as to it. I wish particular attention to this. It adjoins the original Missouri Compromise line, by its northern boundary; and consequently is part of the country, into which, by implication, slavery was permitted to go, by that compromise. There it has lain open ever since, and there it still lies. And yet no effort has been made at any time to wrest it from the South. In all our struggles to prohibit slavery within our Mexican acquisitions, we never so much as lifted a finger to prohibit it, as to this tract. Is not this entirely conclusive that at all times, we have held the Missouri Compromise as a sacred thing; even when against ourselves, as well as when for us?...

But next it is said that the compromises of '50 and the ratification of them by both political parties, in '52, established a new principle, which required the repeal of the Missouri Compromise. This again I deny. I deny it, and demand the proof. I have already stated fully what the compromises of '50 are. The particular part of those measures, for which the virtual repeal of the Missouri compromise is sought to be inferred (for it is admitted they contain nothing about it, in express terms) is the provision in the Utah and New Mexico laws, which permits them when they seek admission into the Union as states, to come in with or without slavery as they shall then see fit. Now I insist this provision was made for Utah and New Mexico, and for no other place whatever. It had no more direct reference to Nebraska than it had to the territories of the moon. But, say they, it had reference to Nebraska, in principle. Let us see. The North consented to this provision, not because they considered it right in itself; but because they were compensated—paid for it. They, at the same time, got California into the Union as a free state. This was far the best part of all they had struggled for by the Wilmot Proviso. They also got the area of slavery somewhat narrowed in the settlement of the boundary of Texas. Also, they got the slave trade abolished in the District of Columbia. For all these desirable objects the North could afford to yield something; and they did yield to the South the Utah and New Mexico provision. I do not mean that the whole North, or even a majority, yielded, when the law passed; but enough yielded, when added to the vote of the South, to carry the measure. Now can it be pretended that the principle of this arrangement requires us to permit the same provision to be applied to Nebraska, without any equivalent at all? Give us another free state; press the boundary of Texas still further back, give us another step toward the destruction of slavery in

[6] The current state of Oklahoma

the District, and you present us a similar case. But ask us not to repeat, for nothing, what you paid for in the first instance. If you wish the thing again, pay again. That is the principle of the compromises of '50, if indeed they had any principles beyond their specific terms—it was the system of equivalents.

Again, if Congress, at that time, intended that all future territories should, when admitted as states, come in with or without slavery, at their own option, why did it not say so? With such a universal provision, all know the bills could not have passed. Did they, then—could they—establish a principle contrary to their own intention? Still further, if they intended to establish the principle that wherever Congress had control, it should be left to the people to do as they thought fit with slavery, why did they not authorize the people of the District of Columbia at their adoption to abolish slavery within these limits? I personally know that this has not been left undone, because it was unthought of. It was frequently spoken of by members of Congress and by citizens of Washington six years ago; and I heard no one express a doubt that a system of gradual emancipation, with compensation to owners, would meet the approbation of a large majority of the white people of the District. But without the action of Congress they could say nothing; and Congress said "no." In the measures of 1850 Congress had the subject of slavery in the District expressly in hand. If they were then establishing the principle of allowing the people to do as they please with slavery, why did they not apply the principle to that people?

Again, it is claimed that by the Resolutions of the Illinois legislature, passed in 1851, the repeal of the Missouri Compromise was demanded. This I deny also. Whatever may be worked out by a criticism of the language of those resolutions, the people have never understood them as being any more than an endorsement of the compromises of 1850; and a release of our Senators from voting for the Wilmot Proviso. The whole people are living witnesses, that this only, was their view. Finally, it is asked "If we did not mean to apply the Utah and New Mexico provision, to all future territories, what did we mean, when we, in 1852, endorsed the compromises of '50?"

For myself, I can answer this question most easily. I meant not to ask a repeal, or modification of the fugitive slave law. I meant not to ask for the abolition of slavery in the District of Columbia. I meant not to resist the admission of Utah and New Mexico, even should they ask to come in as slave states. I meant nothing about additional territories, because, as I understood, we then had no territory whose character as to slavery was not already settled. As to Nebraska, I regarded its character as being fixed, by the Missouri compromise, for thirty years—as unalterably fixed as that of my own home in Illinois. As to new acquisitions I said "sufficient unto the day is the evil thereof."[7] When we make new acquaintances, [acquisitions?] we will, as heretofore, try to manage them somehow. That is my answer. That is what I meant and said; and I appeal to the people to say, each for himself, whether that was not also the universal meaning of the free states.

And now, in turn, let me ask a few questions. If by any, or all these matters, the repeal of the Missouri Compromise was commanded, why was not the command sooner obeyed? Why was the repeal omitted in the Nebraska bill of 1853? Why was it omitted in the original bill of 1854? Why, in the accompanying report, was such a repeal characterized as a departure from the course pursued in 1850? and its continued omission recommended?

I am aware Judge Douglas now argues that the subsequent express repeal is no substantial alteration of the bill. This argument seems wonderful to me. It is as if one should argue that white and black are not different. He admits, however, that there is a literal change in the bill; and that he made the change in deference to other senators, who would not support the bill without. This proves that those other senators thought the change a substantial one; and that the judge thought their opinions worth deferring to. His own opinions, therefore, seem not to rest on a very firm basis even in his own mind—and I suppose the world believes, and will continue to believe, that precisely on the substance of that change this whole agitation has arisen.

I conclude then, that the public never demanded the repeal of the Missouri compromise.

[*Lincoln then argues that at the founding, slavery was considered simply as an unavoidable part of American life. It existed when the United States was formed. It was dealt with as a necessary evil, not as a positive good. It was not mentioned in the Constitution, but hidden away.*]

The earlier Congress, under the Constitution, took the same view of slavery. They hedged and hemmed it in to the narrowest limits of necessity.

In 1794, they prohibited an out-going slave trade—that is, the taking of slaves from the United States to sell.

In 1798, they prohibited the bringing of slaves from Africa, into the Mississippi Territory—this territory then comprising what are now the states of Mississippi and Alabama. This was ten years before they had the authority to do the same thing as to the states existing at the adoption of the Constitution.

In 1800 they prohibited American Citizens from trading in slaves between foreign countries—as, for instance, from Africa to Brazil.

---

[7] Matthew 6:34

In 1803 they passed a law in aid of one or two state laws, in restraint of the internal slave trade.

In 1807, in apparent hot haste, they passed the law, nearly a year in advance, to take effect the first day of 1808—the very first day the Constitution would permit—prohibiting the African slave trade by heavy pecuniary and corporal penalties.

In 1820, finding these provisions ineffectual, they declared the trade piracy, and annexed to it, the extreme penalty of death. While all this was passing in the general government, five or six of the original slave states had adopted systems of gradual emancipation; and by which the institution was rapidly becoming extinct within these limits.

Thus we see, the plain unmistakable spirit of that age, towards slavery, was hostility to the principle, and toleration, only by necessity.

APPENDIX F

A Comparison: Secession Dates and Slave Population[1]

Order of Secession (by date)	Slaves in Population (by percentage)
1. South Carolina	South Carolina (57%)
2. Mississippi	Mississippi (55)
3. Florida	Louisiana (47)
4. Alabama	Alabama (45)
5. Georgia	Georgia (44)
6. Louisiana	Florida (44)
7. Texas	North Carolina (33)
8. Virginia	Virginia (31)
9. Arkansas	Texas (30)
10. North Carolina	Arkansas (26)
11. Tennessee	Tennessee (25)

In the case of six of the eleven seceding states (South Carolina, Mississippi, Alabama, Georgia, Virginia, and Tennessee), the chronological order in which they seceded corresponded to their rank among the seceding states based on the percentage of slaves in the total state population. Florida and Louisiana exchanged places, but there was a small difference in the percentage of slaves in each state and Florida preceded Louisiana out of the Union by only two weeks. Much the same can be said for North Carolina and Texas. On the whole, there is a correlation between the percentage of slaves in the total state population and the speed with which a state seceded.

---

[1] Data derived from https://eh.net/encyclopedia/slavery-in-the-united-states/, based on *Historical Statistics of the United States, Colonial Times to 1970*, U.S. Census Bureau, https://www.census.gov/library/publications/1975/compendia/hist_stats_colonial-1970.html.

Dates of Secession

1. South Carolina (December 20, 1860[2])
2. Mississippi (January 9, 1861)
3. Florida (January 10, 1861)
4. Alabama(January 11, 1861)
5. Georgia (January 19, 1861)
6. Louisiana (January 26, 1861)
7. Texas (February 1, 1861)
8. Virginia (April 17, 1861)
9. Arkansas (May 6, 1861)
10. North Carolina (May 20, 1861)
11. Tennessee (June 8, 1861)

[2] Two different dates are used for South Carolina's Secession Declaration, December 20 and December 24. The state seceded on December 20 with an initial ordinance, but the longer statement included in this collection as Document 23 wasn't issued until December 24.

APPENDIX G

Suggestions for Further Reading

Donald, David Herbert. *Liberty and Union: The Crisis of Popular Government, 1830–1860*. Boston: Little, Brown & Company, 1978.

Douglass, Frederick. *Narrative of the Life of Frederick Douglass*. New York: Dover Publications, Inc., 1995.

Fehrenbacher, Don E. *Prelude to Greatness: Lincoln in the 1850's*. Stanford: Stanford University Press, 1962.

______. *The South and Three Sectional Crises*. Baton Rouge: Louisiana State University Press, 1980.

Foner, Eric. *Free Soil, Free Labor, Free Men: The Ideology of the Republican Party before the Civil War*. New York: Oxford University Press, 1970.

______. *Politics and Ideology in the Age of the Civil War*. New York: Oxford University Press, 1980.

Guelzo, Allen C. *The Crisis of the American Republic: A History of the Civil War and Reconstruction Era*. New York: St. Martin's Press, 1995.

Holt, Michael F. *The Rise and Fall of the American Whig Party: Jacksonian Politics and the Onset of the Civil War*. New York: Oxford University Press, 1999.

Holzer, Harold. *Lincoln President-Elect: Abraham Lincoln and the Great Secession Winter 1860–1861*. New York: Simon & Schuster, 2008.

Jaffa, Harry V. *Crisis of the House Divided: An Interpretation of the Issues in the Lincoln-Douglas Debates*. Chicago: The University of Chicago Press, 1959.

______. *A New Birth of Freedom: Abraham Lincoln and the Coming of the Civil War*. Lanham: Roman & Littlefield Publishers, 2000.

McPherson, James M. *Battle Cry of Freedom: The Civil War Era*. New York: Oxford University Press, 2003.

Oates, Stephen B. *The Approaching Fury: Voices of the Storm 1820–1861*. New York: HarperCollins, 1997.

Peterson, Merrill D. *The Great Triumvirate: Webster, Clay, and Calhoun*. New York: Oxford University Press, 1987.

Potter, David. *The Impending Crisis, 1848–1861*. New York: Harper and Row, 1976.

Pressly, Thomas J. *Americans Interpret Their Civil War.* Princeton: Princeton University Press, 1954.

Randall, J.G. and David Donald. *The Civil War and Reconstruction.* Boston: Little, Brown and Company, 1969; 2nd edition.

Rozwenc, Edwin C. (ed.). *The Causes of the Civil War.* Boston: D.C. Heath & Co., 1972.

Stampp, Kenneth M. (ed.). *The Causes of the Civil War.* New York: Touchstone, 1986; 3rd edition, 1991.

———. *The Peculiar Institution: Slavery in the Ante-Bellum South.* New York: Vintage Books, 1956.

Stowe, Harriet Beecher. *Uncle Tom's Cabin.* Ware, Hertfordshire: Wordsworth Editions Limited, 1995.

Trefousse, Hans L. (ed.). *The Causes of the Civil War: Institutional Failure or Human Blunder?* Malabar, Florida: Krieger Publishing Company, 1977; updated edition, 2002.